Nazarii Gutsul, Kristina Khrul (Eds.)

Multicultural Societies and their Threats

Osteuropa
East Europe

Band / Volume 10

LIT

Multicultural Societies and their Threats

Real, hybrid and media wars in Eastern and South-Eastern Europe

edited by

Nazarii Gutsul and Kristina Khrul

LIT

Cover image: Maksym Muzyka – Savur Mohyla,
Donetsk region, Ukraine

Bibliographic information published by the Deutsche Nationalbibliothek
The Deutsche Nationalbibliothek lists this publication in the Deutsche Nationalbibliografie; detailed bibliographic data are available on the Internet at http://dnb.d-nb.de.

ISBN 978-3-643-90825-4

A catalogue record for this book is available from the British Library

Klosbachstr. 107
CH-8032 Zürich
Tel. +41 (0) 44-251 75 05
E-Mail: zuerich@lit-verlag.ch http://www.lit-verlag.ch
Distribution:
In the UK: Global Book Marketing, e-mail: mo@centralbooks.com
In North America: International Specialized Book Services, e-mail: orders@isbs.com
In Germany: LIT Verlag Fresnostr. 2, D-48159 Münster
Tel. +49 (0) 2 51-620 32 22, Fax +49 (0) 2 51-922 60 99, e-mail: vertrieb@lit-verlag.de
In Austria: Medienlogistik Pichler-ÖBZ, e-mail: mlo@medien-logistik.at
e-books are available at www.litwebshop.de

Foreword

This edited volume is the result of the hard and long work of many authors, who were guests or participants of the workshop 'Multicultural Societies and Their Threats. Real, Hybrid and Media Wars in Eastern Europe', which took place at Justus-Liebig-University of Giessen from the 15th until the 19th of June 2016. This book represents an attempt of the authors and editors to compare different 'frozen conflicts' from different regions like former Yugoslavia, Transnistria, South Ossetia, Abkhazia, Nagorno-Karabakh, Crimea and Donbas.

Through active participation in discussions with university professors and other colleagues, our authors – predominantly advanced and active students at Belarusian, German, Polish and Ukrainian universities – worked on their analyses of the influence of media on conflicts, of the role of regional identity and external actors in the conflict process, and of official statements for peace building.

Most of the articles are written from the perspectives of the political, sociological, historical and diplomatic sciences. Our main goal was to formulate security measures through analytical comparison, which would offer peaceful solutions to current conflicts in the region of Eastern Europe. Our findings are presented in this volume.

This research would not have been realized without the funding and support of the German Academic Exchange Service (DAAD), the German Federal Ministry of Education and Research (BMBF). We are also very grateful for the support of this project by the following: Justus-Liebig-University of Giessen (JLU), Giessen Center for Eastern Europe Studies (GiZo), Professor Hans-Jürgen Bömelburg (Department of Eastern European History at the JLU), the participants of the workshop 'Multicultural Societies and Their Threats. Real, Hybrid and Media Wars in Eastern Europe', research assistant Kristina Khrul, co-editor Nazarii Gutsul and correctors Jacqueline Composanto and Maximilian Brisach.

The contents of the articles do not necessarily reflect the opinions of the editors and correctors. The authors are responsible for the correct use and citation of their sources.

Content

Introduction

Today the keyboard is mightier than the bullet. International media-communities play a key role in the construction of the military conflicts in the world. But why is the media so reluctant to acknowledge the Russian role in the Ukrainian war in the Donbas[1]? What do we know about the peace-processes in the Caucasus and former Yugoslavia? The articles from this book try to explain the terminology we use to describe the war-conflicts in Eastern and South-Eastern Europe. The authors reinterpret such nomenclatures as *'frozen conflicts'*, *geopolitics*, *power of media*, *'hybrid warfare'* and others.

Most of the topics have been presented during the workshop in Giessen from June 15-19th, 2016. During this event the advanced bachelor, master and PhD-students discussed their opinions on these modern conflicts, like hybrid and media wars, especially in multicultural societies. This publication aims to collect the different views of the participants and guests of the workshop and to provide information about threats to multicultural societies in the post-socialist territories in modern Eastern and South-Eastern Europe.

The main goal of this project was to analyze different kinds of conflicts in multicultural regions through examples from former Yugoslavia, Transnistria, South Ossetia and Abkhazia, Nagorno-Karabakh, and find effective safeguards for the societies in Crimea and the Donbas. You can see how this goal was reached by reading the issues in this volume.

Structurally, this book is composed of five parts. In the first three parts, our co-authors focused on the 'key regions', which were separated into 'cases' for: Yugoslavia, the Caucasus and Ukraine. In the next part, the articles are presented to show the conflicts from the historical and geopolitical expectations of external actors. The fifth part can be seen as a conclusion for the whole volume, because there was an attempt to compare all analysed cases.

The book's first section packages the 'frozen conflicts' from the former Yugoslavia. It starts with the article by **Angelina Yurkova** (Belarusian State University of Minsk), who presents the evolution of the situation in

---

[1] All Ukrainian geographical names will be written according Ukrainian transcription.

Kosovo starting from the war of 1998-1999 and goes into relations between Belgrade and Pristina. She points out that the conflict of Kosovo was internationalized strongly by 'occidental and oriental blocs', and the independence of this not-recognized Balkan state was possible with the support of international global actors. Some countries see the way Kosovo took as a possibility towards autonomy for other territories.

The second article from this case, written by **Tetiana Levoniuk** (Belarusian State University of Minsk), discusses self-proclaimed state formations: Kosovo, South Ossetia and Abkhazia. The author shows us three different proclamations of independence and addresses their similarities (e.g. involvement of 'world powers', disintegration of a multiethnic federations and involvement of a 'stranded minority') and differences (e.g. use of force, number of recognizers and level of internationalization of the conflicts). Moreover, in the article there is a comparison of full-fledged recognition for the observed cases.

The following section of this volume is about the Caucasus region. The article by **Frederick Schröder** (Free University of Berlin) is focused on the Mission of the OSCE in Nagorno-Karabakh. The author starts with a historical overview of the emergence of the conflict in this region, describes the actors involved in the conflicts and a path towards a solution. Special attention was paid to the OSCE's role and the challenges for the German Chairmanship in 2016.

The biggest regional case of this book is about the war in Ukraine, which consists of three topics. The first article is dedicated to the construction of the Donbas regional identity in political and media discourses, which was analyzed by **Yuliya Abibok** (National University of Kyiv-Mohyla Academy). She describes the historical development of the regional identity ('donetskiye') and identifies some stereotypes about the Donbas in national and regional Ukrainian media. These include: 'mafia style', 'hard-workers', 'pro-Russian', 'anti-Ukrainian', etc. The result of this analysis concludes that the elites from the Donbas try to use the mythology about the region for their own needs, which contributed, to some extent, to the isolation of this part of the country.

The next article, written by **Demian Shevko** (National University of Ostroh Academy), explores the current conflict between Russia and Ukraine. The author defines this conflict as *hybression* (hybrid aggression), and gives an overview of other possible terms for hybrid warfare. Moreover, he gives examples of hybrid wars in history and shows that the current Russian aggression against Ukraine is not the first example of Russian hybrid war. The article also explains the idea of the 'Russian world' and mentioned the main features of hybression (the masking of military contingents, military success through a minimum use of military force, weakening the opponent from the inside, 'changing of influences' and the illusion of 'non-involvement').

Anastasiia Lykholai's (National University of Ostroh Academy) article focuses on the media coverage of the 'pre-war period', mainly the Euromaidan incident, from the views of the Ukrainian news program TSN (TV-channel '1+1'), the Russian Vesti (TV-channel 'Russia 24'), and the German Tagesschau (TV-channel 'das Erste'). This descriptive media analysis explores the reporting about the events from November 2013 until February 2014. The main point of this article is based on the assumption that different medias show the same news in different ways to reach their own goals.

The book's last two sections – additional and comparative – are composed of articles that give additional information about 'frozen conflicts' from historical, geopolitical and diplomatic perspectives and thereby contribute to the comparative feature of this volume by adding multi-faceted views to the main topic. The additional part is based on four items. **Ivan Basenko's** (National University of Kyiv-Mohyla Academy) article compares the propaganda clichés from the Word War I with the Russo-Ukrainian confrontation over the Donbas and Crimea. The author argues that the propaganda itself is not a new phenomenon and analyses two historical cases of using propaganda. He observes some similarities between these cases, like personalization (Kaiser Wilhelm II vs. Vladimir Putin) and intention to 'enemy atrocities' (crimes against civil population in both cases).

Olga Rusova (National Mechnikov University of Odesa) explains the role of the Weimar Triangle States (France, Germany, Poland) in the settlement of conflicts in the post-Soviet territories, with Russia as the key factor. She identifies and discusses about two of the most broad-scale conflicts in the former USSR: the wars in Georgia (2008) and in Ukraine (2014) with a special focus on the consequences of these conflicts: the economical sanctions against Russia. In the end of her article, Rusova writes about the future of the Weimar Triangle and about the current condition of the European security system.

The next article is by **Olena Starikova** (University of Lodz), and it describes Ukraine's position in the Russo-Ukrainian geopolitical agenda and explains what the 'Russian world' means as an imperialist geopolitical paradigm. At the beginning of the article, the author describes two applied geopolitical schools – the German and the Russian ones – and illustrates the place which Ukraine has in the 'Russian world' according to the Russian school of geopolitics. Possible scenarios are also given for the development of the crises in the Eastern part of Ukraine.

The last article from this chapter is written by **Olga Zhuravskaya** (Belarusian State University of Minsk). The author explains the Belarusian stance on conflicts in CIS-member-states. According to the neutral position of this country, Belarus was a mediation platform in some clashes and a *donor of security* in the region. Today, Minsk tries to play a significant role in the peace-process in Ukraine.

The last chapter of this book is dedicated to one comparative issue written by **Kristina Khrul** (Philipps-University of Marburg). This article includes the analysis of the 'frozen conflicts' in the states with problematic international recognition. The author grounds her study on disintegration conflict theory and used language to make a comparison. With the help of this analysis, she tries to answer the question: 'how did the official language recognition of national minorities change after the collapse of the USSR and Yugoslavia?'

This short overview of the current volume shows how covers many different topics, which used different terms and had different methods of analysis. As it was said in the foreword, the contents of the articles, as well the research methods and terminology, do not necessarily reflect the opinions of the editors and correctors. We would like to thank all of the co-authors and correctors for their work. We hope that this casebook, as an international publication, will contribute to the better understanding of multicultural societies in Eastern and South-Eastern Europe and their threats in a globalized world.

Editors,
Giessen

Case Yugoslavia

The Evolution of the Situation in Kosovo: Political Status and Contemporary Approaches

Angelina Yurkova

Abstract: *Through the examples of Kosovo and Metohija, this article concerns itself with problems such as territorial boundaries, recognition of independence of the state, difficult bilateral relations, self-recognition of the people and international mediation in search of compromise. The final decision of the political status of Kosovo is impeded by the existence of two international blocs of countries, i. e. countries 'for' and 'against' an independent Kosovo. Also important are the internal inconsistencies between Kosovo and Serbia, including their ethnic population. The structure of the article gives a possibility to examine the problem through its evolution up to the contemporary situation, its internationalization, and its possible future prospects.*

Keywords: *Kosovo, Serbia, independent state, political status, mediation, measures*

A. The evolution of the situation in Kosovo from the period of the war of 1998-1999 to the extent of the proclamation of independence in 2008

I. The new war after the 'Cold War' or 'the game in the Cold War'

From the very start it should be noted that the end of the 'Cold War' does not mean the end of military conflicts, rivalries and hatreds between states and the installation of world order. The clearest example of this is the region of South-Eastern Europe, in particular the territories of the former Yugoslavia.

In fact, many researchers even name the Balkans 'the powder keg of Europe' because of a huge number of military conflicts in the region. After the 'Cold War' the states, forming part of Yugoslavia, began to fight for their independence, and a number of referendums were held in support of separation from Yugoslavia (for example Slovenia, Bosnia and Herzegovina, and Croatia). However, the process of disintegration of Yugoslavia was not peaceful or easy due to ethnic oppositions, unwillingness of central government to lose control of the territories and the policy based on ideology of Serbian ethnic nationalism, religious confrontation and separatist movements inside the former Yugoslavian Republics. The conflict in Kosovo can serve as an example which demonstrates the difficult process of a state's collapse, and the successive destiny of each of its parts.

The 'resolution' of the Kosovo armed conflict, as well as how Kosovo obtained its independence and how Kosovo Albanians gained their right to self-determination shows two approaches to the problem of a divided territory inside a sovereign state. We must consider the confrontation between the Serbian minority and the Albanian majority on a domestic level through the instability of state institutions. Furthermore we must look at the position of the European Union in forming legal norms and standards, as well as a divided recognition of Kosovo's political status. These approaches could be conditionally named as occidental and pro-Russian. The occidental approach comes from the majority of western countries, which have become the adherents of Kosovo independence, having regard to the mission of NATO in the Kosovo war (Bieber and Daskalovski, 2003). The pro-Russian approach is different, since Kosovo is the territory of the former socialistic state, Yugoslavia, and the relations between the USSR and Yugoslavia were historically characterized by difficulties. This could be a consequence of Russia's opposition to Kosovo's political status, even when this status was not recognized by other states, such as the People's Republic of China.

It is important to state the internationalization of the conflict, which is characterized by difficult tensions between world actors. And these tensions have greatly influenced the internal situation in Kosovo. But first of all, the aforementioned approaches to the resolution of the existence of an independent Kosovo should be examined, starting with the occidental one.

The crucial role belongs to NATO, which has been leading a peace-support operation in Kosovo since June 1999, supporting an international campaign to build peace and security in the area. Partly NATO's 78-day air campaign was aimed against Milosevic's regime, but KFOR's (*Kosovo Force*) original objectives were to deter renewed hostilities, establish a secure environment to ensure public safety and order, demilitarize the Kosovo Liberation Army, support international humanitarian efforts and coordinate with international civil presence (NATO, 2016). Even in the first months of 1999 it became evident that the war between the Kosovo Liberation Army and the Yugoslav Army was at risk of developing into an 'ethnic cleansing' of the Kosovar Albanians, who constituted over 80% of the province's population. As the official NATO source admit: 'KFOR derives its mandate from United Nations Security Council Resolution (UNSCR) 1244 of 10 June 1999 and the Military-Technical Agreement between NATO and the Federal Republic of Yugoslavia and Serbia. KFOR operates under Chapter VII of the UN Charter and, as such, is a peace enforcement operation' (*NATO*, 2016). It is indispensable to say that UNSCR 1244 also covers the aspect of unity and indivisibility of Serbia (Peci, Dugolli, Malazogu, 2006), which would become an argument for the infringement of the principles of international law concerning Kosovo. Besides, this very resolution established the UN mission which is called the United Nations Interim Administration Mission in Kosovo (UNMIK). The Organization for Security and Cooperation in Europe (OSCE) became UNMIK's pillar for institution building. And finally, under Security Council Resolution 1244, the European Union Rule of Law Mission in Kosovo (EULEX) started its work and coordination with the UN (United Nations Resolution 1244, 1999).

After all, the occidental group can be seen as a new bloc of mostly western countries, which are part of regional and/or international organizations, and they have their own vision to resolve the conflict in Kosovo, which differs from the perception of the problem by '*oriental*' (in particular post-Soviet) countries.

The NATO mission was condemned by the countries of the Commonwealth of Independent States. For the Russian Federation such a resolution of the conflict was nothing else but the aspiration of the US for imposing its will and increasing its authority. Moreover, the oriental bloc, supported by India, China, and Brazil, considered this mission as return to acts of force in the resolution of conflicts. They stressed the importance of non-intervention norms as the essential basis of the UN and of present international security. Then, the relations between NATO and the EU were regarded as a competition more than a cooperation. But in general, the occidental bloc should not intervene in internal affairs of Serbia, in accordance to the opinion of the oriental bloc (Scvoznikov, 2011); it was up to the Serbian administration to find the right solution.

Thus, was it a new war after the 'Cold war'? Or 'the game in the Cold War'? In a strategic sense, Yugoslavia lost its importance when compared with other areas of the world, and consequently no longer attracted economic and political support from the West. But still Yugoslavia was strongly influenced by the West. Kosovo was the area of post-Cold War actions between post-military blocs, mostly because of the disintegration of the world order. The French Professor Didier Bigo had an idea about security expert's attempts to explain the new system of international relations (Zbigniew Brzezinski, Semuel Hantington, Francis Fukuyama). The explanation lies in the wish of world actors to find a new enemy, or a new area of opposition, so they can stay as leaders and decisions makers in different regions of the world (Tsygankov, 1998). That is why the intervention of international and regional organizations, which unite other actors around them, to resolve the conflict in Yugoslavia, particularly in Kosovo, can be explained by the willingness to stay as the superpower, and the force which all regions should reckon with.

The conflict in Kosovo could not be researched without consideration of the situation in the world. The problem is not the development of new states after Yugoslavia's collapse, but the existence of bipolarity in the perception and forces in the world order.

II. The Proclamation of Independence: Two Approaches to the Problem.

The UN Resolution 1244 guaranteed the indivisibility of Serbia. Nevertheless in 2008 the Albanian Government of Kosovo and Metohija declared its independence without the approval of the non-Albanian population or the Government of Serbia (United Nations Resolution 1244, 1999). Again two concepts or approaches to the proclamation of independence of Kosovo can be emphasised.

The occidental bloc, including the United States and the majority of EU countries, supported the decision. Whereas the oriental bloc, including the Russian Federation and People's Republic of China, considered it an infringement of international law. The Serbian delegation applied to the General Assembly of the UN with the request to examine the legitimacy of such a proclamation (Scvoznikov, 2011); however the final decision was not favorable for Serbia and oriental bloc.

It is important to note that several judges of the International Court of Justice (ICJ) expressed their opinion on the decision of the General Assembly. In particular, the Vice President of the ICJ, Peter Tomka (Slovakia), considered it within the competence of the Security Council to make this decision, being beyond the scope of the General Assembly; otherwise Pristina and Belgrade should elaborate the final status of Kosovo. The judge Bruno Zimma (Germany), claimed there were two questions which should be answered: not only whether the proclamation of independence contradicted international law, but also whether it corresponded to it (ibid). Therefore, the conclusion can be made that the final decision of the UN was not elaborated appropriately. But if the Security Council had worked on this conflict, there would not be a result because of the veto power in the council.

Russia's position concentrated on the fact that the population of Kosovo did not have the right of self-determination. Then, it was confirmed that all the countries should adhere to resolution 1244. Besides, Russia did not consider the violation of human rights in Kosovo during the 1990s as an excuse for a one-sided proclamation of independence in 2008. The recognition of this independence by the occidental states was at variance with international law fixed in the UN Charter, the Declaration of principles of the international law, and the final act of the Conference on Security and Cooperation in Europe 1975. All of these documents were about peaceful resolution of international disputes, the respect of territorial inviolability, and the principle of non-intervention in the internal affairs of a state (Chatham House, 2008; Scvoznikov, 2011).

Accordingly, the right to self-determination has become the bone of contention between the two blocs. The occidental countries believed that the Albanians of Kosovo could use their right to self-determination which is affirmed by the Charter of the UN. The oriental countries, particularly Russia, have their own arguments, which are quite convincing. First of all, in the Kosovo conflict there is no reason to claim the presence of foreign occupation, because this territory was a part of Serbia from the beginning of the twelfth century, excluding the time of the Ottoman Empire. Even juridical foundations, such as a 'colonial regime' or 'racial discrimination,' cannot be used. Since 1945, Kosovo had the status of an autonomous region and its people had both the freedom of conscience and religion. Furthermore, the Albanians have already realized their right to self-determination, being citizens of the sovereign state of Albania (Scvoznikov, 2011).

Probably all these arguments were aimed to stop the creation of a 'Greater Albania,' which could mean, in the opinion of Russia, further Islamization of Europe.

Despite the strength of the arguments of the oriental bloc, it seems that the world has almost accepted the new state. Member states in the UN began to recognize it and it also became a member of international organizations. In 2008 Kosovo's then Prime Minister Hashim Thaci read the Declaration of Independence, which states that Kosovo dedicates itself to peace and stability in the region and seeks good relations with its neighbours. The declaration furthermore states that Kosovo was created along the lines of the UN plan drawn up by special representative Martti Ahtisaari, and calls for Kosovo's supervised independence by an international presence (European Forum for democracy and solidarity, 2015). Meanwhile, the relations between Kosovo and Serbia were certainly difficult. The Kosovo conflict has definitively become a subject of concern for the world community, however it is up to Kosovo and Serbia to resolve it. That is why their relations should be analyzed in the period after the unilateral proclamation of independence of Kosovo.

B. Relations between Kosovo and Serbia and the role of the European Union

There is no doubt that the Government of Serbia was deeply against Kosovo's independence. Belgrade continued to support the Serbian majority in northern Kosovo, which kept that area out of the control of authorities in Pristina. By 2011 the tension increased. For example, in order to enforce a trade boycott of Serb goods, the Pristina Government sent special police to the border crossings with Serbia in the North. The reaction of Kosovo Serbs was certainly negative and violent with the series of skirmishes and roadblocks between North and South. Consequently, the situation in the rest of Kosovo was frustrated (Lehne, 2012). The problem was to avoid the escalation of the crisis, which was quite possible.

As a result, it was almost impossible to reach an agreement without a mediator, the role of which the European Union has taken. The fact is that Serbia did not want to link its ambitions to join the EU with its policy on Kosovo. But the condition of the EU toward accession directly depended on Belgrade improving relations with Kosovo. In the opinion of the EU, it was against its interests to incorporate unresolved territorial disputes and 'frozen conflicts' into the EU. As a matter of fact, such an admission for Belgrade could block Kosovo's further progress toward the EU.

The first attempt to construct a dialogue between Kosovo and Serbia was made in 2011. Its character was not just technical but highly political, incorporating heavy-duty mediation by the EU. Every meeting was accompanied by hostile rhetoric between the parties, high drama in the media, and accusations of treason from the opposition; therefore it did not give the hoped for results (European Union external action, 2016).

Then, the EU facilitated a High-Level Dialogue between Belgrade and Pristina, which resulted in the historic 'First agreement of principles governing the normalization of relations' (Brussels Agreement) reached on 19 April 2013. Its 15-point text focuses on two goals: creating an Association/Community of Serb majority municipalities (ASM) in the north of Kosovo, vested with autonomy regarding economic development, education, health, urban and rural planning; while also removing the parallel Serbian structures and integrating the police and judiciary in the Kosovo system. The agreement also states that neither side can block the other's entry into the EU (European Parliamentary Research Service, 2016).

In August 2015, Belgrade and Pristina concluded yet another round of 'landmark' agreements. They signed four new deals: on the establishment of an Association/Community of Serbian Municipalities, on energy, on telecoms, and on the opening of the Mitrovica Bridge.

It can be seen, that the EU has managed to prevent the conflict between Kosovo and Serbia from escalating. Also, the EU has taken some steps to improve its bilateral relations with Kosovo and Serbia. For instance, on 27th October 2015, the EU signed a Stabilisation and Association Agreement (SAA) with Kosovo (*Commission Staff Working Document*, 2015). This is a milestone on Kosovo's path towards a European future, which provides a comprehensive framework for closer political dialogue and economic relations between Kosovo and the EU, including the opening of EU markets to Kosovo products. The European Union Rule of Law Mission in Kosovo (EULEX), which was launched on the basis of a decision by 27 EU Member States in February 2008, assists and supports the Kosovo authorities in the rule of law, specifically in the police, judiciary and customs areas. Concerning EU-Serbia relations, the Stabilisation and Association

Agreement (SAA) between Serbia and the EU came into force in September 2013 (European Union external action, 2016). And the process of Serbia's admission to the EU continues.

At the same time, the United Nations Interim Administration Mission in Kosovo (UNMIK), which was established by the Security Council Resolution 1244 (1999), continues its constructive engagement with Pristina and Belgrade, all communities in Kosovo and regional and international actors.

Finally, NATO continues to offer strong political support to the Belgrade-Pristina Agreements, and KFOR stands ready to support its implementation – by ensuring a climate of peace and security – within its current mandate (NATO, 2016).

However the current situation in Kosovo, which was complicated by the election of the new president Hashim Thaçi on 26th February (United Nations Security Council, 2016), increases tensions between Kosovo and Serbia. During the sessions of the Assembly of Kosovo in 2016, opposition lawmakers (UN meetings coverage and press releases, 2016) released tear gas canisters in the Assembly hall and opposition supporters protested outside the building. On 8th March, four opposition party activists were arrested in Pristina for attempting to halt the official escort of the Prime Minister.

Undoubtedly, the EU has taken many steps to enhance its relations with Kosovo and Serbia. Due to European Commission report, the leaders of Serbia and Kosovo have shown 'political courage and maturity' (*Commission staff working document*, 2015) in tackling difficult issues jointly, as well as a commitment to better relations. But Kosovo is at an early stage in achieving the capacity to cope with competitive pressures and market forces within the Union. It is also at an early stage of alignment with European standards, such as public procurement, statistics and financial control, democratic institutions, gender equality, cooperation between the government and civil society, judicial system, the controlling organized crime and Islamic extremism. But Serbia is unlikely to join the EU until at least 2020. The main criterion required is a complete normalization of the relations with Kosovo (ibid). However, the question of new admissions to the EU is not currently prioritized, because the EU needs to implement a new global strategy, institutional reforms, a rethinking of its purpose. Augmenting the number of member states could make the acceptance of EU decisions more difficult, and also make the EU more unequal considering the developmental differences between all of its members. In general, despite the difficulties on the path of Kosovo and Serbia's admission to the EU, the Union has continued its interest in stabilising Serbia and its neighbours due to Russia's attempts to gain more influence in the region.

C. The regulation of Kosovo's final status

I. Political status of Kosovo

The proclamation of independence of Kosovo and Metohija was analysed earlier, but the problem of political status stays unsolved nowadays. Certainly, a huge number of measures should be taken to resolve the main problem of world recognition of Kosovo's independence, as the conflict is not totally frozen despite the Serbian-Kosovo agreement. There are multiple forces that make a decision on Kosovo's status difficult. There is the question of state sovereignty and power. At the same time, there are also opposing groups within international bodies. But since the population of Kosovo is not always satisfied with the extent of international involvement in the conflict, the international community needs to continue to find a compromise. In addition, Kosovo is not the only state which would like to be recognized (South Ossetia, Northern Cyprus, Transnistria, Gibraltar, the Falklands, Northern Ireland), that is why it is difficult to predict if other states would use the complete recognition of Kosovo as precedent for their independence as well.

The Kosovo Government is not able to exercise control in the North. By investing money, they tried to involve the Serb citizens in Kosovo institutions. However, this has not resulted in increased willingness of Serbs in north Kosovo to accept the Kosovo institutions and, with that, an independent Kosovo. During the past years, the Serbs in Serbia as well as in Kosovo have harshly criticised the failure of UNMIK and KFOR to protect the Serb population in Kosovo. Improving the situation of the Serbian communities was a main point of the status negotiations, and remains an important topic held under close scrutiny by the international community (Chatham House, 2008).

As of 20th October 2015, 111 UN states have recognised the independence of Kosovo and it has become a member country of the IMF and World Bank. In the EU, 23 out of 28 member states recognise its independence; Spain, Cyprus, Greece, Slovakia and Romania have not done so, mainly due to issues with minorities and separatist movements in their own respective countries (European Forum for democracy and solidarity, 2015). Obviously the majority of EU countries would like to keep the same political line on Kosovo's status, but the above-mentioned countries prefer to support the Serbian position. It is very controversial because the UNMIK and the EULEX do not have an internal consensus on how to find the common solution between two blocs, occidental and oriental. Besides, Kosovo and Serbia could not become the EU members. In the first case, five EU countries would block Kosovo's admission, and in the second case, the other 23 EU countries would not allow Serbia to join the EU without the recognition of Kosovo. There were repeated attempts by Russia to discuss the problem under the auspices of the UN, specifically in the Security Council. But the decision would then be blocked using the veto power. There is an impression that not only the conflict is frozen but also the final resolution of it.

II. Measures to be taken

In general, how can the problems of political status be resolved? And which measures are the most realistic to take in the case of Kosovo?

Firstly, the agreements between Kosovo and Serbia, which were adopted in 2013 and 2015, should be implemented completely, and further dialogue should be encouraged by international mediators. Here it is essential to mention that for Kosovo-Serb relations it could be better to have the support of the UN or the EU, while external control of the Kosovo Government could be weakened on the condition that Kosovo will reach all necessary criteria adopted by the world community. This concerns the problems of terrorism, organized crime, corruption, human rights, democratic institutions, displaced people, etc[1]. In addition, because of the continued international involvement in the province, Kosovo remains a protectorate, not an independent state, in spite of its recognition by more than 100 states.

[1] There is a concern about terrorists using Kosovo for recruitment and training.

Secondly, by talking about two approaches to the problem, the oriental and occidental blocs, we should remember we no longer live in the Cold War, which is why a compromise in Kosovo's future should exist. The problem is that some countries, in particular Russia, emphasize that no one has the right unilaterally to revise the resolution 1244. However, rather than justifying their position through arguments that skirt around resolution 1244, and rather than prolonging the interplay between law and politics in Kosovo's recognition, the world community should develop the decision to completely recognize Kosovo in a way that would not give precedence for other territorial disputes. Politics will always play a pivotal role in the recognition of states, and perhaps, because the status quo is politically untenable, Kosovo could be a case of 'bending the law for a good cause' (Chatham House, 2008).

Current law permits extend self-determination only in limited circumstances, preferring instead to resolve minority claims through autonomy within an existing state. Indeed it was to preserve territorial integrity, that recognising governments purported Kosovo as an exceptional situation and thus served as a warning to other aspirant groups that their claims would not receive similar support. Besides, self-determination is a right to which all are entitled, and therefore a right which states are obliged to vindicate. As a matter of fact, there is an idea of earned sovereignty (ibid) as a means of resolving disputes about secession. For example, the development of Kosovo since 1999, a fulfilment of the UNMIK standards, can be a useful argument to support Kosovo's independence.

Thirdly, there is a need to end factionalism and pursue further dialogue (ibid), which means not only that resolution 1244 (1999) does not suit the current reality, but also that accusations using the past could not ever be a solution in Kosovo-Serbia relations. For example, when there is a discussion of the crimes against Kosovo Albanians, Serbia objects to the use of the word '*genocide*'. The Serbian Government also demands a certain emphasis on history. They emphasize that 200,000 people have been displaced in Kosovo (ibid), many crimes were committed by the Kosovo liberation forces in the 1990s and 2000s and there were attacks on cultural landmarks in Kosovo.

The next difficult solution should regard the status of North Kosovo, where the population mostly consists of Serbs. Despite relatively autonomous status and some benefits to the population in this region, there is a huge opposition against the Kosovo Government, which makes carrying out a referendum, for example, meaningless. But this case differs a lot from other cases in the world such as North Cyprus or the Basque Country, because the Serbian population already have their own country. Therefore, it would be quite reasonable to make North Kosovo the legal territory of Serbia. Otherwise, the tension between the Kosovo Government and the opposition in North Kosovo will inevitably continue to exist.

Last but not least, there are other measures which should be taken to find an ultimate resolution to this problem. The process of admitting Kosovo and Serbia into the EU can only be continued after necessary reforms, which are under discussion now. Furthermore, it is essential to integrate the Kosovo police into the international community, including INTERPOL, to guarantee the security of Kosovo. Finally, the platforms for discussion between Kosovo and Serbia should be ensured by international organizations, including the UN.

The necessity to recognize Kosovo prevails because the majority of states have already recognized it, and Kosovo will soon be a member of more international organizations. But again, this situation is not a precedent for universal resolution of political status for all territorial disputes; it is a more or less realistic option to find a consensus.

The Kosovo problem is one challenge for the global community. The military conflict was resolved by international intervention and it has become obvious that the final settlement should be made by international actors in cooperation with the national governments of Kosovo and Serbia. If such a final resolution is found, it could become an example for other territorial disputes, showing real cooperation in order to find a compromise. It also exemplifies how international actors should unite in the face of difficult conflicts, instead of disputing about their own power or benefits. They should concentrate on 'soft' power rather than a 'hard' one, because it is one of the pillars of the modern system of international relations. This system should be safeguarded by each participant and developed only in a positive and effective way.

References

Bieber, F.; Daskalovski, Z. (2003): Understanding the war in Kosovo. London: Frank Cass.

Chatham House (ed.) (2008): Kosovo: International Law and Recognition. A Summary of the Chatham House International Law Discussion Group meeting held on 22nd April 2008. Retrieved from https://www.chathamhouse.org/sites/files/chathamhouse/public/Research/International%20Law/il220408.pdf.

European Commission (2015): Kosovo 2015 Report. Retrieved from https://ec.europa.eu/neighbourhood-enlargement/sites/near/files/pdf/key_documents/2015/20151110_report_kosovo.pdf.

European Forum for democracy and solidarity (2015): Kosovo. Retrieved from http://www.europeanforum.net/country/kosovo.

European Parliamentary Research Service (2016): Serbia and Kosovo: Normalisation of relations. Retrieved from http://www.europarl.europa.eu/RegData/etudes/ATAG/2016/579079/EPRS_ATA(2016)579079_EN.pdf.

European Union external action (2016): What is EULEX? Retrieved from http://www.eulex-kosovo.eu/?page=2,16.

Lehne, S. (2012): Kosovo and Serbia: Toward a Normal Relationship. Retrieved from http://carnegieendowment.org/files/Kosovo_and_Serbia.pdf.

NATO (2016): NATO's Role in Kosovo. Retrieved from http://www.nato.int/cps/en/natolive/topics_48818.htm.

Peci, L.; Dugolli, I.; Malazogu, L. (2006): Negotiating Kosovo's Final Status. Retrieved from http://www.sciencespo.fr/ceri/sites/sciencespo.fr.ceri/files/artpdm.pdf.

Scvoznikov, A. N. (2011): The Kosovo problem: historic-juridical aspects. In: The Journal of Samara Humanitarian Academy 1 (9), p. 17–26.

Tsygankov, P. A. (1998): International relations: sociological approaches. Moscow: Gardarika.

UN (1999): United Nations Resolution 1244. Retrieved from http://www.unmikonline.org/Pages/1244.aspx.

UN (2016): Intensive Effort Needed to Spur Economic Growth, Opportunity in Kosovo, Special Representative Tells Security Council. Retrieved from http://www.un.org/press/en/2016/sc12265.doc.htm.

UN (2016): Report of the Secretary-General on the United Nations Interim Administration Mission in Kosovo. Retrieved from http://www.un.org/en/ga/search/view_doc.asp?symbol=S/2016/407.

The Recognition of Self-Proclaimed State Formations: General and Particular

Tetiana Levoniuk

Abstract: *The subject of unrecognized and partially recognized states, as well as the development of the main criteria for their recognition has always been highly relevant. But it has acquired special significance after the proclamation of Kosovo's independence, followed by South Ossetian and Abkhazian. So what are the similarities and differences of self-proclamation in these cases? What approaches to their recognition by the international community exist and what are the prospects for their further development in international relations? This article is an attempt to give the most comprehensive answer to the issues in question.*

Keywords: *self-proclaimed states, recognition, Kosovo, South Ossetia, Abkhazia*

Introduction

The subject of unrecognized and partially recognized states, as well as the development of the main criteria for their recognition, has always been a highly relevant issue. But despite these states' growing impact on regional security and stability, our understanding of '*de facto states*' is still limited. Only one thing is unchangeable: recognition from others, which provides them with a legal standing in the international system, is central to the foreign policy of these states. In other words, 'statehood remains the top prize' for these entities (Broers, 2014, p.146).

According to the Montevideo Convention on the Rights and Duties of States, 'the state as a person of international law should possess the following qualifications: a permanent population; a defined territory; government; and capacity to enter into relations with the other states' (Montevideo Convention on the Rights and Duties of States, 1933, p. 3). Surprisingly, having built feasible institutions which are supported by the general population living in the territory under their control, but without international recognition, many 'de facto states' have survived for decades beyond the international state system. And they still continue to seek external sovereignty and try to survive against all odds and controversies.

Therefore, it is important to point out that the issue of recognizing such states has acquired a special significance since the proclamation of Kosovo's, South Ossetian's and Abkhazian's independence. So what are the similarities and differences in these three cases? What approaches to the recognition of these territories by the international community exist and what are the prospects for their further development in international relations?

In mid-February 2008 Kosovo and Metohija (officially, a part of Serbia), unilaterally declared its independence, thus aggravating a long history of ethnic conflict. However, despite violating UN Security Council resolutions, many states have recognized Kosovo's independence.

Predictions that this case might expand in the post-Soviet space have become a reality. The recognition of Kosovo's independence has been followed with great interest in other 'de facto states', whose leaderships hope that this case will set a precedent and hence increase their chances of international recognition. Russia has also supported this interpretation due to its fierce criticism of the acceptance of Kosovo's independence by the United States, the United Kingdom, Germany and France.

In the same month, Russian president, Vladimir Putin, while commenting on the situation in Kosovo at a press conference, said the following: 'We are always being told that Kosovo is a special case. This is all lies. There is nothing so special about Kosovo and everyone knows this full well. It is exactly the same situation as an ethnic conflict, with crimes committed on both sides and a complete de facto independence. We need to decide on a common set of principles for resolving such issues' (Transcript of Annual Big Press Conference, 2008). But, after Russia rejected Kosovo's self-proclamation of independence, on 26th August 2008, Russia unilaterally recognized the independence of South Ossetia and Abkhazia immediately after the 'five-day war' with Georgia.

The situation also did not change after the UN General Assembly, at the request of Serbia, asked the International Court of Justice (ICJ) to give an advisory opinion on the question: 'Is the unilateral declaration of independence by the Provisional Government of Kosovo's institutions consistent with international law?' On 22nd July 2010, the ICJ issued the following verdict from The Hague: 'The declaration of unilateral independence of Kosovo on 17th February 2008 did not violate international law'. It also restated that 'international law does not prohibit declarations of independence' (Kabanov in: Akaba, 2011, p. 9). Nevertheless, some countries have continued to support the territorial integrity of Serbia, insisting that the international legal precedent may have a negative impact on the resolution of ethnic conflicts around the world.

The Russian diplomats had lambasted the West for their 'precedent' of recognizing Kosovo from 2007-2008. But after recognizing South Ossetia and Abkhazia, Moscow has shifted its position. They gave an unconvincing argument that there were insufficient grounds to recognize Kosovo as a special case, in legal terms 'casus sui generis'. However, the special circumstances in South Ossetia and Abkhazia, mainly preventing a humanitarian catastrophe and realizing self-determination, are sufficient for their recognition (Allison, 2008). In the following part these two cases will be compared by what they have in common and what makes them different.

Common features

Predictably, in spite of the existing 'specificity' of the Kosovo issue, people made analogies between the above-mentioned cases. The majority of Western countries strongly support Kosovo's independence, while the Caucasian republics, obviously, rely on Russian help. And this is precisely the first similarity: there is an involvement between 'world powers', influencing the situation through external forces.

Secondly, these cases all resulted from conflicts during the transitional context following, or accompanying, the disintegration of a multiethnic federation (respectively, Yugoslavia and the USSR). Undoubtedly, all three entities had a certain degree of autonomy during the Soviet era.

Thirdly, they all involved a 'stranded minority' that expressed demands for joining its kin-state, or alternatively becoming independent. Furthermore, there were similar claims to independence, based on self-determination and popular will. In all cases, the mother countries did not recognize the smaller group, and, in fact, tried to abolish any autonomous power, which led to armed conflicts.

Moreover, these conflicts are marked by human suffering and a large number of refugees. Thus, the 'five-day war' in the South Caucasus displaced 192,000 people including both Ossetians and Georgians (Amnesty International, 2008). As of May 2014, 20,272 persons remained displaced, with their return being blocked by de facto authorities (United Nations, 2014). And since 1999, the Republic of Kosovo, which has seen ethnic conflicts between Serbs and Albanian separatists, still has more than 200,000 ethnic Serbs within it.

Furthermore, information wars accompanied these conflicts. Both sides used information to make the outside world sympathetic to their side. For instance, the UN Court eventually ruled that Serbian troops did not carry out genocide against ethnic Albanians during Slobodan Milosevic's campaign in Kosovo from 1998-1999 (BBC News, 2001). However, in contrast to this, the Russian media claimed that the 'genocide' of thousands of people was taking place in South Ossetia during the initial hours of the war in August 2008.

In its turn, the fact cannot be denied that Western mass media did not present a clear political analysis in their reports on the Kosovo conflict. That is why the conflicts resemble each other in some way. In total, the level of violence, including the number of refugees and the death rate, has certainly been exaggerated in order to mislead public opinion and attract sympathy.

Another similarity, evidently, is the declaration of independence of Kosovo and the South Caucasus republics, which was passed by the UN Security Council.

Then, there is the failure in political dialogue between the conflicting parties. Serbia still considers the Kosovo Republic as a part of its territory, named the Autonomous Province of Kosovo and Metohija, and does not recognize the independence of the state. Georgia, in its turn, does not recognize the independence of Abkhazia and South Ossetia and considers them to be in its own territory. Since 2008, there have not been fundamental shifts in their relationships, and political dialogue is still unsuccessful.

And the last similarity between these two stories is absolutely clear: the reality in the conflict regions has not changed in favor of Serbia or Georgia, which defend their right to return the breakaway territories under their control.

Thus, these are some general similarities between Kosovo / Abkhazia and South Ossetia. While this does not prove that the two cases should immediately be considered in the same context, at the same time, it suggests that none of the cases are unique or exceptions to the general rule. Therefore, these cases obviously have common features, while still being individual.

What makes them different?

As previously mentioned, the cases of Abkhazia and South Ossetia share some similarities with the case of Kosovo, but what makes them different?

First of all, Russia used force against Georgia in the absence of the public support of even its closest partners. Thereafter, Russia unilaterally adjusted the borders that emerged after the collapse of the Soviet Union.

However, the proclamation of Kosovo's independence took place with the support of several dozen states. On November 2015, 108 countries had recognized Kosovo, including all G-7 states, 23 of 28 EU member states, and an increasing number of states from the Americas, Africa, and Asia. A number of international organizations have admitted membership to Kosovo, including the World Bank, the International Monetary Fund, the European Bank for Reconstruction and Development, and the International Olympic Committee (U.S. Department of State). But South Ossetia and Abkhazia were only recognized by Russia, Nicaragua, Venezuela, Nauru and several other non-recognized territories.

Secondly, Russia's recognition of Abkhazia and South Ossetia in the aftermath of the war in August 2008 plunged the 'de facto states' in the region into a new legitimacy crisis by changing the very meaning of recognition. For elites in Abkhazia and South Ossetia – who had ruled since the early 1990s by assuring eventual recognition by the international community, – Russian diplomacy imposed 'unipolar recognition', a return to a bygone bipolar world, in which small nations served as proxies in 'great power games'. 'They became mere beneficiaries of a tactic in the fray of great power plays, in which they had no role and over which they had no control' (Broers, 2014, p.153).

Moreover, the conflict in Kosovo has been, from the very beginning, internationalized, and diplomatic efforts to resolve it were carried out in the framework of the UN, OSCE and other international institutions. However, the decisions on the Caucasian conflict were taken on a bilateral or quadrilateral level. Although, for example, activists from the 'de facto South Caucasus states' drew analogies between the UN-mediated process in Kosovo and the UN-mediated Geneva talks.

In addition, Kosovo functioned under the auspices of the UN (which is an undeniable fact), while Abkhazia and South Ossetia were under the rule of regimes that were globally seen as controlled by Moscow. Nowadays the

European Union's Special Representative in Kosovo and the European Union Rule of Law Mission (EULEX), which has replaced the UN mission in Kosovo (UNMIK), continues to implement its mandate. At the same time, international engagement in the South Caucasus had declined considerably. 'The departure of the UN mission, UNOMIG, was a moment that made little difference to the governments in Tbilisi and Moscow, but it was a big blow for Abkhazia, which lost its only permanent international presence' (de Waal, 2015).

Furthermore, Serbia, unlike Georgia, does not cooperate with the United States or other countries participating in the military operation against it, which promote the idea of Kosovo's independence on the international arena. Furthermore, Serbia was not a part of any integration associated with countries that inclined it to peace by force.

But in the neighborhood of Russia and Georgia, which was a part of the CIS at the time of the '*August conflict*', is paradoxical. Russia, in fact, was the state which carried out an independent military operation against a neighboring country and acted as the only lobbyist of the independence of its breakaway territories. Then, in the last years before the war, Georgia led in the growth of military spending, much of which was invested in retraining and re-equipping the Georgian military. Georgian forces were increasingly engaged in coalition operations in both Kosovo and Iraq, gaining considerable experience of complex military operations. The development of effective military capability also changed Georgian leadership's calculations regarding forceful solutions to conflicts.

Moreover, there were no conditions that allowed the militarization of Serbia. Significant damage to the Serbian army during the NATO operation in 1999 and the introduction of various international restrictions excluded the possibility of Belgrade's new military operations in the region.

Apart from that, the loss of Kosovo opened Serbia to the possibility of implementing its foreign policy's main priority: integration into the European Union. Serbia restored its relations completely with almost all the countries that have recognized Kosovo's independence.

Today, it is a candidate country for EU membership and in December 2015, Serbia and the EU opened the first two chapters of the negotiation dossier on the country's accession to the European Union: Chapter 32, on financial control and Chapter 35, on other business: Item 1, on normalisation of relations between Serbia and Kosovo (Accession conference with Serbia: First two chapters opened, 2015). Moreover, in the course of the April 2016 parliamentary elections, the Serbian Progressive Party (SNS), led by the current Prime Minister of Serbia, Aleksandar Vučić, gained a victory; the party supports the European integration of Serbia (BBC News, 2016).

For its part, the loss of Abkhazia and South Ossetia has reduced the chances of Georgia's accession to NATO. And diplomatic relations have not been greatly restored between them and Russia.

Nowadays, Georgia is a candidate for NATO membership, but the conflicts on the border with Abkhazia and South Ossetia are still important, while there is no such situation in Serbia's case. After all, according to the NATO Charter, a country that has unresolved conflicts on its territory cannot join the Alliance. Thus, Georgia, in comparison with Serbia, loses more by having 'frozen conflicts' on its territory since 2008.

In addition, there is another case in the Caucasus unlike Kosovo. South Ossetia's authorities still have not decided on the principles of its statehood. Therefore, South Ossetia does not exclude the possibility of joining the Russian Federation as an autonomous entity. In 2017 this 'de facto state' plans to hold a referendum on joining Russia (Sharkov, 2016).

However, for all practical purposes, Russia controls South Ossetia's leadership and all strategically sensitive appointments in its cabinet and security services. A majority of South Ossetia's population have Russian passports. That is why the inclusion of this 'de facto state' into the Russian Federation will not change anything largescale.

Thus it follows from all the above, that the differences between the two cases are more important than their similarities, and, as mentioned, they do not indicate the uniqueness of one of the cases.

So, is it still relevant to compare Kosovo/ South Ossetia and Abkhazia cases and try to guess whether Kosovo is unique, becoming a legal precedent for other 'de facto states'? Is the process of recognizing the independence of states relevant for today's realities and not the result of political speculations of great powers in pursuit of their own interests? And, finally, what are the prospects for further development of Kosovo/ South Ossetia and Abkhazia? These questions will be answered in the next part.

Future political status

Today, it can be stated that in the case of Kosovo many measures have been taken for its future productive development. These include the UN Mission in Kosovo (UNMIK), followed by the European Union's Special Representative in Kosovo, and later the European Union Rule of Law Mission (EULEX) replaced this and continues to implement its mandate. For instance, on 14th June 2016 two-thirds of the parliament of Kosovo voted for the extension of EULEX until 14th June 2018 (*b92*, 2016).

Although there are still many steps that should be taken to resolve the main problem of Kosovo, particularly the recognition of its independence by the world. However, internal problems still exist in this self-proclaimed state, which must be resolved by its government, and the countries against Kosovo's independence are still not ready to recognize it, even in the European Union.

Kosovo's integration into the European Union depends on its progress. 'There is lack of economic development in Kosovo, underdeveloped democratic standards and impeded democratic functioning of the state. Kosovo's slower progress makes the integration process with the EU more challenging than it was for the countries in the region' (Kosovo-EU Relations: The History of Unfulfilled Aspirations, 2015, p. 33). Also, Kosovo does not have contractual relations with the European Union and Kosovars still need a visa to travel within Western European countries.

It cannot be said that EU-Kosovo relations are considerably well-developed. Despite EU efforts, it has not succeeded in taking an unique stand towards Kosovo's status. This is the main obstruction to the productive development of formal relations between the EU and Kosovo. In addition, Kosovo itself does not try its best for admission to the EU. That is why 'without a change of attitude from both sides, the realization of Kosovo's aspirations for a European future will remain only pretty political rhetoric' (ibid., p. 34).

Furthermore, what will be the future status of the self-proclaimed South Caucasian states? Is a reconciliation between Georgians and Abkhazians, as well as Georgians and Ossetians possible at all? Theoretically, yes. But the situation is tremendously complicated by the ever-present Russian factor, which cannot be ignored. Undoubtedly, Moscow tightly controls every aspect of economic and political life in the above-mentioned areas. Georgia's relations with its breakaway territories remain stalled and furthermore, if South Ossetia will become officially a part of Russia in 2017, nobody will be surprised.

Concerning the recognition of these states, it seems that their independence will continue to be recognized under Russia's egis by countries that are either: allies of Moscow, with no territorial problems of their own; or small countries with no close ties to the post-Soviet space that are interested in some type of Russian support. However, an additional two or three countries, which recognize these entities, will not change the overall picture.

So, the most probable scenario for Abkhazia and South Ossetia is isolation and support only by Russia. But 'de facto states' and Georgia's membership in NATO remain a permanent topic of discussion. Perhaps new leadership in Russia, or a radical policy shift of the current leadership, could promote the rapprochement of Abkhazia and South Ossetia with Georgia. But any path for this region have too many global factors involved. Thus, these territories are certainly lost to Georgia for the foreseeable future.

Besides, Georgia's current government is trying, to a certain extent, to normalize relations with Russia. It primarily supports the strengthening of Russian-Georgian economic relations. Today, for example, Russia is still the leader among importers of Georgian wine. At the same time, the interests of other players (the EU, the United States) in this conflict resolution are weak. For this reason, they are unwilling to invest sufficient diplomatic efforts in it. The strategy of engagement, which is supported by the European Union, as time shows, is not so successful as a line of conduct. Its main aim, to be honest, is to prevent the possible escalation of the conflict, but it will not lead to any sort of reconciliation between the conflicting parties. Moreover, pledging enduring support for Georgia's territorial integrity is impractical now when Abkhazia and South Ossetia are even further outside of Georgian sovereignty than they were before the war (Cooley and Mitchel, 2010).

One more thing should be noted: Kosovo is more likely to become a full-fledged state, in contrast to South Ossetia and Abkhazia, whose status, in the foreseeable future, will not be recognized by most countries of the world. Although, due to the complex dynamics of the political processes both worldwide and in that region, it is extremely difficult to guess the future settlement of the conflicts in Georgia. One point, however, can be stated with certainty: the process of developing a peace policy will take several more years or even an entire decade.

Conclusion

'Formation and recognition of states serves as an indispensable precondition for an entity's status as a sovereign state in international relations' (Fabry, 2010). This is often the result of a long confrontation between the two principles of international law: the right of nations to self-determination and the territorial integrity of the state. However, the leading countries of the world play an important role in this process.

'It seems that today recognition is a political act that has hardly to do with any legal norms' (ibid.). Everything depends on the policies of the major powers, which have their own interests and are the ones that determine the direction in which 'de facto states' develop. That is why the cases of Kosovo/ South Ossetia and Abkhazia and their comparison are still relevant and significant in this context.

Today it can be stated that international relations can often be faced with political decisions based on 'we and they' or 'our and their' antagonisms. This phenomena is correlated with the policy of double standards, once imposed by the USA, and now clearly traced on the example of the recognition of Kosovo, South Ossetia and Abkhazia. That is why, according to the opinion of Alice Lacourt (Chatnam House, 2008), 'ultimately, whether or not to recognize Kosovo's secession was a political question for individual states to decide'. Western countries, allies of the USA, supported the decision to recognize Kosovo as an independent state, but because they were unsympathetic to Russia, did not do that in the Caucasus. As a result, nowadays both sides (Western countries and Russia) strongly insist on the legality of their actions and do not intend to retreat.

At first, Russia claimed the Kosovo precedent was an impetus for the recognition of Abkhazia and South Ossetia. Then in 2014, the Russian authorities used this so-called precedent as one of the justifications for the recognition of the Republic of Crimea's independence, unilaterally seceded from Ukraine and later adopted by Russia.

In fact, it is quite unlikely that Russia's recognition of these entities in August 2008 would have ever occurred without the US-led recognition of Kosovo in February 2008. Thus, the Kosovo problem called into question and led to a revision of the fundamental principle of international law: the principle of the inviolability of borders.

As can be seen, today a collision of central powers exists on the international arena, which is manifested in the situation with Kosovo and the Caucasian territories and drawn into the sphere of certain blocks. In such conflicts, 'major players' strive to achieve their interests and their relations are based on the principles of a '*zero-sum game*'. The West adheres to the Euro-Atlantic community and Russia is the counterbalance. Therefore, there are occidental and pro-Russian approaches to the recognition of Kosovo, Abkhazia and South Ossetia, since the majority of Western countries have accepted Kosovo's independence, but do not recognize the state in the Caucasus.

Therefore, the cases of these 'de facto states' affect international legal criteria regarding secession and recognition of the independence of states. No universal standards have been developed under international law to provide a precise definition of the principles and criteria for recognition of new states. In practice, highly politicized criteria are used, some of which have little in common with categories under international law. This selective approach towards recognition of new entities (like the USA with Kosovo and Russia with South Ossetia/ Abkhazia) does not facilitate the peaceful resolution of conflicts.

That is the reason why recognition of states will continue to be vigorously debated, with supporters and opponents of recognition each citing international law and also historical and political grounds for their positions. This may lead to situations that endanger stability and security. Therefore, in order to withhold a precedent in the future and stabilize the institute of recognizing the independence of states, the international community and, primarily, the 'leading world powers' must start to develop an effective international process to recognize states under international law. This will help current realities and put an end to any controversy or disputes on the status of unrecognized states. It is high time to consider a bold, new approach.

References:

Allison, R. (2008): Russia resurgent? Moscow's campaign to 'coerce Georgia to peace'. In: *International Affairs*, p. 1145–1171.

Amnesty International (2008): Georgia/Russia: Civilians in the line of fire: the Georgia-Russia conflict. Retrieved from https://www.amnesty.org/en/documents/EUR04/005/2008/en/.

BBC (2001): Kosovo assault 'was not genocide'. Retrieved from http://news.bbc.co.uk/2/hi/europe/1530781.stm.

Broers, L. (2014): Mirrors to the world: the claims to legitimacy and international recognition of the de facto States in the South Caucasus. In: *The Brown Journal of world affairs*, p. 145–159.

Chatnam House (2008): Kosovo: International Law and Recognition of Kosovo. Retrieved from https://www.chathamhouse.org/sites/files/chathamhouse/public/Research/International%20Law/il220408.pdf.

Cooley, A.; Mitchel, L. A. (2010): Engagement without Recognition: A New Strategy toward Abkhazia and Eurasia's Unrecognized States. Washington. In: *The Washington Quarterly* (59-73).

European Council, Council of the European Union (2015, December, 14): Accession conference with Serbia: First two chapters opened. Retrieved from http://www.consilium.europa.eu/en/press/press-releases/2015/12/14-accession-conference-serbia/.

Fabry, M. (2010): Recognizing states: International society and the establishment of new states since 1776. New York: Oxford University Press.

International Alert (2011): The policy of non-recognition in the context of the Georgian-Abkhaz conflict. Retrieved from http://www.international-alert.org/resources/publications/politics-non-recognition-context-georgian-abkhaz-conflict#sthash.1PfFPohB.dpbs.

Kosovo Foundation for Open Society (2015): Kosovo – EU Relations: The History of Unfulfilled Aspirations? Retrieved from http://kfos.org/wp-content/uploads/2013/04/Kosovo-EU-Relations-The-History-of-Unfulfilled-Aspirations.pdf.

Montevideo Convention on the Rights and Duties of States (1933). Retrieved from https://www.ilsa.org/jessup/jessup15/Montevideo%20Convention.pdf.

Serbia election: Pro-EU Prime Minister Vucic claims victory (2016). In: *BBC*. Retrieved from http://www.bbc.com/news/world-europe-36122928.

Sharkov, D. (2016): Separatist Georgian Region to Vote on Joining Russia in 2017. Retrieved from http://europe.newsweek.com/separatist-georgian-region-vote-joining-russia-2017-464375?rm=eu.

Tanjug, Beta (2016): Council of European Union extends EULEX mandate. Retrieved from http://www.b92.net/eng/news/politics.php?yyyy=2016&mm06&dd=15&nav_id=98319.

Transcript of Annual Big Press Conference (2008). Retrieved from http://en.kremlin.ru/events/president/transcripts/24835.

United Nations (2014): Status of internally displaced persons and refugees from Abkhazia, Georgia, and the Tskhinvali region/ South Ossetia, Georgia. Retrieved from http://www.un.org/ga/search/view_doc.asp?symbol=A/68/868.

U.S. Department of State: The Case for Kosovo. Retrieved from http://www.state.gov/p/eur/ci/kv/c24701.htm.

Waal, Thomas de (2015): Crimea, Russia and Options for Engagement in Abkhazia and South Ossetia. Retrieved from http://carnegieendowment.org/2015/11/26/crimea-russia-and-options-for-engagement-in-abkhazia-and-south-ossetia-pub-62122.

Case Caucasus

The OSCE in Nagorno-Karabakh: Can the 2016 German Chairmanship of the OSCE Make a Difference?

Frederick Schröder

***Abstract**: In this paper, the author attempts to make one short historical overview of the conflict in (and over) Nagorno-Karabakh. It will also explain which challenges the OSCE had – especially Germany, as the chairman in 2016 – in finding solutions to this conflict.*

***Keywords**: OSCE, Nagorno-Karabakh, conflict solution*

In 2016, Germany took over the chairmanship of the OSCE. Since Germany wants to foster dialogue, restore trust and enhance long-term security in Europe, it is emphasizing crisis and conflict management in the OSCE area. The conflict in Nagorno-Karabakh is also part of the agenda, since new tensions arose in 2016. Even though another ceasefire was brokered on the 5th of April 2016, conflict is still likely to break out again. This article will examine whether the German chairmanship can help solve the conflict and what possible obstacles can emerge.

1. Historical Review of the Nagorno-Karabakh Conflict

The Nagorno-Karabakh conflict is an armed conflict between two states – Armenia and Azerbaijan – over the region of Nagorno-Karabakh. Between 1988 and 1994, tensions arose and between 20,000 and 30,000 people died while nearly 1.5 million people became refugees and had to flee (Lindenstrauss, 2015, p. 97).

To understand the conflict in detail, it is necessary to take a closer look at the history of Azerbaijan, Armenia and especially of the region of Nagorno-Karabakh. The historic dimension of the conflict is very important because both parties use their history to legitimize their claims in the region and to justify their actions.

Already the name '*Karabakh*' gives a hint about the history of the region because it contains the Turkish word 'Kara', which means 'black' and also 'Bao', which means 'garden' in the Persian language. The ending 'Bakh' is a russification of the English word 'bag', while 'Nagorno' simply means 'mountainous' (Bashlinskaya, 2010, p. 13). So the name already indicates that the history of the region was mainly influenced by Persia, the Ottoman Empire and Russia.

The claims of Azerbaijan and Armenia date back even further and are difficult to prove. The Armenians argue that Nagorno-Karabakh belonged to an Armenian kingdom in the 4th century BC. In contrast, Azerbaijan believes that there are descended from tribes of Caucasian Albanians, who lived in the region from 2000-1000 BC (ibid.).

After the Ottomans and Persians conquered the region, the Russian empire expanded. This led to two Russo-Persian wars, which concluded with peace treaties: The Treaty of Gulistan in 1813 and the Treaty of Turkmanchai (Cornell, 1999, p. 5). The treaties ended the Russian victory over Persia, and Nagorno-Karabakh came under Russian control (Bashlinskaya, 2010, p. 18). Immediately after the treaty of Turkmanchai, Russia began to organise a population exchange. And then many Armenians left Turkey and Persia and came to Karabakh (ibid.). The population exchange led to 130,000 Armenians coming to Karabakh between 1828 and 1830, while big parts of the Azeri population were forced to leave (cf. ibid.). The immigration of Armenians went on, so the amount of Armenians in the region increased from nine percent in 1823 to fifty-three percent in 1880 (ibid.).

After the October Revolution in Russia in 1917, new tensions arose[1]. The power vacuum in the region, created by Russia's absence, led to a civil war, where many Armenians and Azeris in Baku and in Nagorno-Karabakh died (Krüger, 2009, p. 15).

But the Russians were still interested in the Transcaucasian region, so they founded the 'Caucasian Office', which coordinated the Bolshevik infiltration and the Russian invasion of the region (ibid., p. 18). In April 1920, Soviet soldiers conquered Azerbaijan, and in May of the same year, they conquered Nagorno-Karabakh (cf. ibid., p. 20). On 5th of July 1921, the Caucasian Office decided that Karabakh should belong to Azerbaijan, while also having special autonomy rights. According to Babajew (2014, p. 33), Azerbaijan fulfilled this requirement by establishing the 'Nagorno-

---

[1] See more in Cornell (1999).

Karabakhskaya avtonomnaya oblast'[2]. Nagorno-Karabakh remained part of the Azerbaijan Soviet Socialist Republic (ASSR) until 1991.

Glasnost and *Perestroika* led to the emergence of national movements in Nagorno-Karabakh. On the 20th of February 1988, the Soviets of the Oblast decided to ask the Supreme Soviets of Azerbaijan, Armenia and USSR to unite the NKAO with the Armenian SSR (cf. ibid., p. 14). The proposal was rejected, which led to riots and violence in the region (Krüger, 2009, p. 22). The reactions of the Supreme Soviet of Armenia and the National Soviet of Karabakh followed on the 1st of December 1989, by voting for unification. However, Moscow decided to return the administrative power of the region back to Azerbaijan (cf. ibid., p. 24). The next stage of the conflict's growth happened after the dissolution of the USSR.

In 1991, the conflict between Azerbaijan and Armenia lost the stability that kept the conflict contained for years (Cornell, 1999, p. 31). Between 1992 and 1994, they fought a bloody war, which led to many displaced persons and violence against civilians (Waal, 2003, p. 286). Lindenstrauss (2015, p. 98) writes that as a result of the war, Armenia conquered Karabakh as well seven other territories[3] and forced the Azeris to leave[4]. In the end, Armenia captured fourteen percent of Azeri territory, which also meant an ethnic cleansing of these regions (ibid.).

Since 1992, the Minsk Group has tried to solve the conflict. In 1994, a Russian brokered a ceasefire that was signed. But both sides violated it at the line of contact, where both parties face each other today (Paul and Sammut, 2016, p. 1).

In April 2016, the conflict escalated again, leading to the heaviest fighting since 1994 (*BBC News*, 03.04.2016). Because of this, some experts call it the 'Four-Day-War' (Background Briefing on the Nagorno-Karabakh conflict, 16.05.2016). One hundred and ten people died during the fighting and who started the war remains unclear (*Zeit Online*, 17.05.2016). But a ceasefire was signed on the 6th of April. Both Armenia and Azerbaijan are complained about violations and ongoing fighting.

---

[2] NKAO, 7th of July 1923.

[3] Aghdam, Fizuli, Jebrail, Kelbajar, Kubatly, Zengelan, Lachin (s. in Waal, 2003, p. 286).

[4] See more in *BBC News* from 03.04.2016.

2. German Chairmanship 2016

On the 1st of January, Germany took over the chairmanship of the OSCE for the second time (previously in 1991). The German Chairmanship will especially focus on crisis and conflict management in the OSCE area. The plan of the new office is to 'increase activities to resolve the protracted conflicts in the OSCE area by supporting the current negotiating formats and mechanisms for the conflicts in Nagorno-Karabakh (the Minsk Process), Transdniestria (5+2 Talks) and the Geneva International Discussions on the conflict in Georgia' (Federal Foreign Office, 2016, p. 4).

The Minsk Group of the OSCE consists of three Co-chairs: France, Russia and the United States; the permanent members: Belarus, Germany, Italy, Sweden, Finland, and Turkey, as well as Armenia and Azerbaijan; plus the OSCE Troika, which is on a rotating basis. Even though the Minsk Group has tried to solve the conflict, for a long time it did not succeed to find a proper solution for both parties. As can be seen, even a new view of the violence in the region arose in 2016, which led to the 'Four-Day-War'.

While Germany made crisis and conflict management a priority of its chairmanship, can they make a difference as the chairman? To answer this question, the obstacles should be looked at. The first issue Germany will face is below.

a) The main issues of the parties are not solved:

- the status of Karabakh;
- the status of the other 7 regions;
- the right of the return of refugees and IDPs;
- status and size of Lachin corridor[5] (Faber and Kasprzyk, 2003, p. 1).

Furthermore, the parties believe that time is on their side. Azerbaijan thinks they can use time to build a stronger army; Nagorno-Karabakh and many Armenians believe that 'the continuation of the status quo will gradually strengthen their position, since the de facto status will increasingly appear to the outside world to be accepted as the reality on the ground the longer the present stalemate endures' (Hopmann, 2015, p. 173).

---

[5] It connects Armenia and Stepanakert.

b) The Minsk Group itself: The Minsk Group itself was and is criticized because of various reasons. Russia, for example, is criticised in many different aspects. First of all, many experts see Russia as the main benefiter from the current situation, because holding the *status quo* means they still have control over the region (Hedenskog and Korkmaz, 2016, p. 1).

Russia also delivers weapons to both countries and is responsible for ninety percent of the arms supplied to Armenia, but at the same time is also providing Azerbaijan with weapons[6] (cf. Halbach and Smolnik, 2013, p. 29). Furthermore, Russia is the main guarantor of Armenian security. Armenia is a part of the Russian-led Collective Security Treaty Organisation and the Eurasian Economic Union[7]. Moreover, Russia has a base in Gyumri and an airbase in Erebuni near Yerevan (Hopmann, 2015, p. 173). Based on these factors, Russia is accused of being biased towards Armenia.

But also the other Co-chairs of the Minsk Group, France and the USA, are accused of favouring Armenia, because of the large Armenian diasporas in their countries (ibid., p. 172). France is also criticized for not representing the EU in a good way. As one EU official stated: 'We get more information about the Minsk Group from Russia and the United States than we do from France' (Huff, 2011, p. 35). But not only are the Co-chairs criticized, some experts also think that representatives of Nagorno-Karabakh and of the Azerbaijani IDPs should be part of the negotiations (cf. Halbach and Smolnik, 2013, p. 29).

c) External Actors: The number of external actors who are able to influence the conflict is very high. A reason for that is the strategic importance of the Caucasus regions for energy supplies and its location in general. Not only the members of the Minsk Group are interested in the conflict, but also Turkey, Iran and Israel.

Turkey is supporting their 'brother nation' Azerbaijan and announced publicly that 'Turkey will stand shoulder to-shoulder with Azerbaijan against Armenian aggression and occupation until the end of time' (Hedenskog and Korkmaz, 2016, p. 2). President Erdogan stated that 'Karabakh will

---

[6] 60 percent of arms supplies between 2007 and 2011.

[7] Many experts think that Armenia was pressured to cancel negotiations with the EU to join the EEU (Hopmann, 2015, p. 173).

surely be returned to its rightful owner, Azerbaijan, one day' (Huff, 2011, p. 35).

Because of tensions with Azerbaijan (nowadays and historically), and a rivalry in the energy sector, Iran is supporting Armenia (Cornell, 1999, p. 3). As Azerbaijan and Israel both regard Iran as an existential threat, Israel is supporting Azerbaijan and is fostering deeper cooperation and supplying weapons (Lindenstrauss, 2015, p. 71). Allegedly, Azerbaijan is using Israeli drones in Nagorno-Karabakh (Gibbons-Neff, 05.04.2016). As can be seen, there are many actors with different strategic and personal interests in the region, which make it very difficult for the OSCE to negotiate and broker between the parties.

d) Weakness of the OSCE: Another issue regarding the Nagorno-Karabakh conflict is the weakness of the OSCE. First of all, the OSCE is not able to fulfill its task to observe the Line of Contact properly, because only six international observers are allowed (and 11 regional posts)[8]. They must observe 20,000 troops on either side, facing one another across a 175-kilometre line (Waal, 01.08.2010). The observers are not based in the region and must announce their visits to the Line of Contact, separating Armenian and Azerbaijani forces in advance (Kucera, 08.04.2016). Moreover, an OSCE arms embargo has been in force since 1992 (*SIPRI*), which Russia ignores. But also other state like Israel or Turkey is delivering weapons to the conflict parties.

3. Conclusion

As presented in the current issue, the conflict in Nagorno-Karabakh is a very difficult one to solve. It is very hard to convince the two countries to come to a solution, because both countries see Nagorno-Karabakh as part of their heritage and history. The keeping of this territory plays an important role for the national identity of both sides. Every solution that has been presented to them and aimed towards cooperation between the two countries, was seen as a zero-sum game from both sides.

[8] See p. 33 in *Survey of OSCE field operations*, 2016.

Furthermore, the main questions of the conflict are not answered yet, which means every effort trying to avoid these topics while negotiating the conflict is doomed to fail. The number of external powers and actors is another important aspect of the OSCE's failure. These powers often try to satisfy their own needs and interests and are working against each other. For some powers, like Russia, even the status quo of having a conflict is best, which makes it very difficult to have progress in the conflict and the region.

This also leads to the weakness of the OSCE, because Russia, Armenia and Azerbaijan, as members of the OSCE, have the right to decide what OSCE activities will happen in Nagorno-Karabakh. Consequently, the OSCE is a consensus-based organisation – it cannot be ignored or pushed. That is the main reason for having such a small amount of observers for such a huge amount of soldiers and a nearly 200 kilometre line of contact.

Thus, in conclusion, Germany will have a small possibility to have a huge impact on solving the conflict. Furthermore, the international agenda presented a deep confrontation in general between Russia and the West (in Ukraine, Georgia, Transnistria), which should be solved first, before engaging with Russia in Nagorno-Karabakh.

So what can Germany do? At first, small steps have to be taken, rebuild trust and confidence in the OSCE and used the OSCE as a platform to cooperate with Russia again. Regarding Nagorno-Karabakh, it will be very important that the line of contact and the ceasefire will be respected. Only then can further steps be made to reach a resolution to the conflict. In summary, has to be concluded that the conflict in Nagorno-Karabakh will be a difficult one to solve because of the number of problematic issues and external actors.

References

Armenien und Aserbaidschan versprechen Friedensgespräche (2016). In: Zeit Online, 17.05.2016. Retrieved from: http://www.zeit.de/politik/ausland/2016-05/berg-karabach-waffenruhe-armenien-aserbaidschan-john-kerry.

Babajew, Aser (2014): Weder Krieg noch Frieden im Südkaukasus. Hintergründe, Akteure, Entwicklungen zum Berg-Karabach Konflikt. Baden-Baden: Nomos.

Bashlinskaya, Aydan (2010): Die völkerrechtliche Bewertung des militärischen Konflikts zwischen Armenien und Aserbaidschan um Berg-Karabach. Das Krisenmanagement durch die Vereinten Nationen, die Europäische Union und die OSZE. 1. Aufl.: Nomos (Schriftenreihe des Zentrums für Europäische Rechtspolitik der Universität Bremen (ZERP), 60).

Cornell, Svante E. (1999): The Nagorno-Karabakh Conflict (46). Retrieved from: https://is.muni.cz/el/1423/podzim2012/MVZ208/um/35586974/Cornell_The_Nagorno-Karabakh_Conflict.pdf.

Faber, Jan-Mient and Kasprzyk, Andrzei (1993): How Should the OSCE Deal with the Nagorno-Karabakh Conflict? In: Helsinki Monitor (Volume 14, Issue 1), p. 1–6.

Federal Foreign Office (2016): Renewing dialogue, rebuilding trust, restoring security. The priorities of the German OSCE Chairmanship in 2016. Retrieved from: www.diplo.de/GER2016OSCE.

Gibbons-Neff, Thomas (2016): Israeli-made Kamikaze drones spotted in Nagorno-Karabakh conflict. In: Washington Post, 05.04.2016. Retrieved from: https://www.washingtonpost.com/news/checkpoint/wp/2016/04/05/israeli-made-kamikaze-drone-spotted-in-nagorno-karabakh-conflict/.

Halbach, Uwe and Smolnik, Franziska (2013): Der Streit um Bergkarabach. Spezifische Merkmale und die Konfliktparteien. Berlin. Retrieved from: https://www.swp-berlin.org/fileadmin/contents/products/studien/2013_S02_hlb_smk.pdf.

Hedenskog, Jakob and Korkmaz, Kaan (2016): he interests of Russia and Turkey in the Nagorno-Karabakh conflict. Retrieved from: https://www.foi.se/download/18.1b4084ea15549d027d14b79/1466509555042/RUFS+Briefing+No.+35+.pdf.

Hopmann, P. Terrence (2015): Minsk Group Mediation of the Nagorno-Karabakh Conflict: Confronting an 'Intractable Conflict'. In: OSCE Yearbook 2014, p. 167–179.

Huff, Ariella (2011): The role of EU defence policy in the Eastern neighbourhood (Occasional Paper 91).

Krüger, Heiko (2009): Der Bergkarabachkonflikt: Eine juristische Analyse. Dordrecht [u.a.]: Springer.

Kucera, Joshua (2016): Nagorno-Karabakh: Trying to Separate Fact from Fiction, 08.04.2016. Retrieved from: http://www.eurasianet.org/node/78216.

Lindenstrauss, Gallia (2015): Nagorno-Karabakh: The Frozen Confict Awakens. In: Strategic Assessment (Volume 18, No. 1), p. 97–108.

Nagorno-Karabakh violence: Worst clashes in decades kill dozens (2016). In: BBC News, 03.04.2016. Retrieved from: http://www.bbc.com/news/world-europe-35949991.

Paul, Amanda and Sammut, Dennis (2016): Nagorno-Karabakh and the arc of crises on Europe's borders.

Stockholm International Peace Reasearch Institute (SIPRI) (2012): OSCE arms embargo on Nagorno-Karabakh (Azerbaijan). Retrieved from: https://www.sipri.org/databases/embargoes/eu_arms_embargoes/azerbaijan, zuletzt aktualisiert am 02.10.2012, last checked on 06.12.2016.

The Secretariat Conflict Prevention Centre (2016): Survey of OSCE field operations. Retrieved from: http://www.osce.org/secretariat/74783?download=true.

U.S. State Department (2016): Background Briefing on the Nagorno-Karabakh conflict. Vienna, Austria. Retrieved from: http://www.state.gov/r/pa/prs/ps/2016/05/257263.htm.

Waal, Thomas de (2003): Black Garden. Armenia and Azerbaijan through Peace and War. New York and London: New York University Press. Retrieved from: https://raufray.files.wordpress.com/2010/11/0814719449.pdf.

Waal, Thomas de (2010): Remaking the Nagorno-Karabakh Peace Process, 01.08.2010. Retrieved from: http://carnegieeurope.eu/2010/08/01/remaking-nagorno-karabakh-peace-process-pub-41367.

Waffenstillstand in Berg-Karabach brüchig (2016). In: euronews, 08.04.2016. Retrieved from: http://de.euronews.com/2016/04/08/waffenstillstand-in-berg-karabach-bruechig.

Case Ukraine

The Construction of Donbas Regional Identity in Political and Media Discourses: Implications of the Conflict

Yuliya Abibok

Abstract: *This article examines Ukrainian and Donetsk local media discourses about Donbas in the pre-war period (2006-2008 and 2010). The aim of this work is to define Donbas myths and stereotypes through regional and all-national perception, identify the main Donbas discourses and their historical and social background, and to estimate a role of national media in promoting and cementing the Donbas regional identity. Discourse analysis of both regional and national media texts is implemented to achieve this aim.*

Keywords: *Donbas, Donetsk, media discourse, regional identity, myths and stereotypes, division, war*

Introduction

The 2013-14 Euromaidan protests in Kyiv, which were followed by the annexation of Crimea and a war in Eastern Ukraine, actualized the old problem of 'two Ukraines' (Hrytsak, 2007), which was widely discussed after the 2004-05 '*Orange Revolution*'. The Orange Revolution, and the election campaign that preceded these events, clearly showed the division between the assumed pro-Russian and pro-Western parts of the country. As Luhansk professor Illia Kononov (*Regionalni identychnosti v suchasniy Ukraini*, 2007, p. 13) noted, each of them had their own 'project' for the Ukrainian state: one was based on professional and social identification, the other on ethnicity.

There were several popular explanations of the Ukrainian division. Almost all Donbas researchers pointed towards historical conditions, since different parts of modern Ukraine belonged to different states and empires, with different social experiences and under different ideological influences (Hrytsak, 2007; Osipian, 2006, 2012, 2015; Sereda, 2007; Zhurzhenko, 2014). The Russian and then Soviet influence was longer and stronger in the East of Ukraine. But this theory does not give a complete explanation to different identities and attitudes toward Kyiv in the territory of 'pro-

Russian' Southeast Ukraine. That is why some other researchers (Zhurzhenko, 2014; Zimmer, 2004, 2007; Pop-Eleches and Robertson, 2015) insist on a key role of local elites in shaping regional identities and political loyalties.

The Russian role, primarily the role of Russian media, was also an obvious subject of study (Osipian 2006, 2012, 2015; Zhurzhenko, 2014[1]). At the same time, the role of assumed pro-Western political elites and central Ukrainian media was not researched. Thus, Lviv sociologist V. Sereda (Sereda, 2007) published a study in 2007, which shows a completely opposite evaluation of historical events using Lviv and Donetsk newspapers. So now, this article is an attempt to study and compare both national and regional political discourses about Donbas in a pre-war period. The purpose of this study is to analyze how Ukrainian national media engaged in the 'war of identities' (Zhurzhenko, 2014, p. 250) between the 'two Ukraines'.

Donbas Identity: Prehistory and Development

Different researchers noted that two of the most Eastern regions of Ukraine, Donetsk and Luhansk regions, which are also known by the common name of Donbas,[2] were at the same time the most pro-Russian or pro-Soviet (Walkowitz, 1993; Zimmer, 2007; Hrytsak, 2007; Sereda, 2007). The new Ukrainian identity was still on its formation stage there, and the regional Donbas identity was the strongest one. As Kerstin Zimmer notes, 'while many key local figures would characterize their region as multiethnic, it would be more accurate to view it as nonethnic' (Zimmer, 2004, p. 5-6). The strong regional identity created during the Soviet time and shaped in Ukraine's independence years became the most powerful and reliable mobilization tool for Donbas political and business elites, which helped them to stay in power in the region since the middle of the 1990s (Zimmer, 2007).

---

[1] See also a Wilson's (Wilson, 1995) research about Ukrainian and pro-Russian historical arguments about Donbas belonging.

[2] Sometimes this definition is used for only Donetsk region, but geographically not only Donetsk and Luhansk, but also parts of Kharkiv and Dnipro (former Dnipropetrovsk) regions belong to Donetsk Coal Basin.

Donetsk, which was the main city of Donbas before the war in Eastern Ukraine, was founded in 1869 as a small settlement around a metallurgical plant. Numerous other settlements near plants and mines arose across the Donbas region. The rapid industrial development of this territory followed economical processes in the Russian Empire. But the imperial period of Donetsk history did not have a direct impact on the creation of local identity. The different small settlements were united to a single city (called Stalino) and to the single Donetsk oblast only in 1930s. The Donbas workers did not form a joint group. Instead there were many separate, and even rival, groups: plant workers, miners, Ukrainian peasants, Jewish merchants and tavern keepers, and other workers were grouped according to their regions of origin (Kuromiya, 2002). Migration was very common as many miners came to Donbas from Russian and Ukrainian villages only as seasonal workers. As Hiroaki Kuromiya notes, even in the time of the Bolshevik Revolution the local population was politically indifferent.

The imperial past played its role in shaping the Donbas identity only in Soviet time, when it was common practice to compare it with Soviet realities. For example, the famous Donbas workers poet Pavel Besposhchadnyy portrayed the area in completely dark tones, while under the Soviet rule the region became one of the 'locomotives' of the national economy and – especially – of the national ideology. The name Stalino itself did not mean the Soviet dictator, but the shortened form of Vladimir Lenin's definition of revolution as a 'steel locomotive' which he led. Actually the name Stalin (later – Stalino) was given to the young town in 1924 in honor of Lenin (Hrytsak, 2007, p. 38). The rapid industrialization of the 1920s, the Stakhanovite Movement in the 1930s – which started from Donbas, – and the post-war rebuilding of the city in the late 1940s and 1950s, created a strong basis for a regional self-identification. Later, in the 1960-70s, local workers felt even more special when the First Secretary of the Communist Party in the Donetsk regional committee, Vladimir Degtiaryov, made Donetsk the exemplary Soviet municipality. It was in Degtiaryov's time when Donetsk received its image (at least, internally) of 'the city of the million roses'. The miners had the highest salaries in the region and enjoyed the status of the Soviet aristocracy (Walkowitz, 1993, p. 1, 4).

Other developments, which were very important for the Donbas identity, were related to a national policy of the post-Stalin USSR. Since the end of the 1950s, it was not necessary to teach children in Ukrainian. The Ukrainian schools quickly disappeared in Donbas. Ukrainian dissident Ivan Dziuba in his famous feuilleton 'Internationalism or Russification?', written in 1965 (Dziuba, 2005), described in detail an incremental de-Ukrainization of Ukraine, when the Ukrainian language was artificially made the language of a conservative and culturally backward village. While Donbas was a highly urbanized region, there was no constant inflow of migrants from rural areas, as in, for example, Western Ukraine (Hrytsak, 2007, p. 43). Thus, the Ukrainian language quickly disappeared not only from the public space, but also from private communication in Donbas' cities and towns.

Even the late Soviet years showed all the danger of the Donbas workers' identity when miners strikes started in 1989. It is hard to measure the impact of the strikes on the breakdown of the USSR, but researchers (Walkowitz, 1993; Hrytsak, 2007, p. 45-46) point out that there was at least some impact. The Donbas miners were taught that they were the main state class and in the main city grew dissatisfied with their current working condition becoming aware of their right to demand more. Paradoxically, as Walkowitz (Walkowitz, 1993, p. 3-4) underlines, through their strikes the miners destroyed not only the USSR, but also the basis of their own identity and glory. The new country did not favor proletarians, but entrepreneurs. The economic decline of 1990s hit the former 'aristocracy' especially hard. And the unexpected Ukrainization sparked anger among Donbas people. Walkowitz writes that for many Donbas inhabitants, the independence brought restrictions rather than freedom (ibid., p. 3).

This was the initial ground for later political division in Ukraine. The new country proposed a form of lost glory to Donbas. The Ukrainian national ideologists wanted to see the region as a victim of forced Russification and genocide of Ukrainians by the Soviet regime, while locals saw themselves as the powerful economical avant-garde (Zimmer, 2007, p. 104). In the beginning of the 2000s, the region still lived in its Soviet past. As Zimmer concluded (ibid.), there were no historical alternatives to the Soviet version and no alternative vision of Donbas' future. Because local political and business elites formed a strong conglomerate and benefited from the status-quo, an appearance of competitive discourse seemed to be impossible.

During and after the 2004 presidential campaign, Donbas became even more strongly isolated because of a reciprocal hostile rhetoric. One side still propagated the Donbas Soviet identity, as well as spread the old Soviet myths about 'fascists' in the West of Ukraine and the alleged forced Ukrainization of Donbas. The other side described the Donbas elites as 'mafia', 'bandits' and 'Moscow puppets', and the Donbas population as marginalized and lumpenized. One way or another, both sides showed the people in Donbas, that they were somehow exceptional. For Donbas itself, it was not so important whether their exclusiveness was positive or negative, that is why the external 'criminal' discourse was also accepted domestically. One of the cases analyzed in this work is about a speaker, who is one of the most active internal promoters of the uniqueness of Donbas in the media. In a speech, they used criminal jargon and then commented: 'as our specially genteel Donetsk inhabitants are used to saying' (Izmaylov, 2008).

The presidential polls showed that both Donbas and Halychyna looked at the people from 'rival' regions as adversaries who want to forcefully change the other's identity by establishing their own order (*Regionalni identychnosti v suchasniy Ukraini*, p. 17-18). The direct contacts between the two regions were not active, and people from both acquired knowledge about 'others' mostly from Ukrainian and local media (ibid.). This all explains why it was so easy for Donetsk elites and Russian spin-doctors to make the local population believe that right-wing activists from the Maidan movement posed a real threat to them (Kudelia, 2014, 2016). As Kudelia (ibid., ibid.) notes, the law abolishing local languages, including Russian, could have been seen in Donbas as a clear sign of an upcoming violent reprisal for the 'Donetsk president', pro-Russian attitudes, etc.

Donbas Discourses in Ukraine before the War

Regional Discourses in a National Frame

A text published in April 2008 by the then-popular website Obkom will be used for this analysis. The text includes a number of symbols and stereotypes about the Donetsk region, used by both Donetsk and Kyiv mythmakers. It also clearly shows a conflict between opposite narratives: 'pro-Donetsk' and 'anti-Donetsk' ones. The website Obkom was created by journalists who lived and worked in Donetsk before moving to Kyiv. The text consists of two parts, which were published separately by the common headline: 'Ones don't fall down far from Mertsalov's Palm' (Mironov,

2008 a, b). The headline has two references. The first one is a Russian saying 'An apple doesn't fall down far from an apple-tree'[3]. The second is the history of the Mertsalov's Palm[4] – the widely known Donetsk symbol.

The author of the Obkom article begins with the statement that 'lords (or expressers) of Donetsk's 'collective conscious' confidently move towards establishing the myth of the unquestioning "God-chosenness" of the local people'. The cause of this article was a Donetsk regional council press release, in which the deputy head of the Council proposed to build a hydro park 'like in Kyiv' in the Kleban-Byk nature reserve in the Donetsk region. The Obkom correspondent wonders why the future Donetsk hydro park must be exactly 'like in Kyiv': there were many better ones. However, the author does not specify where better ones are; the Kyiv *hydro park* is the only known one in Ukraine. The second problem with this message for Obkom was that there was a big radioactive graveyard recently found near the Kleban-Byk, and the Council deputy speaker did not mention this.

In this short piece of the article three main discourses appeared. First, the Donetsk claimed its 'capital status', as it is mentioned further. Second, there was an extremely bad ecological situation in the region and the Donetsk elite disregarded the problem. And third, there was a conflict between the elite and common locals.

Obkom cites the headline of another message about the proposed hydro park, this time from the local newspaper. The headline was: 'Why can't we be as good as Kyiv? The Donetsk region will have its own hydro park'. The author wonders again why journalists are silent about the radiation

---

[3] The English analogue is 'Like father, like son'.

[4] The idea for Mertsalvo's Palm came from a late 19th century local businessman, who wanted to promote Donetsk through new symbols. The 'palm' was made from a railroad rail by a worker of Yuzivka Metallurgical Plant named Aleksey Mertsalov. The palm won the grand prize in Paris 1900 Exposition Universelle, which is why it was chosen as one of the new symbols. A special foundation was created for Mertsalov's Palm. Later, the foundation became a matter of public dispute between its founder and local authorities. The founder accused some authorities' figures of forcibly taking over the foundation – a kind of action, which was later widely acknowledged as a 'brand style' of Donetsk elite. Mertsalov's Palm changed the owner in favor of the authorities.

near the Kleban-Byk. Do not they care? The author mocks another publication of the same Donetsk newspaper, in which alternative places were discussed in Donetsk. One of the alternates mentioned is 'enclosed from the noisy city by three gob piles and a branch railway line, which runs from DMP (Donetsk Metallurgical Plant. – Y. A.)'; another is 'the Drinking ponds near the coking plant'. The Obkom correspondent, originally from Donetsk, writes that he would not advise someone to rest there. 'I remember this clearly, there were many more places in Donetsk, where beaches were well-developed and dead fish didn't lie by shoals along a shore at the height of the swimming season'.

After this, the author changes the topic again and focuses on the personality of the Donetsk writer, Mr. Yasenov, and local mentality. The discourse about marginalized and criminalized local population appears. Mironov, the Obkom writer, quotes Yasenov's recent interview where he said that 'a Donetsk local is the type who grew up in huts and backstreets. Even people who lived in the city center didn't have an alternative. The culture of suburbs and backstreets – that's all that was given to Donetsk. This couldn't redound upon a genotype' (Izmaylov, 2008). The Obkom correspondent writes later: 'Statements like this (about not fostering a culture of hard work, criminal elements, and grabbers who earned a fast buck in the mines) happened to be read and listened to enough, both earlier and nowadays. But is there any use of casting the blame on historical predetermination, on the "genotype"? Doesn't it understate a particular and major intelligentsia's "contribution" to shaping the "Donetsk type" of the current generation of the "Donetsk people"?' (Mironov, 2008 a).

The question is also, is there any use of comparing themselves with Kyiv or another city? Obkom quotes another of Mr. Yasenov's statements from the same interview, about people from Lviv and Donetsk. Mr. Yasenov considers Lviv people to be 'angry' and 'bitter', albeit more clever than Donetsk ones, which are more 'warm', and as 'warm' as people in Dnipro[5] or Odesa. The Obkom correspondent sees this as a declaration of Donbas exclusiveness (Mironov, 2008 a, b). At the same time, Mr. Yasenov talks about 'two Ukraines,' where Odesa and Dnipro are in the same 'camp' as

[5] The city Dnipropetrovsk was renamed in 2016 under a 'decommunization' process and today is called Dnipro.

Donetsk and are more preferable for him than Donetsk, because they are 'maybe even warmer'.

Meanwhile, Obkom notes that 'both in Soviet times and now' not every Donetsk visitor gets the impression that Donetsk people are 'warm' (Mironov, 2008 b). (But Yasenov specifies this warmth as 'hospitable, polite, benevolent, attentive, helpful, composed etc'). 'For quite a big number of people, Donetsk inhabitants at all times make a shocking impression'. The author does not provide any examples. He further criticizes 'methods of studying people who live out the Donbas borders' (Mironov, 2008 b). Therefore, while Yasenov 'draws together' Donetsk, Dnipro, and Odesa (namely, the whole Southeastern Ukraine), the Obkom author 'cuts down' Donbas from the rest of Ukraine. It is also important to mention that while Yasenov speaks only about Donetsk in his interview and notes that he does not know the rest of the region well enough, Obkom extends his observations to the whole Donbas, which consists of the Donetsk and Luhansk regions.

The Obkom correspondent sees Yasenovs' statements as similar to the older claims made by Donetsk journalist Rimma Fil. Fil was an editor-in-chief of the newspaper *The Donetsk News*, owned by local oligarch Rinat Akhmetov and close ally to Viktor Yanukovych. Obkom quotes Fil's article about her meeting with Western Ukrainians in the 2003 pre-election period: 'And the country is not big, but the difference between us, as a classic wrote, is of a huge size. All the power of anger and hatred toward us, the Donbas people, I felt every second and every hour. They, the intelligent people, simply belched anger when they themselves started to speak about us' (cited by Mironov, 2008 b). Obkom also provides another quote from Fil's text: 'We are workers. We need deeds. Our Donbas, where people mine heat for the entire country by the sweat of their brow, where people gnaw out the future for them and children by their teeth. Calm. Peaceful. Where people are used to work a sweat but not to reap someone's harvest' (ibid.).

The text itself is highly emotional and thus manipulative and consisting of traditional Soviet and modern Donbas metaphors and symbols: do not speak but do, work in hard and dangerous jobs for the country's well-being, and create a peaceful future for the children (as if there was a danger of war). At the same time, Obkom writes that 'Fil didn't go without the same old praise of her townsmen, in contrast to the rest of Ukrainians, who are nothing but handicapped villains'. In this case, the Obkom correspondent also draws the conclusion of Donbas exceptionalism from all of Ukraine, when Fil speaks only about Donbas or compares it with Western Ukraine, but not the entirety of Ukraine[6]. Obkom notes that Viktor Yanukovych and other Donbas representatives had also made speeches like this. Many journalists use the definition 'the Donetsk nation', which will be analyzed here in one more text.

The next publication Obkom points to belongs to another Donetsk journalist, Oleg Izmaylov (2008 a), who was also the interviewer of Yevgeniy Yasenov. Izmaylov asked several colleagues and friends 'whether they consider Donbas a special place'. As he writes, 'almost all replied immediately and with such passion, which was difficult to expect even from such patriots as Donetsk inhabitants. The fact that also brought joy was that almost all who replied didn't strike an attitude of sour flag-wavers. This justified the reputation of Donbas people as those who used to think critically and even with a healthy European skepticism. Maybe the mining and metallurgical culture, in which we all had grown up, exert a specific influence, after all'. Actually one of the most widespread stereotypes about the Donbas people is that they are easily manipulated and agree to do everything they are asked rather than critically thinking. The author does not specify what 'mining and metallurgical culture' means and which exact influence it may exert. Many of those who were asked could not easily be called Donetsk patriots, since they left the city and lived somewhere else. It is also not clear why the author decided that Donetsk inhabitants are exceptional patriots. At the same time, the author actually claims that his respondents, as a group, are exceptional as well given their relation to Donetsk.

The answers include all the main myths promoted by Donetsk elites or accepted by the Donetsk people from outside: the most hard-working men and the most beautiful women, strength, impudence, entrepreneurial spirit, unique talent, geniality of local people, and also gruffness, gloom, despondency, the lack of education and culture exist at the same time. Some respondents wrote that Donetsk was made exceptional by Ukrainians from

---

[6] Usually it means Halychyna or only the city of Lviv as its 'capital'.

other regions who imposed on it an image of 'oligarchs', 'bandits', 'depressive miners' and 'separatists territory', and that it should be a 'capital' of 'Russian Ukraine' or even a part of Russia.

The Obkom correspondent ironically notes that this vox populi result is a reason to create *The Society of Donbas Lovers* (Mironov, 2008 b). Indeed, Oleg Izmaylov (2008 b) in his blog post describes his idea of this society. In the text he also uses the term, 'the mining and metallurgical culture', which led to the appearance of the 'Donbas phenomenon' with 'extraordinary people' and 'the specific state of life and value of being'. Obkom quotes: 'It's time to realize that without an understanding of the role of the Donbas, its inhabitants' place in history, in modern world, it would be hard to us to save our mental and other acquisitions for tomorrow' (Mironov, 2008 b).

The Obkom correspondent points out that Donbas 'new patriots' blame their specific history and 'genotype' on all local problems. But this criticism is impossible to compare well with their praises of local spirit, mentality and habits. In fact, the author combined the opinions of several persons who in reality have opposite points of view. The full text of Oleg Izmaylov's interview (Izmaylov, 2008) with Yevgeniy Yasenov clearly shows these contradictions. The first question v whether Yasenov's interest to Donetsk history started, 'only from local patriotism, love to the home place', or from something else – shows that its author completely excludes the possibility that Yasenov could have any other primary motives except the local patriotism, not to mention a possible absence of patriotism. But Yasenov replies that he just loved history, and then Donetsk history, and only then Donetsk itself. Further on, Izmaylov asks Yasenov to point to some 'moments' in Donetsk history, which help it stand out from other industrial cities, but Yasenov only recalls some dates important for Donetsk development, including 'the time of development of post-industrial Donetsk with new architecture, which puts it to the common row with other cities as if making it equal to those having much more years' (Izmaylov, 2008). Izmaylov argues: 'Not all the cities which have more years are within their right to match to Donetsk' (ibid.).

The city's age becomes the source of painful reflections when Yasenov laughs at Donetsk 'patriots' who are proud of every local 'nondescript shed', 'only because it was build in the 19th century' (ibid.). During the interview, Yasenov constantly tries to keep his distance from local myth-making. He says that before himself, no one discussed Donetsk's past 'in an easily-accessible form', and no one tells it nowadays. He notes: 'They prefer to play in a serious history. Although I think that actually one should present history in a maximally facile, popular manner. As such it has more truth, paradoxically, because it has less ideology' (ibid.).

Izmaylov tries to receive a confirmation of Donetsk uniqueness again: 'It has been said that people are the best of what is in Donbas' (ibid.). It looks like a last attempt when previous ones, when talking about the history and architecture, failed. Yasenov still does not agree: 'Both the best and the worst. Then again, as always and everywhere' (ibid.). Izmaylov does not give up: 'Dmitriy Mendeleev, after a visit to Yuzovka and the vicinity wrote in his notebook: 'You see these people, simple-minded and nice, look directly into eyes and believe in their future… I feel fairly free with them, with this people, and I speak with them somehow more freely, and even a child understands me here, I enjoy myself with them, my heart is with them.' How would you comment on Dmitriy Ivanovich's words?' (ibid.). Yasenov replies that 'Dmitriy Ivanovich said what a Russian intellectual of 19th century should say. These words have more emotions than truth' (ibid.).

But then the statements quoted by Obkom, about Lviv, Donetsk people's 'warmth', and specific local 'genotype', followed. Yasenov finally specifies negative and positive characteristics of the Donetsk people, as he sees them. It looks like he finally admitted to the uniqueness of these people. At the end, Izmaylov asks Yasenov to describe his vision of Donetsk in twenty years. Yasenov says that he would like to see Donetsk with architecture like in Barcelona; with its own subway; without depressive suburbs, stench in the city center, widespread tuberculosis and all the negative characteristics of local people. However, he understands that it is impossible in twenty years. Yasenov states: 'I want Donetsk to be the world city rather than Donbas' capital […]. Because I awfully love this rubbish pile and people who naturally fall to swarm here. The fact that sometimes they produce true miracles – that's what is the most amazing. That's what I love about Donetsk people first of all, that's why they are unique' (ibid.).

Two more Obkom articles were also quoted in the previous one. The first has a headline: 'You can't improve 'donetskiy' by Hermitage' (*Obkom*, 07.06.2006). The definition "donetskiy" was widely used by Ukrainian media since the 2004-05 Orange Revolution and initially referred to Viktor

Yanukovych's allies originally from the Donetsk region. Then it started to identify any person from this territory. Although it had a negative connotation, local people started to use it as well to identify themselves. Even an Obkom writer, who notes that 'Russian language in a 'donetskiy's' mouth – that's the kind…', marks himself as "donetskiy" in the same text (*Obkom*, 07.06.2006). This case may show that Donbas' inhabitants identified themselves not only with their region, but also with their public representatives in Kyiv.

In another case, Obkom published a report about the anniversary of the Donbas Community in Moscow, written by the head of the Donbas Community in St. Petersburg, Sergey Lisovskiy, who personally sent the text to Obkom. The Obkom correspondent notes that 'there are completely normal people living in Donbas', but they have very dubious representatives, and 'because of their efforts you get a very back-alley impression about Donbas' (*Obkom*, 07.06.2006). Here is another attempt to draw a line between the Donbas elite and common Donbas people.

Lisovskiy's text consists of exaggerated Donbas and Soviet symbols and myths. Lisovskiy calls Donbas 'a part of God's kingdom on the Earth', 'its own civilization', 'territory of love, from where sprouts of new technologies and global management solutions will start to grow', the 'Great Donbas' and the region where 'the future of the planet is arising' (ibid.). The word 'work' ('trud' in Russian) and its derivatives are one of the most frequent in the text: Lisovskiy uses it 14 times; the author even writes 'trud' with a capital letter. The text ends by the most famous citation from the Donbas proletarian poet Pavel Besposhchadnyy 'No one has ever forced Donbas to knees, And no one gets to force' (ibid.).

The second linked text, published in the summer of 2007, is about the 75th anniversary of the Donetsk region (Kosyachkov, 06.07.2007). The text starts with a quotation of then Prime Minister Viktor Yanukovych's congratulatory text. Yanukovych writes that 'the Donbas people a long time ago became a personification of all the best of what Ukraine has, a brilliant symbol of what we as a nation are able to achieve' (ibid.). Later this first idea of unification, when the then prime-minister saw Donbas in a national context, is confronted by divisive statements by people in Donetsk. They should be 'free to celebrate our holidays and to praise our history in a way we understand this, but not in a way someone will dictate' (ibid). Actually, Yanukovych was the second person in the state after the president and had all the power not to let anyone 'dictate'; there were no restrictions for any celebrations in Donbas. But it was a time close to the start of a parliamentary campaign and the prime minister was seemingly using an old, successful political strategy. Obkom also notes that the Dnipro, Kharkiv, Vinnytsia and Odesa regions had had their 75th anniversaries before the Donetsk, but none of them held such a huge celebration.

Meanwhile, Obkom itself uses statements which are seemingly divisive. For example, Obkom quotes the congratulation by then Speaker of the Ukrainian Parliament, Alexander Moroz, when he says that on a map Donbas looks like the open palm of a hand. The Obkom correspondent writes that it looks rather like an outstretched hand (in the meaning of begging) 'or even as a gang sign' (the allusion to criminal roots of Donbas elite or even the common Donbas inhabitants).

Then the author wonders whether the Donetsk coat of arms, with a fist and sledgehammer in it, reminds Moroz of the events of October 2004 at the Central Electoral Commission headquarters where the supporters of Yanukovych's competitor, Victor Yushchenko, were beaten by hammers, or the killing of journalist Ihor Alexandrov in the Donetsk region[7]. The Obkom correspondent also mentioned the killing of the famous Ukrainian poet and dissident Vasyl Stus[8]. Obkom also notes that the 'complete' Donetsk coat of arms appeared in the autumn of 2004, during the presidential campaign, and that is why the word 'fascist' emerged in its official description. Finally, the author laughs at the latest Sergey Lisovskiy text where it is written that 'our region's destiny (Donbas and St. Petersburg. – Y. A.) is somehow similar'. Obkom writes: 'What makes the destinies similar is not specified. Maybe it is that 'donetskiye' like 'piterskiye'[9] managed to steamroll the entire country'.

Consequently, the Obkom and Oleg Izmaylov's texts show the confrontation and commixture of two different Donbas discourses – namely the local and the national ones. They both include a number of internal and external

---

[7] Alexandrov was beaten to death by baseball bats in 2001 after the start of whistle-blowing broadcasts about criminal ties of Donetsk elite; the head of the regional administration at that time was Viktor Yanukovych.

[8] Stus lived and studied in Donetsk but left it long before his death; he was killed in Soviet Russia prison in 1985.

[9] Russian president Vladimir Putin and his closest allies are from St.Petersburg.

myths and stereotypes about the region, which shape the sense of Donbas and – especially – Donetsk exclusiveness. It is also important to mention that the representatives of the Kyiv discourse (Obkom writers) also have a Donetsk background. That is why in some parts of their texts they showed themselves – intentionally or not – as mediums of the same identity (even if they criticize it) as the Donetsk writers.

National Discourses

For the next analysis three national and assumed independent media were selected: the websites *Ukrayinska Pravda* and *Obkom*, and also the *Zerkalo Nedeli* weekly newspaper. This choice is because the first and the last ones were the most reputable media outlets in Ukraine in those time while Obkom was still the web-site the most strongly focused on Donbas issues. All their publications (but not news messages) in 2010 were studied to find examples using characteristic definitions about Donbas people.

The year 2010 was chosen as it was the first year of Yanukovych's presidency, when there was no election campaign for the near future and the interest to Donbas must have been high. Two interviews were excluded from the analysis; they were with political actors and local Donbas correspondents (as the idea was to analyze not regional, but national discourse). The reason why only one Zerkalo Nedeli article was analyzed is this: the newspaper had a correspondent in Donetsk. This analysis studied seven of Obkom's and nine of Ukrayinska Pravda's articles. In total, seventeen articles for analysis were found in three media outlets.

All of these news sources mentioned the region or specific town of Yanukovych or his allies, but not for other officials or politicians. They always mentioned when a person was from Donbas because it is an additional characteristic. The second common feature is that journalists (and, supposedly, their audience) see the special definition of 'donetskiye' and Donbas as a common word with the whole specter of its 'traditional' meanings. But for Ukrayinska Pravda writers 'donetskiye' mean, first of all, people with anti-Ukrainian or pro-Russian sentiments. Some Zerkalo Nedeli correspondents also think this. And for Obkom these are people with criminal past and mafia-style habits and behavior. For example, Ukrayinska Pravda writes (soon after the Yanukovych victory): 'Indeed, no one so far spits in face of Donbas and Crimea inhabitants – on the contrary, the triumphant

Southeast got an opportunity to spit in face of Halychyna inhabitants. Therefore the Southeastern electorate observes with approval a dismantling of democratic institutions and Yanukovych's clumsy attempts to turn into the Ukrainian Putin' (Dubynyanskyy, 2010 c). Obkom, writing about the new president, notes: 'Yanukovych used to show signs of his intellectual ingenuity, when he loved publicly to boast of a clever mot, a kind of "I'll rip your arms off" or "I will sear with a hot iron", but all this modest Donetsk glamour quickly bored' (Rybnikov, 2010 d).

For Obkom the words related to Donbas representatives are: 'super suit "Adidas"[10]', "brazing torch[11]", "yoot", "gang", "dons[12]", "thug", "tough guy"' (Nyekhlyudov, 10.02.2010; Rybnikov, 2010 b, 2010 c, 2010 e; Kosmina, 09.12.2010). The website also uses other hints to the president's criminal past or childhood in Donbas (it is not always possible to clarify whether an author means only Yanukovych's criminal past in Donbas or Donbas as a criminal region itself). For example, while Yanukovych was making a decision to sign away highly enriched uranium to the USA and Russia, an Obkom correspondent expressed his doubts that it was a personal decision for Yanukovych. He writes that president did it 'in collusion with a group of persons' (Rybnikov, 2010 a).

All Ukrayinska Pravda articles are focused on pro-Russian attitudes of the powerful representatives of the new state. Their authors underline the political division between the West and East of Ukraine and the fact that politicians and intellectuals from both sides benefit from this division and actively and consciously promote further polarization (Dubynyanskyy, 2010 a, 2010 b, 2010 d, 2010 e, 2010 f; Karasiov, 16.08.2010). They all have a peaceful rhetoric towards common people from both sides, only criticizing elites. One author (Paliy, 2010 a, 2010 b) is sure that Yanukovych will finally unite Ukraine because his electorate already sees that the president acts against the interests of all Ukrainians, except himself and his closest allies. At the same time, he writes that the minister of education, Dmytro

[10] A man in 'Adidas' gym suit – while not in a gym – in Ukraine means a person from a criminal gang or a lumpenized marginal.

[11] Instrument of torture supposed to be used in a period of early post-Soviet 'wild capitalism' in Ukraine, especially in Donbas, where mafia wars often took place.

[12] Short from Donetsk or Donbas, but also a hint to a mafia, traditionally seen as an Italian social phenomenon.

Tabachnyk, who has a reputation of having the fiercest anti-Ukrainian attitude. He 'not only rewrites the history, but also admonishes Ukrainian nation – to which he belongs neither politically, nor ethnically, – who is a hero for it and who is not' (Paliy, 2010 a). It may also look like a racist denial of a non-Ukrainian national (Tabachnyk is a person of Jewish background) or of pro-Russian inhabitants belonging to Ukraine. The article is called 'A Half a Year of Blathering Rattle'. The headline refers to famous saying that 'Donbas doesn't send empty cars', which initially meant that Donbas sends freight wagons exceptionally full of coal, but later the words 'to send empty cars' obtained the meaning of idle talk and sounded like criminal jargon.

The Zerkalo Nedely article (Rakhmaninov, 29.04.2010) is very different from the rest. The author states that 'Yanukovych isn't afraid of violent motions because they are natural for him. People of this temper, men descending from this region don't engage in self-reflection. Many of them have behind them a rough and fairly specific experience of a primitive capital accumulation. With a clear vision about an ends and means balance' (ibid.). The author points out the last fight in the Ukrainian parliament, when Yanukovych's allies behaved with 'unmotivated cruelty' and 'inadequate ferocity'. The Zerkalo Nedely concludes: 'The jokes are over'. Then the author states that Yanukovych acts intentionally to hurt 'the part of Ukraine, which traditionally doesn't vote for him' as painfully as possible (ibid.). This refers to the humanitarian politics of the new president, who favours the Russian language and disapproves of Western Ukrainian heroes. For the Zerkalo Nedely correspondent, who states that Yanukovych 'is sincerely sure that a normal person could not use the Ukrainian language in real life', it is clear that this is the president's long-desired revenge for 'bygone humiliations' (ibid.). In the end, the author calls on his audience to come together around their values, which he associates with a ribbon in the colors of the Ukrainian flag. He writes that 'current developments don't make the final split of the country unavoidable. But they make the choice unavoidable' and that 'fortunately, we have nothing to lose. Because, regretfully, we have built really nothing till yet. To dismantle the construction, which Yanukovych settled down lively, would nevertheless collapse itself'.

In other words, national media in Ukraine from 2008-10 already had two different discourses about Donbas, but in their case both meanings of 'donetskiye' (that is, 'donetskiye' as haters of all Ukrainian and 'donetskiye' as bandits) were clearly negative. The split of the country in two parts, with one of them represented by Donetsk and the second, which was not defined and was often accepted as all the rest of Ukraine, was seen as a matter of fact.

Conclusions

The provided examples show that until 2008-10, the Donbas myths and stereotypes became a visible part of regional and national political, as well as media, discourses. The Donbas (and Donetsk) myths and stereotypes became so common that were widely used not only in regional, but also in national media without any explanations, as understandable and acceptable to everyone in the country. Donbas was portrayed as a mafia-style region and one of 'two Ukraines'. While the electoral maps showed the blue Southeastern Ukraine and orange West and North[13], it was Donbas (and especially Donetsk as its 'capital') that represented the 'pro-Russian' Ukraine in these discourses. It is worth mentioning that while researchers acknowledge differences in political loyalties and attitudes towards Ukraine and Kyiv in other regions of the Ukrainian East, the views about Donetsk or Dnipro, or Kharkiv inhabitants in the media, for example, are still the subject for future research.

For Ukrainian media, Donetsk became both the symbol of the political split, as well as the relation between political and business elites and Viktor Yanukovych, who was unpopular in the West and Center of Ukraine. Even those authors who tried to keep peaceful attitudes towards common Donbas people were still separating them from inhabitants of other regions.

At the same time, regional media and journalists were involved in painful self-reflection, which was inspired by 'the loss' in the '*Orange Revolution*' and the ongoing demonisation of 'donetskiypoe' from within. The mutual Ukraine-Donbas confrontation politically served both sides in turn. It made the search for a new Donetsk self-identification as a public need for that

[13] By brand colors of dominant political parties symbolics.

region. The local identity was also used as a common explanation of past and current political events related to Donetsk elites.

Donetsk media and their representatives adopted the political myths and stereotypes about Donbas people, both Soviet (about the positive exclusiveness of the region: hard-working people, 'feeding the whole Ukraine') and modern (the 'mafia-style' Donetsk and Donbas).

As a result, both Donetsk and Kyiv made their contribution to the political isolation of the region, which became one of the preconditions of the current war.

References

'Donetskogo' Ermitazhem ne ispravish (2006). In: *Obkom*. Retrieved from http://obkom.net.ua/articles/2006-06/07.1111.shtml.

Dubynyanskyy M. (2010 a, February, 11): Tomu shcho Yanukovych. In: *Ukrayinska Pravda*. Retrieved from http://www.pravda.com.ua/articles/2010/02/1-1/4752875/.

Dubynyanskyy M. (2010 b, April, 16): Humanitarnyy symulyakr. In: *Ukrayinska Pravda*. Retrieved from http://www.pravda.com.ua/articles/2010/04/16/4-938590/.

Dubynyanskyy M. (2010 c, May, 14): Proshchannya z democratiyeyu. In: *Ukrayinska Pravda*. Retrieved from http://www.pravda.com.ua/articles/201-0/05/14/5040462/.

Dubynyanskyy M. (2010 d, May, 20): Znayomtes: opozytsiya. In: *Ukrayinska Pravda*. Retrieved from http://www.pravda.com.ua/articles/2010/05/20/5060074/.

Dubynyanskyy M. (2010 e, September, 24): Trahikomediya pomylok. In: *Ukrayinska Pravda*. Retrieved from http://www.pravda.com.ua/articles/201-0/09/24/5411312/.

Dubynyanskyy M. (2010 f, October, 8): Bezalternatyvna Ukrayina. In: *Ukrayinska Pravda*. Retrieved from http://www.pravda.com.ua/articles/2010/10-/8/5454334/.

Dziuba I. (2005): Internatsionalism chy Rusyficatsiya? Kyiv: Vydavnychyi Dim 'Kyyevo-Mohylyanska Akademia'.

Hrytsak Y. (2007): Istoriya dvokh mist: Lviv i Donetsk u porivnyalniy perspectyvi. In: Lviv-Donetsk: socialni identychnosti v suchasniy Ukraini. Specialnyi vypusk. *Ukraina Moderna*, 12 (2), p. 27–60.

Izmaylov O. (2008, March, 18): Za Rodinu! Za Stalino! Donchanye govoryat o Donetske. Retrieved from http://tattarrin.livejournal.com/3730.html.

Izmaylov O. (2008 a, March, 23): Yevgeniy Yasenov: 'Ya ochen hochu, chtoby Donetsk byl gorodom mira, a ne stolitsey Donbassa'. Retrieved from http://tattarrin.livejournal.com/5554.html.

Izmaylov O. (2008 b, April, 9): Obshchestwo lyubiteley Donbassa. Obsudim? Retrieved from http://tattarrin.livejournal.com/5928.html.

Karasiov V. (2010, August, 16): Labirynty Yanukovycha. In: *Ukrayinska Pravda*. Retrieved from http://www.pravda.com.ua/articles/2010/08/16/5304092/.

Kosmina Y. (2010, December, 9): Ruka Makeyevki. In: *Obkom*. Retrieved from http://obkom.net.ua/articles/2010-12/09.1458.shtml.

Kosyachkov Y. (2007, July, 6): Yanukovych uzhe ne schitayet narod Donbassa voploshcheniyem samogo luchshego v Ukrainye. Drugiye prodolzhayut tak dumat. In: *Obkom*. Retrieved from http://obkom.net.ua/articles/2007-07/06.1430.shtml.

Kudelia S.: Domestic Sources of the Donbass Insurgency. PONARS Eurasia Policy Memo (351), p. 1–7. Retrieved from http://www.ponarseurasia.org/memo/domestic-sources-Donbass-insurgency.

Kudelia S. (2016): The Donbass Rift. In: *Russian Politics & Law* 54(1), p. 5–27.

Kuromiya, H. (2002): Svoboda i Teror u Donbasi. Ukrayinsko-Rosiyske Prykordonnya, 1870–1990-i roky. Kyiv: OSNOVY.

Mironov, A. (2008 a, April, 18): Kak stat ne khuzhe Kieva, ili Ot Palmy Mertsalova nyedalyeko padayut. In: *Obkom*.

Mironov, A. (2008 b, April, 23): Ot Palmy Mertsalova nyedalyeko padayut – II. In: *Obkom*. Retrieved from http://obkom.net.ua/articles/2008-04/23.1254.shtml.

Nyekhlyudov, Y. (2010, February, 10): Vitya 'tri protsenta': uslovno lyegitimnyi lider. In: *Obkom*. Retrieved from http://obkom.net.ua/articles/2010-02/10.1316.shtml.

Osipian, A. (2006): Why Donbass Votes for Yanukovych: Confronting the Ukrainian Orange Revolution. In: *Demokratizatsiya* 14(4), p. 495–517.

Osipian, A. (2012): Regional diversity and divided memories in Ukraine: Contested past as electoral resource, 2004-2010. In: *East European Politics & Societies* 26(1), p. 616–642.

Osipian, A. (2015): Historical Myths, Enemy Images, and Regional Identity in the Donbass Insurgency. In: *Journal of Soviet and Post-Soviet Politics and Society* 1(1), p. 109–140.

Paliy, O. (2010 a, September, 3): Pivroku hurkotinnya porozhnyaka. In: *Ukrayinska Pravda*.

Paliy, O. (2010 b, October, 29): 'Pechenye' 'profesionaliv' abo chomu vyboriv bilshe ne bude. In: *Ukrayinska Pravda*.

Pop-Eleches, G.; Robertson, G. B. (2015): Political Machines and Regional Identities. Evidence from Post-Soviet Ukraine. Retrieved from https://www.princeton.edu/csdp/events/PopEleches01222015/Pop-Eleches-Robertson-Ukraine-patronage-and-region-CSDP-2015.pdf.

Rakhmaninov, S. (2010, April, 29): Nezavisimost dlya 'chaynikov'. In: *Zerkalo Nedeli*. Retrieved from http://gazeta.zn.ua/POLITICS/nezavisimost_dlya_chaynikov.html.

Regionalni identychnosti v suchasniy Ukraini i metody ich vyvchennya. Lviv-Donetsk: socialni identychnosti v suchasniy Ukraini. Specialnyi vypusk. (2007). In: *Ukraina Moderna* 12(2).

Rybnikov, V. (2010 a, April, 16): OBYEPOPA, ili Pyatiletku raspada dosrochno. In: *Obkom*. Retrieved from http://obkom.net.ua/articles/2010-04/16.17-14.shtml.

Rybnikov, V. (2010 b, April, 30): Vitka-syn k otcu prishel. In: *Obkom*. Retrieved from http://obkom.net.ua/articles/2010-04/30.1609.shtml.

Rybnikov, V. (2010 c, September, 17): O polze vorovstva shakhmatnykh figur. In: *Obkom*. Retrieved from http://obkom.net.ua/articles/2010-09/17.1650.shtml.

Rybnikov, V. (2010 d, October, 22): Supermeny i teploye mesto pod yubkoi. In: *Obkom*. Retrieved from http://obkom.net.ua/articles/2010-10/22.1748.shtml.

Rybnikov, V. (2010 e, December, 3): O pravakh ukrainskogo cheloveka. In: *Obkom*. Retrieved from http://obkom.net.ua/articles/2010-12/03.1616.shtml.

Sereda V. (2007): Regional historical identities and memory. Lviv-Donetsk: socialni identychnosti v suchasniy Ukrayini. Specialnyi vypusk. In: *Ukraina Moderna*, p. 160–209.

Swain, Adam (ed.) (2007): Re-Constructing the Post-Soviet Industrial Region: The Donbass in Transition. London: Routledge.

Walkowitz, D. J. (1993): Normal life: Identity and the unmaking of the Ukrainian working class. Retrieved from https://www.ucis.pitt.edu/nceeer/1993-807-10-Walkowitz.pdf.

Wilson A. (1995): The Donbas between Ukraine and Russia. In: *Journal of Contemporary History* 30(2).

Zhurzhenko, T. (2014): A Divided Nation? Reconsidering the Role of Identity Politics in the Ukraine Crisis. In: *Die Friedens-Warte* 89(1/2), p. 249–267.

Zimmer, K. (2004): Ukraine: The Donetsk Factor. In: *Transitions Online*. Retrieved from https://www.ceeol.com/search/article-detail?id=216453.

Zimmer, K. (2007): Trapped in past glory. Self-identification and self-symbolisation in the Donbass. In: Adam Swain (Ed.): Re-Constructing the Post-Soviet Industrial Region: The Donbass in Transition. London: Routledge, p. 97–121.

Why the Conflict between Russia and Ukraine Is a Hybrid Aggression against the West and Nothing Else

Demian Shevko

Abstract: *This paper examines the current general scientific understanding of nonlinear wars and their features in the context of the Russo-Ukrainian relations of last decade. It also aims to analyze the concept of hybrid warfare in the framework of Russia's modern strategic military thinking and to give an exact definition to the Russo-Ukrainian conflict. This has been done by analyzing a number of scientific works and articles on hybrid wars, examining events such as annexation of Crimea and the subsequent, 'indirect' invasion of Eastern Ukraine, and also studying the statements of Russian policy makers.*

Keywords: *Russian-Ukrainian conflict, hybrid warfare, hybrid aggression, 'russkii mir', Vladimir Putin, Crimea*

The Place of Wars in Modern History

War has always been a permanent condition of the human race. While talking about the place of warfare in human history, it is appropriate to mention some interesting figures that clarify the number of wars in history, the total number of casualties and correlation of peace and war years. The following citation was taken from Encyclopedia Of The United Nations and International Agreements is rather prototypical: 'According to estimates based on the period from 3600 B.C. until 1960, mankind has known only 292 years of universal peace, and in the remaining 5268 years has faced 14,513 armed conflicts taking 1240 million human lives' (Osmanczyk, 1990, p. 1018). But with destruction, military conflicts also brought technological and cultural progress to societies. The geopolitical map of the world often changed fundamentally after the end of big wars. The *Versailles-Washington* and *Yalta-Potsdam* systems of international relations are an excellent confirmation of this.

As the years passed, the forms and methods of war changed. It is difficult to put it in words better than Sun Tsu did: '… just as water retains no constant shape, so in warfare there are no constant conditions' (Sun Tsu, n.d.). The 20th century became a turning point in methods of warfare. This is because of other unprecedented developments in information (and other) technologies and means. It was also due to the philosophical comprehension of the two world wars that called into question the existence of mankind in itself. The end of the 'Cold War' also seriously influenced the format of international relations and the style of warfare. The world transfered from a bipolar to a unipolar one. This was followed by a quick transformation to a multipolar world with several dominant centers with different potentials.

In these conditions hybrid warfare turned into one of the main instruments of influence in international relations. Its indistinct nature disperses the attention of world leaders and societies. Also, it allows states to wage 'hidden' wars and reach geostrategic goals without formal violations of fixed international rules. Technology and globalization had a significant transformational effect on warfare in the 21st century. Military force is no longer regarded as the determining factor of victory or defeat.

In the 21st century, the main geopolitical conflict of the world gradually developed along a 'Russia – the West (mainly USA and NATO)' axis (MacAskill, 2016). Owing to a coincidence of circumstances and a range of factors (which we will analyse below), the Russian Federation actively started to strengthen and resume its geopolitical impact in the world. It especially strives to reach domination in post-Soviet territories. The well-known 'Brzezinski formula' is about the impossibility of restoring Russia's power without control over Ukraine, explaining Russia's special attention to this country (Brzezinski, 1998).

For some time, Western leaders were successful in 'not noticing' and 'closing eyes' to the decisive and aggressive actions of Vladimir Putin's Russia in the international arena. However, the confrontation between the largest state of the world and the largest state in Europe, which started in 2014, drew the attention of the whole civilized world. With all the information presently available, this conflict could be characterized as a hybrid aggressive war by Russia towards Ukraine (Horbulin, 2015, January).

Background of the Hybrid War Phenomena

It is difficult to say when and where the first hybrid war took place and even if there is such information. Numerous examples of hybrid type warfare reach back to ancient times.

The oldest known military treatise in the world, The Art of War by Sun Tsu, brilliantly illustrates many aspects of the modern hybrid war concept (Sun Tsu, n.d.). Scythian fighting techniques included false retreats, sudden raids behind enemy lines, destroying food stocks, stealing cattle and burning the vegetation, and they could be easily characterized as hybrid (Eliseev, 2013). The same applies to the Athenian strategy in the Peloponnesian War against the more powerful Sparta (Kagan, 2004). Much later, in the Peninsular War of 1808-1814, a 'hybrid army'[1] of Spanish guerillas united with regular British and Portuguese forces generated decisive military impacts on Napoleon's Grand Army (Chartrand, 2004).

Dr. Harlan K. Ullman shares the idea that hybrid wars are as old as war itself. In particular, he notes that hybrid warfare was 'very much in evidence' at the beginning of the 20th century. Lenin and the Soviet state used hybrid elements to seize its young neighbors (Estonia, Ukraine, Finland and others). In those days, informational warfare meant occupying and controlling telephone communications. During the First World War, cyber components boiled down to code breaking and either tapping into or disrupting the undersea telegraph cables that linked London, Paris and Berlin with their overseas bases and colonies. Economic sanctions were imposed by unrestricted submarine warfare and blockades. Propaganda labeled the enemy as barbarians committing countless atrocities against innocent civilians (Ullman, 2015). During World War II, the Soviet Army integrated and synchronized irregular units of ill-equipped partisans with its conventional military forces, aiming to generate multiple hybrid-type effects from 1941 to 1945 (McCulloh, Johnson, 2013).

Therefore, attributing the hybrid warfare as a phenomenon simply of innovation is not fully valid. At the same time, we should understand that the current interpretation of hybrid warfare differs significantly from previous thought. Hybrid elements of war never played principal roles of fighting in

---

[1] Hybrid in a sense that it was composed of non-professional Spanish troops and regular British and Portuguese formations.

the past. They served as a supporting component, an useful addition to the actions of regular troops while victory was achieved by traditional (conventional) means and methods.

Prior to the events in Ukrainian in 2014, the term ‘hybrid warfare’ was widely used to describe the strategy practiced by the Hezbollah in the 2006 Lebanon War. The Hezbollah movement, of which its forces had been trained, equipped and inspired by Iran, surprised Israel with its complex combination of guerrilla and traditional military tactics. Hezbollah used advanced weaponry and communication systems normally associated with the armed forces of developed countries. Furthermore, Hezbollah made effective use of the Internet and other media resources for information and a propaganda campaign that influenced global opinion during the course of the conflict (McCulloh, Johnson, 2013).

A hybrid warfare phenomenon which occurred in the modern sense appeared during the ‘Cold War’. The war had a hybrid nature in many ways. No one fought in the same way as the First or Second World War. However, periodically in different parts of the world – in Korea, Vietnam, Cuba, Angola, Nicaragua, Afghanistan – hybrid confrontation between the East and the West took place. On the one hand, this confrontation was quite composed: the ideological and economic competition of two world systems – capitalism and socialism. On the other hand, it had the vivid traits of a hot war in the arms race. It was also bloody enough. Human casualties during civil and local conflicts were on the conscience of either the USSR or the USA (Centre for Global Studies “Strategy XXI”, 2016).

In September 2010, the U.S. Army Chief of Staff, General George Casey, provided the following description of hybrid threats in the operational environment: ‘There are not going to be clear threats and clear solutions… I don’t see us ever getting back to that. And, the hybrid threats are fuzzy… but, basically what they’re saying is: people that oppose us (one) aren’t going to confront us head on, and (two) they are going to come at us asymmetrically – as you would expect any enemy to do. And they’re going to use every means available to them – and one of the things we saw in Lebanon in 2006 was that you have non-state actors now that have the instruments of state power… and as we saw on September 11th that can produce catastrophic results’ (Fleming, 2011).

Fifty years earlier, the Colonel of the Tsarist Army, who fought in First World War and later against the Bolsheviks in the Russian Civil War, set up a surprisingly similar concept of future wars as Casey's concept. Evgeniy Messner, the most prominent Russian military theorist of the 20th century, immigrated to Latin America after the Second World War. In Argentina, he focused on the conceptualization of the covert conflicts of the 'Cold War'. He noticed the emergence of new phenomena and formulated the theory of *hybrid war* (*Myatezh Voina*) in his fundamental work 'The Face of Modern War', published in 1959 in Buenos Aires (Messner, 1959; Klus, 2016). Messner wrote 'One should stop thinking that war is when they fight, and peace is when they don't fight. States can be in the state of war without obvious fighting… Modern form of war is rebellion. It is a deviation from dogmas of classical art of war… Violence (intimidation and terror) and guerrilla warfare is the main arms in this war… using in the war of guerrillas, wreckers, terrorists, saboteurs, propagandists will acquire immense sizes' (Messner, 1959). In his work we can also find an interesting quotation regarding wars of the future: 'In the past wars annexation of territory was considered as most important. In future, wars' annexation of souls of the enemy-state will be considered more important' (Messner, 1959).

Definition Gap

Despite the big interest in the Russo-Ukrainian conflict in Western scientific literature, there is still a debate on how to define events that Ukraine and the world faced from early 2014. This debate stems from a gap in terminology and the absence of a generally accepted definition (Fleming, 2011). The annexation of Crimea and follow–up developments in Eastern Ukraine led to a search for terminology to describe the character of the conflict (Kofman, Rojansky, 2015). Most Western observers use the neutral term *Russo-Ukrainian crisis*, while others argue about shades of the concept of *hybrid warfare*, focusing on one or another of its components. Their opponents claim that it is an internal conflict, denying its bilateral nature. The overall image of this phenomenon that emerges from the literature is rather vague. There is not any consensus among scholars on the exact or unique definition of hybrid warfare. Not surprisingly, many terms for this phenomenon arose. *New age war. Postmodern war. Unconven-*

tional war. Nonlinear war. Diffuse war. Creeping War. Proxy-war. Asymmetric war. Ambiguous war. Network-centric warfare. Rebellion war. These and other terms, the most appropriate of which still to be determined, reflect the different features of the hybrid war phenomenon that Ukraine has been confronted with in recent years (Centre for Global Studies "Strategy XXI", 2016).

Google search shows hundreds of results covering the issue. More and more attention is paid to the problems of *hybrid warfare* in international political science, military science and even in the relevant official documents of NATO, the EU, the USA, Russia and other countries.

The term 'hybrid' became a very common way to describe contemporary warfare among commentators and scientists during the 2000s, particularly because of the growing sophistication and aggressiveness of violent non-state actors and the increasing potential of informational and cyber warfare. For instance, in 2007 a leading analyst of the concept, Frank G. Hoffman, defined hybrid threats in his paper 'Conflict in the 21st Century: The Rise of Hybrid Wars' as: 'Any adversary that simultaneously employs a tailored mix of conventional weapons, irregular tactics, terrorism and criminal behavior in the same time and battlespace to obtain their political objectives' (Hoffman, 2007).

In his article, the US Army Chief of Staff George C. Casey characterized a hybrid threat as an adversary that incorporates 'Diverse and dynamic combinations of conventional, irregular, terrorist and criminal capabilities' (Casey, 2008). The U.S. Army codified the term in its 2011 operations doctrine as 'The diverse and dynamic combination of regular forces, irregular forces, criminal elements, or a combination of these forces and elements all unified to achieve mutually benefitting effects' (Fleming, 2011).

Western definitions of hybrid warfare are also similar to the Chinese theory of *unrestricted warfare*. This concept is elaborated in detail in the book *Unrestricted Warfare,* which was published in 1999 by two colonels of the People's Liberation Army (PLA). It proposes methods of warfare to enable countries like China to confront an opponent with superior military technology such as the USA. Senior Colonel Qiao Liang and Senior Colonel Wang Xiangsui present innovative alternatives to traditional military engagement using a wide and unrestricted variety of tools. Similar to the concept of hybrid warfare, unrestricted warfare involves the use of a multitude of means, both military and non-military, to strike back at an enemy during a conflict. Among other things, authors assert: 'The existence of boundaries is a prerequisite for differentiating objects from one another. In a world where all things are interdependent, the significance of boundaries is merely relative' (Qiao Liang, Wang Xiangsui, 1999).

The hybrid war concept was used in particular by specialists analyzing Russian aggression against Georgia in 2008[2], where Russia made use of a mix of its regular armed forces, South Ossetian and Abkhazian militias, and Russian special operations forces operating as 'local defense' troops. In fact, during its preparation for the invasion in Georgia, Russia worked out and tested a considerable part of its hybrid war tools (Dikiy, 2016). However, only the Russo-Ukrainian war has shown all these tools are not just isolated instances, but a very well thought out and elaborated set of political, informational, ideological and military measures aiming to occupy the victim country.

Therefore, with all possible conceptual limits in mind, the definition of *hybrid warfare* could be put as: *a set of diverse and dynamic combinations of conventional, irregular, terrorist and criminal capabilities, as well as non-military means of combined character that could be applied in a rapid and adaptive manner to the enemy (victim-country)... and the act of aggression itself generates uncertainty among international actors* (Centre for Global Studies "Strategy XXI", 2016).

The Nature of Russian Hybrid Warfare

Though *hybrid warfare* is a Western term and not a Russian one, since the creation of the Soviet Union, the theory and practice of 'hybrid conflict' has been considered by Russian rulers as the most effective method to submit neighboring states to the dictates of the Kremlin. Although *hybrid war* is not an invention of Putin's regime, new achievements of current Russian

[2] Most Russian and some Western observers stick to the point that Russia played a supportive role in this conflict, however author regards it as a part of Russian propaganda campaign. Chronicle of Russian-Georgian war could be checked by Ukrayinska Pravda (08.08.2011).

military and political thought are based on templates of the old Soviet practice (Magda, 2015).

The fundamentals of Russian hybrid warfare are contained in the decree of the Political Bureau of the Central Committee of the Russian Communist Party (of the Bolsheviks) on the issue of active intelligence from February 25th, 1925. This security document anticipated clandestine 'special units' instead of 'active intelligence in its present state' in the territories neighbouring the USSR. They were organised 'for preparation of destructive work during wartime in the rear area of the enemy'. It was indicated that while 'units have informative and preparative nature, they should be able to transfer into combat units in due moments,' but 'in no circumstances they should be affiliated with the Party' (Voronov, November 2014).

Soviet Russia first practiced hybrid warfare in the 1920s-1930s against neighboring countries such as, Poland, Ukraine, China, and countries in Central Asia. Stalin's format of hybrid warfare was known as military subversive activities. For example, during the 1920s-1930s, special groups wearing Polish military or police uniforms acted in Eastern Poland. They looted and burnt local settlements, private premises, captured trains, discrediting the central government and tried to start revolts in regions with non-Polish populations. Diversionists and terrorists did not carry out the main tasks, and a 'people's revolt' did not happen (Voronov, October 2014).

During the 'Cold War', the USSR acted in a number of countries through the support of left and national liberation movements. In exchange for such 'cooperation', these groups were provided not only with weapons and money, but also with the help of military councillors and Special Forces units for conducting military operations masked under the 'people's struggle with Western puppet regimes' (Sergiychuk, 2002).

The unnoticeable and hidden use of military men from one country in another is one of the most determinative factors of successful hybrid operations. The sudden appearance of 'little green men' in Crimea in 2014 and later of 'servicemen on leave' in Luhansk and Donetsk regions brought all Western politicians to a standstill (Magda, 2015). But this aspect of Russia's present hybrid war against Ukraine rests upon absolutely concrete Soviet experience. Even the use of armed forces under the pretence of volunteers took place in the Korean War of 1950-1953.

Stalin and Mao's collaborative actions resulted in a redeployment to Korea of between 1 to 3 million Chinese and about 40 thousand Soviet military men. Of course, they were all volunteers. While the Chinese were the basis of ground formations, the Soviet 'volunteers' formed the backbone of air and air defence forces. All Soviet military men were well masked like Chinese soldiers: they wore Chinese uniforms, had Chinese pseudonyms and appropriate documents, plus their airplanes were marked with symbols of the Air Forces of Chinese People's Liberation Army (CPLA) (Yakunov, 2015). According to the data gathered by Ukrainian researcher Oleksandr Kotlobovskyi, 22 Soviet pilots that took part in the Korean War were given the title Hero of the Soviet Union (Babakov, 2000).

Furthermore, 1,500 Soviet officers and generals acted in the ranks of the CPLA. Officially they were registered as war councillors, but in reality they were in full command of units and divisions. Chinese officers played the role of interpreters. Many experts believe that these councillors played, to a large extent, a decisive role in the conflict in the Korean peninsula ("Centre for Global Studies Strategy XXI", 2016). The USSR kept back and denied the participation of its military in the war, officially declaring that Soviet troops had not taken part in the Korean War.

Kremlin 'volunteers' also appeared in Syria. And this happened long before 2015. In 1956, they were directly involved in combat actions on the Syrian-Israel front and other armed conflicts: in June 5-13, 1967 ('6-day war'); in March-July 1970 ('war of starvation'); September-November 1972 ('air war'); October 6-24, 1973 ('Yom Kippur War') (Shama, 2015).

So called 'interfronts' or international fronts, created by the KGB of the USSR in the late 1980s and early 1990s, were the latest modification of military subversive activities of the Soviet period. They were conceptualized as a counterbalance to national civil movements that started to appear in the union republics as a result of democratization of society and 'perestroika'. The last chief of the KGB, Vadim Bakatin, wrote in his book *Getting Rid of the KGB*: 'The Committee for Security was one of the originators of the creation of "international fronts" in union republics which kicked against relations with the Centre. An evil logic of "divide and rule" stimulated the split of society in these republics into two uncompromising camps and led to the escalation of social tension… A scheme worked: "if you don't want to obey – you will get an interfront that will cause strikes, put borders of the republic under question, as well as the overall legitimacy of the elected in this country". Interfront activities were presented by the KGB as the manifestation of true will of all people' (Bakatin, 1992).

It is possible to quote other works of USSR military specialists of different times that gained attention of the General Staff of the Armed Forces of the Russian Federation and numerous theoreticians of the '*Russian world*' concept.

But not only representatives of the Soviet General Staff stood behind the genesis of Russian 'hybrid warfare'. As was mentioned earlier, Evgeny Messner, the army officer of the Tsarist Russian Army and a prominent representative of the anti-Bolshevik emigration, also made his contribution to the theory of future warfare. By the way, his role in this process remains largely underestimated by Western commentators (Klus, 2016).

Certain parts of the hybrid warfare toolbox were developed and used in practice by ideologists, propagandists and special service officers after the collapse of the Soviet Union. Even though Russia's participation in the Armenian-Azerbaijani War (1992-1994) and the Tajikistani Civil War (1992-1997) could be viewed as an old Soviet scheme of 'outside interference in an independently developed conflict.' Even armed conflicts in Transnistria (1992), Abkhazia (1992-1993) and South Ossetia were, to a large extent, provoked outside by the Kremlin government of that time (Dikiy, 2016). It is noteworthy that in the course of these conflicts a methodology for the international legitimization of Russia's military aggression was worked out and tested for the first time. Legitimization consists of invasion forces that first act unofficially and without any distinctive insignia, and masked under local paramilitary formations. After obtaining some military success, they become legitimated as a 'Russian military peacekeeping contingent' in the course of international negotiations (Dikiy, 2016).

The two Russian-Chechen wars (1994 and 1999-2001) also had clear signs of a 'hybrid conflict' due to the legitimization of obviously illegal Russian actions. Clear examples of this are the violations of 1996 Khasavyurt peace treaty and the overthrow of the Ichkerian government, which was elected in the international community elections that took place under OSCE control in 1997 (Dikiy, 2016). This method, which is also widely used in the aggression against Ukraine, uses the inability of the legitimate government of the victim-country to control that territory through different armed formations in its country.

Russia worked out several other very important components of modern hybrid warfare through its aggression against Georgia in 2008. Firstly, it created the propagandist image of the enemy (the victim-country). Secondly, it determined weak points in the system of international common security and neutralized the interference of Western countries in the conflict.

In February 2013, the Head of the General Staff of the Armed Forces of the Russian Federation, General Valeriy Gerasimov, published a program article 'Science Value is in Prevision' (Gerasimov, 2013). The article came out as a result of the long work of Russian military analysts and specialists. It was an answer for how to restore Russia's geopolitical influence without levying a 'great war'. Gerasimov's article, and his previous report to the Academy of Military Sciences, became a peculiar point of no return in Russian military and political management's views on modern conflicts. The article described in what way a modern military political conflict should deploy, what elements should be involved in it and what stages it involves. The report emphasized the increasing role of non-military methods to pressure the enemy, firstly through political, economic and humanitarian elements. Informational warfare was defined as a principal activity during each stage of the conflict, from its initiation to the post-conflict period. Special attention was drawn to such 'asymmetric measures' as the activity of the special forces, the construction of internal opposition and also the unceasing increase of informational influence on the opponent (Gerasimov, 2013).

Therefore, Russian hybrid warfare had developed a fundamental suite of tools in broad lines by 2014. Its elements had been successfully tested in the course of a range of regional conflicts. However it was in the war against Ukraine when the armoury of 'hybrid warfare' was used in a full and consistent manner.

What Does Russia Want?

The successful seizure of Crimea and subsequent intervention in Eastern Ukraine should not be treated as a sudden and unexpected violation of international law. There are reasons to believe that Russia has been preparing a hybrid war against Ukraine, at least during the last decade. And these presumptions are confirmed not only with publications in Russian special military literature (Gerasimov, 2013). In 2014, a combination of several circumstances took place that allowed Russia to sharpen the situation on the European continent.

The collapse of the Soviet Union, the dissolution of the Warsaw Pact and other global processes that took place in the world at the end of the 20th century caused fundamental changes of the world's political map. A new geopolitical situation was settled. Current Russian elite consider these changes as the destruction and not the collapse (as is accepted outside of Russia) of Soviet Union[3]. Unlike a collapse, which is a natural process, destruction is an artificial one. By the Kremlin's belief, this was specially prepared and implemented by the countries of the West, and headed by the USA (Kuzio, 2016).

Just after the Soviet Union came to an end, a large part of the Russian political elite started talking about Ukraine and other former USSR republics as 'temporarily' lost territories (Magda, 2015). Favourable political, economic and social conditions to achieve Russia's uncompromising dominance in the post-Soviet territories started to appear with Vladimir Putin's accession to power.

According to Putin's convictions, the USSR was destroyed by a non-military hybrid method (*Lenta.ru*, 21.01.2016). The idea that the Union could be reconstructed by the same non-military methods predominated in the Kremlin for a long time. Such geopolitical projects as the *Single Economic Space*, *Eurasian Economic Community*, and *Eurasian Customs Union* were aimed at spreading and strengthening Russia's influence in the region.

Furthermore, as time went by, the idea arose that a reconstruction of a modern hybrid superstate, something between the Russian Tsarist Empire and the Soviet Union, would be able to compete as an equal with the USA. This spread among and strengthened Russian leadership (Dugin, 2014; Prokhanov, 2012). Also, some illusional obsession about the special historical mission of Russia and Russian culture in the global world – especially towards neighbouring states – took place. The hype in the main Russian state media of such marginal 'Russian world' concept theorists as Aleksandr

[3] Putin's famous Munich speech is a proof of this statement. For more detailed information please check the book of Russian sociologist Olga Kryshtanovskaya 'Anatomy of Russian Elite' (2005).

Dugin and Aleksandr Prokhanov is the obvious proof of this obsession. These and the other pseudo-philosophers actively promote idea that, according to the Kremlin's ideology, geographical and historical spaces of Kyivan Rus are identical to Soviet-Russian ones (Kuzio, 2016). They include the historical territories of Eastern Slavs – that is Ukraine and Belarus. They believe that Ukrainians and Belarusians are a part of a 'single nation', certainly a Russian one, which was artificially separated and opposed each other many times because of the enemies of Russia (*Gordonua.com*, 17.08.2015).

As described by the famous British Russianist, James Sherr: 'Today's Russian state has inherited a culture of influence deriving from the Soviet and Tsarist past. It bears the imprint of doctrines, disciplines and habits acquired over a considerable period of time in relations with subjects, clients and independent states' (Giles, 2016).

Mainly non-military economical and humanitarian methods to reconstruct the 'great country' brought no results. Except for Belarus and some Central Asian countries, the former Soviet bloc members were not willing to share their sovereignty and chose an independent way to develop. From the Kremlin's viewpoint, the West's continuing expansion on Russia's virtual living space resulted in this situation (Snegovaya, 2015).

The joining of the European Community and NATO by Eastern European countries and the Baltic States was taken very painfully by the Kremlin. Eventually Ukraine and Georgia reached a certain amount of progress in the negotiations with the EU on the Association Agreements and talks about the possible quick entry of these states to the NATO. Then Russia decided to give a serious geopolitical answer. Since then, the weakening of NATO and the EU became a strategic task of the Russian Federation.

World leaders did not take Putin's words seriously when he said the collapse of Soviet Union as 'the greatest geopolitical catastrophe of the century' (Sanders, 2014). As a result, more aggressive Russian politics appeared again more openly on the international scene in February 2007, when the Russian President gave his famous Munich Speech. In this speech, Putin declared that Russia would no longer accept the unipolar and U.S.-oriented model of international relations, and that Russia would implement its own independent foreign policy in pursuit of its geopolitical interests (Snegovaya, 2015).

Soon after, the Russian-Georgian war took place. Western leaders reacted feebly and placed the main blame for the conflict upon the victim of the aggression: Georgia. This assured Russian leaders of the efficiency of such policy (Bowker, 2011). Russia not only evaded sanctions but was also able to strengthen its position owing to high prices for hydrocarbons. The large amount of funds from the oil and gas export to Europe ensured an abrupt rise in the Russian economy and supported the financing of such projects as the modernization of the army and the creation of a modern worldwide propaganda system (Snegovaya, 2015).

But renewing the geopolitical balance of Soviet Union times is not Putin's only goal for Russia. Another high-priority task is reformatting the world's financial and economic systems in such a way that cash flows would be controlled by the countries that generate resources. As long as Russia is the largest and one of the most mineral-rich countries in the world, the resource flows from Russia should return with equivalent financial counter flows under state control. In Kremlin ideologists' judgment, this situation could be achieved by a generation of destabilization and managed chaos through competition between Russia and resource-rich regions such as the Middle East. This will lead to a growth in the prices of energy resources and increase its exportation from Russia (Centre for Global Studies "Strategy XXI", 2016).

The growing political deconsolidation of NATO and the European Union organisations, the existence of numerous problems like Syrian refugees in Europe, Britain's exit from the EU and terror attacks by Islamic extremists in European cities – all of this can play into the hands of Russia. Therefore the Russian Federation supports and lobbies in every possible way the assumption of power of different right-radical, left-radical and populist groups in European countries (*Argumentua.com*, December 2014). Besides, the Kremlin actively exploits former and acting influential politicians from all over the world. In this capacity, former chancellor of Germany Gerhardt Schroder, acting Prime Minister of Hungary Victor Orban, acting Prime Minister of Slovakia Roberto Fico, former President of Serbia Voislav Kostunica, president of Czech Republic Milos Zeman, leader of National Front in France Marie Le Pen and many others could be mentioned (*Argumentua.com*, December 2014).

Everything abovementioned provide evidence that hybrid warfare did not become the main instrument of Russian neo-imperialism policy on accident. Vladimir Putin and his government are very well aware of the tremendous gap between Russian and Western economic potential and military development. This very fact predetermined why the hybrid model was chosen as the single possible option that causes damage to Western democracies in a way that is not identified as an act of war against them.

Hybrid aggression against Ukraine in 2014 became a very important step in this geopolitical confrontation with the West for Russian leadership. The subsequent intervention in Syria in 2015 allowed the criminal, but loyal to the Kremlin, Bashar Assad regime to remain in power and triggered the movement of a million refugees from the Middle East to Europe.

These actions prove an understanding of the complex nature of multi-layered hybrid warfare, which Russia is carrying out against the West. The European Union is a principal object of this policy since the Kremlin considers it to be a vulnerable element of the transatlantic system of security and cooperation.

'Russkii Mir' Concept as Ideological Matrix of Hybrid Warfare

Hybrid aggression against Ukraine is one of the most important parts of Russia's foreign policy, of which the final goal is the creation of a so called 'Russkii mir' (Russian world). Aleksandr Dugin formulated this goal as the following: 'Imperative of Russia's geopolitical and strategic sovereignty involves not only restoration of lost regions of the "Near Abroad", not only renewal of allied relations with the countries of Eastern Europe, but also including in a new Eurasian strategic coalition states of the continental West (first of all, Franco-German bloc which tends toward liberation from Atlantic supervision of the pro-American NATO), and of the continental East (Iran, India, and Japan)... Access to the cold seas of the North and the East should be completed with access to the warm seas of the South and the West, and only in this case Russia will become geopolitically "completed"' (Dugin, 2014).

The project of 'Russkii mir' became an ideological matrix of restoring influence in the world as a whole, in the post-Soviet space and in Ukraine in particular. This project has a circular structure with the centre being the

Kremlin and a radiating number of 'concentric circles', each of which corresponds to different levels of removed control from Russia's side (Dikiy, 2016).

According to this project, the Russian Federation is located in the very centre of the 'Russian world'. In the course of the last sixteen years of Vladimir Putin's rule, his control over this state gained a total and authoritative nature. The project of the 'Russian world' provides Russia with multiple assets. It creates a rigid vertical power of government while liquidating civil society institutions and independent mass media. And there is a formal imitation of election procedures, but with an authoritarian governance and the absence of real opposition. The constant working of the state ideological propaganda apparatus, with the absence of independent media, along with the conservation of a resource-oriented economy with a full dependence from the state is also predefined. This goal has been almost achieved by the Kremlin (Belkovskii, 2012).

The former USSR countries make the next circle of the 'Russian world'. The gradual achievement of the same degree of control by the Kremlin, which reaches the same territory of the Russian Federation is planned. The 'Russian world' project supposes a set-up of fully controlled puppet regimes in these states with the formal reservation of 'independent status'. Gradually, these countries should lose all features of sovereignty except the coat-of-arms, the flag and the anthem (Dikiy, 2016).

It is widely accepted that the most important element of this circle of the 'Russian world' is Ukraine, a formerly principal part of the Russian Empire and the USSR (Stürmer, 2015). Therefore, it is very important for Russia to keep Ukraine in its sphere of influence and not allow its integration into a hostile Europe.

The next 'layer' of this 'Russian doll' world includes the countries of Central and Eastern Europe – these are mainly former members of 'Warsaw Pact', including the Balkan countries and Greece. This also includes a set of 'second and third world' countries, which are India, Brazil, Turkey, Iran, Israel, Syria and some other Middle Eastern countries. The relations for these types of states would support Russia on international policy issues. At least Russia should have a 'veto right' for all of the serious foreign policy decisions of these states (Dikiy, 2016).

The continental states of Western Europe, such as Germany, Austria, Spain, Portugal and Scandinavian countries form the next level, which would become a 'neutral buffer' between Russia and Anglo-Saxon countries. A super soft control would be applied to these countries. It should be carried out by pulling political elites' representatives into corrupt practices, and the direct and indirect bribery of local media. Presumably, local corporations will use the preferences in joint economic projects with Russian companies, so that Moscow in its turn could use these corporations to lobby in their countries in favour of Russia.

Dismantling NATO and The European Union is necessary to successfully implement the described project. Not surprisingly, the Russian Federation makes a great effort and contributes many resources to support the so called 'Eurosceptic' groups of all kinds in many European countries. Anti-American and anti-NATO movements are also welcomed. The accomplishment of the 'Russian world' supposes an immense weakening of the West and its split into three parts competing with each other. These are: the USA and Anglo-Saxon world which is deprived of allies within continental Europe; the continental countries of 'Old Europe'; and the countries of Central and Eastern Europe.

This geopolitical spectrum should provide Russia with the role of a 'global player' that competes as an equal and shares 'spheres of influence' with the USA (Dugin, 2014).

Features of Russian Hybrid Aggression against Ukraine

Dutch Major-General and former NATO Security Councillor Frank van Kappen was one of the first Western analysts who called events in Ukraine by their name. On April 26th of 2014 he declared: 'Putin is carrying out hybrid warfare in Ukraine' (Kornienko, 2014).

As it was mentioned above, a set of hybrid warfare means and methods had been worked out and tested in practice by Kremlin political experts and the Russian military by 2014. They were brought together to an unified invasion plan known as the "'Russian spring" project' (Dikiy, 2016). As the hybrid invasion plan into Ukraine was implemented simultaneously in different regions of Ukraine and in a complex manner, it is possible to make certain conclusions concerning a range of distinctive features of Russian hybrid warfare.

The first distinctive feature of hybrid warfare (in contrast to a conventional one) consists in the thorough masking of military contingents at the initial stage. It does not allow the enemy to find out about the aggression. The occupation of Crimea can serve as an example where the attacking party was in an advantageous position, as it concentrated its potential for the appropriate attacks, and the opposing party stayed in a deconcentrated condition (Centre for Global Studies "Strategy XXI", 2016).

The second important feature is that military success is ensured by using minimal armed forces. The victim country and, more importantly, its potential allies have an illusion of a low intensity war that do not threaten the parties involved in the conflict. The very weak reaction of the West during the first phase of the annexation of Crimea may serve as the illustration of this feature (Horbulin, 25.03.2016).

The third feature is that the aggressor tries to undermine the opposing party from the inside, making maximally possible damage to its informational, political, economic and social potentials. Consequently, defensive mobilization and response strikes are blocked or slowed down.

The fourth feature lies in the creation of a comprehensive scheme of 'changing influences', when the potential of the victim country works towards its own weakening and the benefit of the aggressor. A good example of this may be the multibillion dollar Gazprom gas debt that was generated by an unrecognized Transnistrian Republic but officially considered as Moldavian debt (*Moldova.org*, 26.07.2013). Russia tried to force Ukraine to put up money for the occupied regions in Eastern Ukraine according to the same scheme (*BBC*, 18.08.2016).

The fifth feature is the creation of an illusion for the third parties of 'non-involvement' of the aggressor in the 'internal conflict'. The attacking country begins its own peacekeeping operations and induce third parties to provide noninterference policy.

As was stated before, *hybrid warfare* is usually a set of tactics used by a weaker force against a stronger force, or a non-state actor against a state actor. The whole idea of asymmetric war is to defeat a more powerful enemy. What is interesting about the war in Crimea and Eastern Ukraine is that the Russian Federation, despite being the obviously stronger party in this war and having one of the best armies in the world, is fighting as if it were the weaker side. Russian forces use techniques such as: not wearing insignia, mixing in with the civilian population, claiming they are not really there at all, using human shields, drawing fire into large groups, and alienate civilians. These are all classic partisan tactics. However, the use of these type of tactics can be characterized as 'reverse asymmetry', and has its logic because Ukraine is regarded by the Kremlin as a battlefield with the West. The Russian version of hybrid warfare is based on the idea of defense against an imaginary attack. In Ukraine, the case aggressor presents itself as a victim of unfriendly Western policies and claims the right to defend itself from this pretended aggression in the post-Soviet space.

Democratic transformations in the neighbouring countries (the 'Orange Revolution' and the 'Revolution of Dignity' in Ukraine) are interpreted by the Kremlin as elements of hybrid warfare of the West against Russia in its sphere of interests. This is confirmed by the words that Putin said at the board meeting of the Federal Security Service on March 26th, 2015: 'A full set of measures is used in order to restrain Russia – from the attempts of imposing a political isolation and economical pressure to global information war and special services actions' (Tass Information Agency, 26.03.2015).

With concern to the specific nature of Russian type indirect operations in Ukraine, which involve a multiplicity of actors and erode the traditional distinctions between war and peace, *hybrid aggression (hybression) could be defined as a military strategy that implies multidimensional controlled poly-destruction of one state by another through the use of a complex and combined set of military and non-military means and forces on different levels (political, military, economical, informational, humanitarian, etc.) which are concentrated on the goal of extermination of victim's life potentials from inside through regulated external impacts* (Centre for Global Studies "Strategy XXI", 2016).

Periodization of Russian Hybression against Ukraine

Taking everything into account it is possible to distinguish certain phases of preparation, fulfilment and completion of Russia's hybression (hybrid aggression) against Ukraine.

'Zero' phase or 'crypto' war. The period from late 2003 (conflict around Tuzla island (Woronowycz, 2003)) until August 14th, 2013, when Russia imposed unilateral sanctions upon all Ukrainian goods (ZN.UA, 2013, August, 8). The 'zero' phase is an obligatory preparative stage that does not have a certain time limit and may last for unlimitedly long periods of time until favourable conditions for next phases of 'hybrid warfare' appear. This is a hidden form of the gradual, systematic and long-term causing of damage to the enemy in order to exhaust its potential to the maximum by the time that the decision about a classical or hybrid type of aggression will be taken (Centre for Global Studies "Strategy XXI", 2016).

During this phase, Russia tried to achieve the following goals:

– Psychological treatment of Russian society in order to explain the 'necessity' of the armed interference in Ukraine;

– psychological treatment of Ukrainian society in order to weaken the resistance to the invasion;

– establishing a network of pro-Russian agents that would be directly involved during next phases of aggression;

– modification of public opinion and political position in the Western countries in order to legitimate aggressive actions and neutralize international mechanisms of collective security (Dikiy, 2016).

Destabilization phase. The period from August 14th, 2013 to February 23rd, 2014, when Yanukovych escaped from Ukraine. At this stage, Russia enables different extremist groups inside the victim-country. They are supported by a limited number of secret service professionals. These groups destabilize the situation, imitate civil conflict, and create an atmosphere of chaos and anarchy.

At the same time, a broad propaganda campaign is switched on in Russian and Western media-spaces in order to create a certain 'picture' that helps legitimize further actions. The idea of the 'weakness' of the legitimate government and the 'absence of government control' over the state's territory as well as different real and fictitious paramilitary groups is actively pushed forward (Magda, 2015).

Imitation of sovereignty phase (short period of self-proclaimed 'independences' of Crimea, DNR and LNR after referendums). This phase is one of the most important in hybrid aggression. It is characterized by aggression 'from inside' with outside support by the aggressor state. This phase is usually accompanied by the appearance of internal tensions and conflicts, prepared in advance by secret agents, as well as the declaration of separatist regions. 'Self-defense' groups or the 'people's militia' is created under hidden leadership of foreign secret services. A transit from 'natural self-defence groups' to 'legitimate representatives of the will of local population' is highlighted in the media. An increasing number of regular army units camouflaged like 'paramilitary formations' under the control of 'local self-administration' may be involved.

The Russian Crimean campaign became a textbook example of successful hybrid operations at the imitation of sovereignty phase. On the contrary, the 'Novorossiya' project is an example of the collapse, when the Crimean campaign was automatically imposed on the region which had substantial differences from the Crimea (Centre for Global Studies "Strategy XXI", 2016).

*Military phase***.** The period from April 12nd, 2014 (Capture of Sloviansk) to February 18th, 2015 (Conclusion of Minsk II Agreement). During this phase, direct military interference is used. In Eastern Ukraine numerous bombardments of the Ukrainian Army from Russian territory, and the use of regular Russian Army units in the territory of Ukraine were documented. If the internal conflict potential of a victim is 'switched on' properly during the 'destabilization' phase and the victim has been emasculated enough in crypto war, the military phase should pass very quickly (Blitzkrieg) (Centre for Global Studies "Strategy XXI", 2016).

Intra – phase. The period from February 18th, 2015 until the present time. If diffuse invasion and the use of the military component have no success, 'phase shifting' could be implemented. This occurs in the case of the collapse of the blitzkrieg. Actually, it happened in the East of Ukraine.

The Intra-phase of the war is switched on with a parallel resumption of the destabilization phase. Some kind of peaceful process is started (Minsk process). At this time, the military component is minimized, and non-military mechanisms to destroy the victim are activated. Russia tries to legalize representatives of occupied territories through the Minsk process and federalization within the legal framework of Ukraine. As a result, Ukrainian integration with Europe should be 'blocked'.

In case such an algorithm does not work, another scenario is implemented within the intra-phase – the entry of a contingent of regular armed forces under the guise of peacekeeping. As long as the victim-country has a continuing internal conflict (from the aggressor's point of view), it needs resolving. Taking into account the length of the decision-making procedures on the international level, the initiator of the 'peacekeeping operation' may find a faster resolution to the problem in order to prevent civilian casualties.

Stabilization-transformation phase (Crimea during last two years). The final stage is the stabilization-transformation phase. It is a transition phase where all the objectives of the invasion are already achieved and the main problem is definitively to stabilize the occupied territory either by integration (Crimea) or by the creation of a satellite area or several areas with different statuses (Centre for Global Studies "Strategy XXI", 2016).

Summary

The Russian Federation is pursuing a very intelligent, hostile, multi-level policy of weakening the West. The unprovoked, ongoing hybrid aggression against Ukraine that started in 2014, became a new step of this policy. What is clear from the thinking going on in the Russian elite is that 'hybrid warfare' obtained the finished form as a military-political concept, and that this concept was added to the Russian armoury and used against Ukraine. There is no doubt that it may be used against other countries chosen for aggression. Parts of this warfare style, such as informational warfare, are already being effectively used against Western democracies.

The Russo-Ukrainian war has already become the longest and the bloodiest hybrid war in the history of mankind. It put existential challenges in front of the Ukrainian people and state. As for the 4th March 2016, total loses of Ukrainian military aggregated 2683 persons (Lykhoviy, 2016). According to the information of the UN Human Rights Monitoring Mission in Ukraine, there were 2,000 civilians who were killed during the Russian aggression (Pavlov, 2016).

In the 21st century the largest state in the world is assaulting the biggest state in Europe, denying its right to exist as an independent country. In many ways Ukraine is a very demonstrative and symbolic victim. Russian aggression against Ukraine also gave an opportunity for the civilized world to get rid of illusions concerning the governing regime in Russia and to think seriously over the threats of wars of new type. The annexation of Crimea and creation of 'peoples' republics in the East of Ukraine provide plenty information for consideration and research. The key for understanding an effective counteraction to hybrid aggressions lies in understanding the Crimea and Donbas war, but also lies in detailed analyses of the Kremlin policy towards Ukraine during all years of its independence.

References

Babakov, S. (2000): Order was the Following: to Combat only under the Territory of North Korea. In: ZN.UA. Retrieved from http://gazeta.zn.ua/SOCIETY/prikaz_byl_takoy_boi_vesti_tolko_nad_severnoy_koreey.html.

Bakatin, V. (1992): Getting Rid of KGB. Moscow: Novosti.

Belkovskii, S. (2012): The newest Putin. What Russia should wait for? Algoritm.

Bowker, M. (2011): The War in Georgia and the Western Response. In: Central Asian Survey 30(2), p. 197–211.

Brzezinski, Z. (1998): The Grand Chessboard: American Primacy and Its Geostrategic Imperatives. Retrieved from http://www.lib.ru/POLITOLOG/AMERICA/bzhezinskij.txt.

Casey, G. C. (2008): America's Army in an Era of Persistent Conflict. In: Army Magazine.

Centre for Global Studies "Strategy XXI" (2016): Putin Hybression. Non-military aspects of new generation warfare. Geostrategy. Retrieved from http://geostrategy.org.ua/images/Hybression_finversion.pdf.

Chartrand, R. (2004): Spanish Guerrillas in the Peninsular War 1808–14: Osprey Publishing.

Dikiy, E. (2016): Russian hybrid war: Ukrainian experience for Baltic states. Vilnius.

Dugin, A. G. (2014): War of Continents. Current World in the Geopilitical Coordinate System. Moscow: Academicheskii Proekt.

Eliseev, M. (2013): Scythians 'Legendary and Undefeated'. Yauza: Eksmo.

Fleming B. (2011): The Hybrid Threat Concept: Contemporary War, Military Planning and the Advent of Unrestricted Operational Art. Retrieved from http://indianstrategicknowledgeonline.com/web/2753.pdf.

Gerasimov, V. (2013): Science Value is in Prevision. In: Voyenno-Promyshlennyi Kuryer (VPK). Retrieved from http://www.vpk-news.ru/articles/14632.

Giles, K. (2016): Russia's 'new' tools for confronting the West. London: Chatham House.

Hoffman, F. G. (2007): Conflict in the 21st century: the rise of hybrid wars. Arlington.

Horbulin, V. (2015): Hybrid War as a Key instrument of Russian Geostrategic Revenge. In: ZN.UA. Retrieved from http://gazeta.dt.ua/internal/gibridna-viyna-yak-klyuchoviy-instrument-rosiyskoyi-geostrategiyi-revanshu-_.html.

Horbulin, V. (2016, March, 25): Hybrid war: it is just beginning… In: ZN.UA. Retrieved from http://gazeta.dt.ua/internal/gibridna-viyna-vse-tilki-pochinayetsya-_.html.

Kagan, D. (2004): The Peloponnesian War: Penguin Books.

Klus, A. (2016): Myatezh Voina: The Russian Grandfather of Western Hybrid Warfare. In: Small Wars Journal. Retrieved from http://smallwarsjournal.com/jrnl/art/myatezh-voina-the-russian-grandfatherof-western-hybrid-warfare.

Kofman, M.; Rojansky M. (2015): A Closer look at Russia's 'Hybrid War'. Retrieved from https://www.files.ethz.ch/isn/190090/5-KENNAN%20CABLE-ROJANSKY%20KOFMAN.pdf.

Kornienko, S. (2014, April, 26): The Jacket is Bursting at the Seams. In: Radio Svoboda. Retrieved from http://www.svoboda.org/a/25362031.html.

Kremlin's Insruments: Exclusive List of Russian Agentsin European Countries (2014). In: Argumentua.com. Retrieved from http://argumentua.com/stati/instrumenty-kremlya-eksklyuzivnyi-spisok-agentov-rossiiskogo-vliyaniya-v-evropeiskikh-stranakh.

Kuzio, T. (2016): Nationalism and Authoritarianism in Russia. In: Communist and Post-Communist Studies (49), p. 1–11.

Lykhoviy, D. (2016, March, 13): What State Doesn't Say. NOVYNARNIA Found Out Exact Loses of Ukrainian Military in Anti-Terrorist Operation. In: NOVYNARNIA. Retrieved from http://novynarnia.com/2016/03/05/pro-shho-ne-govorit-derzhava-novinarnya-z-yasuvala-tochni-vtrati-v-ato-vsih-silovih-st-ruktur/.

MacAskill, E. (2016): West and Russia on course for war, says ex-Nato deputy commander. In: The Guardian. Retrieved from https://www.theguardian.co-m/world/2016/may/18/west-russia-on-course-for-war-nato-ex-deputy-comma-nder.

Magda, E. (2015): Hybrid War: Survive and Win. Kharkiv: Vivat Publishing.

McCulloh, T.; Johnson, T. (2013): Hybrid Warfare. In: JSOU. Retrieved from http://jsou.socom.mil/JSOU%20Publications/JSOU%2013-4_McCulloh,John-son_Hybrid%20Warfare_final.pdf.

Messner, E. (1959): Fight the Metezhevoyna if You Want a Peace. Retrieved from http://militera.lib.ru/science/0/pdf/messner_ea01.pdf.

Naftogaz will not Pay for Gas for Donbas to Russia (2016, August, 18). In: BBC Ukraine. Retrieved from http://www.bbc.com/ukrainian/business/2016/08/160-818naftogaz_gazprom_donbas_rl.

Osmanczyk, E. J. (1990): The Encyclopedia of the United Nations and International Agreements.

Pavlov, O. (2016, July, 14): UN Gave Number of Killed Civilians During Donbas War. In: Uapress. Retrieved from http://uapress.info/uk/news/show/137886.

Prokhanov, A. (2012): The Tread of the Russian Triumph. Moscow: KNIGO-VEK.

Putin Explained Destruction of USSR by Lenin's Ambitions (2016, January, 21). In: Lenta.ru. Retrieved from https://lenta.ru/news/2016/01/21/leninjiv/.

Putin: Russia Always had and Always will have Adequate Response to Anti-Russion Actions (2015, March, 26). In: Tass Information Agency. Retrieved from http://tass.ru/politika/1857492.

Putin: Russians and Ukrainian are the same nation. We Don't Make any Differences. (2015, August, 17). In: Gordonua.com. Retrieved from http://gordon-ua.com/news/worldnews/putin-ya-schitayu-chto-russkie-i-ukraincy-eto-voob-shche-odin-narod-raznicy-my-ne-delaem-video-94487.html.

Russia uses Transnistrian gas debt as political weapon against Moldova (2013, July, 26). In: Moldova.org. Retrieved from http://www.moldova.org/en/russia-uses-transnistrian-gas-debt-as-political-weapon-against-moldovainterview-238043-eng/.

Sanders, K. (2014, March, 6): Did Vladimir Putin call the breakup of the USSR 'the greatest geopolitical tragedy of the 20th century?' Retrieved from http://www.politifact.com/punditfact/statements/2014/mar/06/john-bolton/did-vladimir-putin-call-breakup-ussr-greatest-geop/.

Senior Colonel Qiao Liang, Senior Colonel Wang Xiangsui (1999): Unrestricted Warfare. Beijing.

Sergiychuk, I. M. (2002): Modern History of Asia and Africa countries (from 1918 to the End of XX Century). VTD Universytetska knyha: Sumy.

Shama, O. (2015): This was already. 60 Years Ago USSR Started to Supply Huge Flows of Weapons to Syria After Secret Talks. In: Novoe Vremya. Retrieved from http://nv.ua/ukr/publications/60-rokiv-tomu-srsr-pochav-postavljati-zbroji-i-miljardni-potoki-sirovini-v-jegipet-i-siriju-74951.html.

Snegovaya, M. (2015): Putin's information warfare in Ukraine. Washington.

Stoltenberg Says NATO's Assistant Package for Ukraine Doesn't Include Arms Supply (2016, June, 15). In: Interfax.com.ua. Retrieved from http://en.interfax.com.ua/news/general/350383.html.

Stürmer, M. (2015): Ohne Kiew fühlt sich Russland nicht als Imperium. In: Die Welt. Retrieved from http://www.welt.de/debatte/kolumnen/Weltlage/article145890502/Ohne-Kiew-fuehlt-sich-Russland-nicht-als-Imperium.html.

Tkachuk, O. (2010): Bloody Morning Stars of Red Partizans. In: Ukrayinska Pravda. Retrieved from http://www.pravda.com.ua/column-s/2010/10/2/5408427/.

Tsu, Sun: The Art of War. Sacred Texts. Retrieved from http://www.sacred-texts.com/tao/aow/aow14.htm.

Ukraine will complain to the Eurasian commission on 'Russian trade blockade' (2013, August, 8). In: ZN.UA. Retrieved from http://dt.ua/ECONOMICS/ukrayina-poskarzhitsya-u-yevraziysku-komisiyu-na-torgovelnu-blokadu-rosiyi-126788_.html.

Ullman, H. (2015): Hybrid War: Old Wine in a New Bottle? Retrieved from http://www.atlanticcouncil.org/publications/articles/hybrid-war-old-wine-in-a-new-bottle.

Vasyliev, A. (2016): Why Ukraine Should Not Rely on UN Peacekeepers. In: Unian. Retrieved from http://www.unian.info/politics/1372747-why-ukraine-should-not-rely-on-un-peacekeepers.html.

Viyna do Viyny. Yak Rosiya napala na Hruziyu (2011, August, 8). In: Ukra-yinska Pravda. Retrieved from http://www.istpravda.com.ua/blogs/2011/08/8/49809/.

Voronov, V. (2014): Hybrid War in Ukraine. Putin's plagiarism of Stalin. Retrieved from http://zakona.net.ua/gibridnaya-vojna-v-ukraine-putinskij-plagiat-stalina/.html.

Voronov, V. (2014): Red Terror for Export. Retrieved from http://www.sov-sekretno.ru/articles/id/4373/.

Woronowycz, R. (2003, October, 26): Russian-Ukrainian Dispute Over Tuzla Escalates. In: The Ukrainian Weekly. Retrieved from http://www.ukrweekly.com/old/archive/2003/430301.shtml.

Yakunov, E. (2015): Chinese vatnik successors. Putin stole Mao's Idea. In: Ukrinform. Retrieved from http://www.ukrinform.ru/rubric-lastnews/1807631-nasledniki_kitayskih_vatnikov_putin_sper_ideyu_u_mao_1706587.html.

The Information Phenomenon in Hybrid Warfare in Ukraine: A Euromaidan Example

Anastasiia Lykholai

Abstract: *This article deals with the question of key characteristics of media war and propaganda in hybrid warfare as a brand-new way of war. The main focus is paid to the major role of information and media as part of a hybrid threat. The article contains short descriptions of some events and illustrates how different media sources highlight some Euromaidan events. For this analysis, one of the most popular media sources in Russia, Ukraine and Germany were chosen, in order to see the way they present the events during this period. The time period covered are the events from 21st November 2013 until 22nd February 2014.*

Keywords: *(Euro)Maidan, hybrid warfare, media war*

Theory

Hybrid war is not a new phenomenon. This type of war is not only carried out by means of guns, weapons and tanks, but by political propaganda, terror, fake information and economic pressure on the opponent. The first characteristic of hybrid war is a war without rules or restrictions. It is unrestricted and unlimited in the particular sense of the rules in use. The unrestricted warfare 'ignores and transcends the boundaries of the battlefield and what is not the battlefield, between what is and what is not a weapon, between military personnel and civilians, between state and non-state actors' (Mihai Marcel NEAG, 2016).

Yevgeny Messner – a former colonel of the General Staff of the Russian army – wrote: 'In previous wars of conquest, the territory was regarded as important. Henceforth, the most important thing will be honored *winning souls* in the warring states. Fighting will not be a two-dimensional surface as of old, not in three-dimensional space, as it was during the time of the birth of military aviation, but four, where the mentality of warring peoples is the fourth dimension' (Messner, 2004, p. 512).

American scientist Bernard Cohen notes that media may not often impose how to think on people, but it can successfully prompt them on what to think about. Nowadays, skillful commanders of modern hybrid warfare actively use media as a means of information weaponry, since they know how powerful it is.

Currently every war can be called 'hybrid', because countries use not only military weapons, but other methods of influence: intimidation, manipulation, control over people, propaganda, giving 'correct' information which helps the *aggressor*, misrepresentation, partial presentation of information, and many other methods. Furthermore, in times of globalization and development of various technologies, information possesses an important role. Enemies want to influence global opinion and the thoughts of each other. The policy of information warfare is usually prepared long before military action takes place, and the audience, which the information will be directed towards, is carefully researched.

In this article, the author tries to look at the problem from an analytical side, without evaluating the events and actions of the involved parties. The analysis has minimal personal influence, and only shows what the Russian, Ukrainian and German media told about the same events. Readers can decide the situation for themselves while seeing what was going on in Ukraine and how the *East* and the *West* reacted to these events. That is why a descriptive analysis is used, as it shows and reports essential events, consists of language analysis, and shows the kind of political rhetoric used by some media and how they influenced people.

Ultimately, for this analysis the most popular media in each country (according to social polls, these media scored one of the highest ratings and are recognized by a majority of the population) were chosen. For Russia, the TV channel 'Russia-24', which is a news channel with an online broadcast shown on the website www.vesti.ru, was chosen. For Ukraine, the TV channel '1+1' with the news program called 'Televiziina Sluzhba Novyn' (TV News Service – TSN – tsn.ua) was chosen. And among German media, the channel 'Das Erste', which is part of the TV-company ARD and the everyday program called 'Tagesschau' (www.tagesschau.de), was selected.

The program TSN was chosen because of relevant daily news, as well as the weekly wrap[1]. The channel Russia-24 was chosen as the only full-time news channel about the federal state[2]. And the channel 'das Erste' has a 10-minutes newscast 'Tagesschau' every hour[3]. These are all TV channels that normally cover all types of incidents, but information was chosen from their official websites and from archives, so all of the sources are online. Often the articles covered the speeches of moderators covering news about these incidents.

Because of the limitation of the article's format, not the main part of the analysis will not be presented, but instead its results will. But first, a short historical review must be given of the Euromaidan events.

Historical Review

In this part of the article, the main periods and events during the 'Revolution of Dignity' will be considered, starting with the Summit in Vilnius. The current media analysis begins with the reporting about the visit of Stefan Fule, the European Commissioner for Enlargement and European Neighbourhood Policy, on 20th November 2013. Already, the reporting on this event happened in some sources in different ways.
The Ukrainian media, TSN, highlighted Fule's following statement: 'I am inspired by the determination of the President Viktor Yanukovych and Verkhovna Rada Chairman Volodymyr Rybak who on 21st November had adopted key laws, including the law about parliamentary elections, the

---

[1] 'In December 2012, the program has set an absolute record, winning audience share of 31.5%' ('1+1' Media group of companies).

[2] 'Daily coverage – 7.8 million people. As a percentage – almost 12%. 'Russia 24' is broadcast in 200 of the largest cable networks and IP-TV networks of the country and the world. Experts call the channel one of the most successful TV start-ups in the history of the industry, which, indeed, is broadcasting from Russia without frontiers' (Litovko, 18.01.2013).

[3] 'The "Tagesschau" was the richest among news channel in 2015, by far the most watched news broadcast on German television. Compared to the previous year, it won 210,000 spectators and was seen every evening on average by 9.11 million viewers. The market share of the main issue at 20:00 was 32.7 %' (Krei, 30.12.2015).

Prosecution Service and the law about the possibility of medical treatment abroad for prisoners' (TSN, 20.11.2013).

On the same day, the Russian media broadcasted that during his visit to Kyiv on 20th November, Stefan Fule received a refusal on the part of President Viktor Yanukovych to sign the Association Agreement this year. It was said that Brussels set very strict conditions for Kyiv and that was the reason for the refusal (Vesti, 20.11.2013).

The German channel 'das Erste' reacted to this incident one day later, but covered it in the 'global way' to show the reaction of the EU (and not of the individual European actors). It was argued that 'Ukraine stands between the EU and Russia. The EU lures with political and economic convergence. Russia's President Putin is vigorously trying to reverse this process – he has other plans. [...] The disappointment was great in Brussels and other EU capitals, when the government of Ukraine declared that it was stopping the conclusion of the Association and Free Trade Agreement with the EU. Over the past few weeks, the Union has continued to focus on the Ukrainian President Viktor Yanukovych. The agreement would have tied Ukraine closer to the EU economically and politically. [...] Not only the EU parliamentarian Elmar Brok sees Russian pressure as a reason for the fact that the Ukrainian President Yanukovych took more and more distance from the agreement' (Tagesschau, 21.11.2013).

After the initial refusal to sign the Agreement by the Ukrainian President, on 21st November one Ukrainian journalist Mustafa Nayem called on people on his personal Facebook page to go to the Maidan Nezalezhnosti[4]. Journalists, community activists, opposition political leaders and other Kyiv citizens came to the Maidan. In other cities of Ukraine (Donetsk, Ivano-Frankivsk, Lutsk, Kharkiv, Khmelnytskyi, Uzhhorod etc.) and citizens from all over the world also gathered in order to support Euromaidan[5].

---

[4] The main square in the center of the Kyiv, that means 'Independence Square'.

[5] Is a wave of demonstrations and civil unrest in Ukraine, which began on the night of 21st November 2013 with public protests in Maidan in Kyiv, demanding a closer European integration.

On the next day, the *Berkut*[6] were brought to Maidan. Police tried to prevent the activists from setting up tents; there were some clashes, which were intensified by provocateurs – so called '*titushky*'[7]. The reporting about these incidents (also about '*Anti-Maidan*'[8], student strikes on 25-27th November) and specially about the actors involved during the first period of the Euromaidan was in the center of the current media analysis.

The second period focused on how students' demonstrations were forcibly broken up, beginning the 'Revolution of Dignity'. It started during the night of 29-30th November, when the Head of the Interior Ministry of Ukraine, Valerii Koryak, ordered to apply force to disperse the Euromaidan in Kyiv. That night there were about 400 activists who were still at Maidan, of which more than 79 were hurt or wounded and most were students. That is why the events of 30th November became a turning point in Ukrainian protests at the end of 2013. It shifted the focus of the protests from pro-European ones to anti-governmental ones, as well as gave them mass character.

On the morning of 1st December, after a terrible night people began to gather at the monument of Shevchenko for the National Assembly and the whole procession went to the Maidan. The exact number of protesters is unknown. The analyzed sources informed about 'a million people' (TSN, 1.12.2013), '5-6 thousand people' (Vesti, 2.12.2013), 'up to one million people' (Eckart Aretz, Tagesschau, 02.12.2013).

The reports of this period were focused on cleaning up Maidan Square, the 'installation of the Christmas Tree' there, the role of St. Michael's Monastery during this time, the life of the Maidan with it's whole infrastructure, clashes between protesters and security forces, etc.

The last explored period could be called the period of radicalization of Maidan events. The start of this period can be seen on 16th January after

---

6 (stands for Golden Eagle) – riot police. It was the system of special police of the Ukrainian militsiya within the Ministry of Internal Affairs. The main stated purpose (in Ukraine) of the national special force was crowd control.

7 (plural) is a term for mercenary agents who supported the Ukrainian police force during the administration of Viktor Yanukovych, often posing as street hooligans with the express purpose of performing illegal acts.

8 a support meeting for the policy of Viktor Yanukovych, started one day before.

the adoption of ten so called 'demonstration laws', which aimed at narrowing constitutional rights and freedoms. Already some days later, it led to the first victims[9] of clashes between protesters, security forces and provocateurs. These victims were later named the '*Heavenly Hundred*'[10]. But the most final and dramatic phase of the Euromaidan was on 18-20th of February 2014, when more than a hundred protesters were killed and a few thousands were injured. There were clashes in the front of the Parliament building, in the Mariinskyi Park, on Hrushevskoho Street and in other places of Kyiv. Most of the analyzed news reports were dedicated to these incident, and also to the 'anti-terrorist operation' of security forces, to the (failed) negotiations of the opposition leaders with President Yanukovych, to the new clashes and to the flight of the president from the country.

As has already been mentioned, in the current article it is impossible to show to the full extent how every analyzed informational source covered each incident, but the main results of this analysis will be presented in the concluding section.

Findings and Conclusion

By comparing Russian, German and Ukrainian TV channels it can be noticed that truly some media did not cover certain incidents in their information programs in a neutral way. Some media showed only close and short shots and some incidents were not even mentioned.

The analysis of the first period showed some trends: Firstly, the Ukrainian media, TSN, described the incidents in more detail than the Russian Vesti or the German Tagesschau. If the first conclusion is more or less evident, than the second gives one cause to claim that, in the analysed Russian media, incorrect information were used (probably intentionally). As the first part is about signing the Association, the reaction to this event was different in the three media sources and they each showed a different attitude of the EU: While Ukrainian TSN and German Tagesschau told that the EU

[9] Sergiy Nigoyan, Armenian by origin, and Michael Zhyznevsky, Belarus were shot. Roman Senik and Oleksandr Badera were deadly wounded and died the next week in hospital.

[10] Protesters who were killed during Euromaidan events (about 100 people were killed on 18-19 February, 2014).

was inspired by the work Ukraine had made, and was disappointed that it had not signed the Association because of the pressure of Russia, the Russian Vesti told that the EU refused the Association. Probably, with this statement the Russian media wanted to show that Ukraine is not significant to the EU, and the only way for Ukraine to develop is to cooperate with Russia. This confirms also that Ukraine is strategically important for Russia, and the loss of influence in Ukraine would be bring negative consequences.

Another remarkable incident, is the reporting about the provocateurs which were called '*titushky*'. Here the information is distinguished in different quantities: Vesti named only a small amount of provocateurs and mentioned them later than the Ukrainian and German media. It can be assumed that the Russian media wanted to hide some facts.

The last example is the number of people protesting at Maidan differs in every media source. In Russian Vesti the number was much smaller. The information about another meeting called 'Anti-Maidan' also differed, while TSN gave full and detailed information, the Vesti concentrated more on the 'Anti-Maidan', than on Maidan, probably to show the people who disagreed with the Association with EU. And 'das Erste' channel did not concentrated on the 'Anti-Maidan' but called it as another meeting.

The analysis of the second part, which deals with breaking up the demonstrations of students, confirmed the conclusion of the first part. The information in the Russian media is very different from the Ukrainian and the German ones. For example, in the cases of the number of participants in Maidan protests, Russian media reported about the smallest number of protesters in comparison with other sources. The potential goal of this informational perversion could be an attempt to create an image of the protest as unpopular and unsupported by the local population.

Another example of dishonest information is also the way media named the events at Maidan. Considering the fact that the *Berkut*, police and '*titushky*' acted aggressively against protesters, even hitting the students, the protests became anti-governmental and not pro-European. Russian Vesti did not show the changing of the main goal and main idea of the protesters, perhaps not to show the disagreement and denial the government. Moreover, while the Ukrainian and German media called these movements a 'revolution', the Russian media did not use this term. Rather, the protests were described as 'preparations for the New Year celebrations' and that everything was peaceful and calm. In the German media there was also information about special police who had fought against students at government's command. And they told about the beginning of the revolution in Ukraine. This confirms the fact that 'das Erste' showed events more neutrally and still provided all the necessary information.

And the last example when information differed in all media is during the period referred to as the adoption of the laws (16.01.2014). The Ukrainian TSN reported that the opposition called this event an 'evil day in history', though some representatives of the government from Yanukovych's party, who ordained these laws, named the people at Maidan terrorists and radicals. That means that prevailing authorities could not find a common language with demonstrating people, and that the protests were truly anti-governmental. The Russian Vesti gladly reported about this event, probably because they wanted to show their support to the Ukrainian government. They also called protesters 'terrorists and nazis'. At the same time, the German channel 'das Erste' reported about 'dictatorial power in Ukraine'.

The analysis of the third part, about the most hellish days of the protests from 18-22nd February, corresponds to the above-mentioned conclusions. Obviously, the Ukrainian media, TSN, described incidents more inline with the accounts of eyewitnesses. They also described the participants as protesters, and the protest was called a 'revolution'. Moreover, it was often reported about the *Berkut*, police and '*titushky*' as aggressive fighters against protesters. They also reported about snipers who were killing people from the roofs.

In the case of the Russian media, Vesti, a tendency to use strong negative terms like 'nazis', 'fascists', 'radicals', 'right-wing extremists', 'maidowns' for participants can be noted, as well as talking about the swastika (fylfot) in their reports. Here, the term 'revolution' was not found, but the protest was described as a 'riot of terrorists and nazis'. Meanwhile, the *Berkut* and '*titushky*' were shown as a neutral side, which delivered security. Nothing was told about snipers and the reported amount of deaths was much smaller than in the reports of the TSN and 'das Erste'. Probably, again, with the reason to create a negative image of the participants and supporters of the Euromaidan and to show the actions of the current government as non-violent.

The German media 'das Erste' was very similar to the Ukrainian media, as they described these days fully and in a detailed way. The Euromaidan participants were called 'protestors' in the program Tagesschau; the protests themselves were characterized as 'the biggest riot against the president'; moreover, it was reported that people wanted to show democracy in a peaceful way. It also told about the *Berkut* and police's violent actions. It could be noted that the German media paid close attention to the snipers killing people and to the deaths during clashes between protesters and security forces.

From the presented analysis, it follows that the analysed TV-channels have different goals and different target groups. The Ukrainian TV channel TSN had a goal to cover the whole picture of the protest, mostly oriented to viewers who identify themselves with an independent Ukraine and probably would support the protest. It is also obvious that the Ukrainian media was much closer to all these events and they could show all of the incidents in details. Nevertheless, the Ukrainian media reported about this period in its own interests.

According to the conclusions about the Russian media, Vesti, it could be supposed that the goal of this channel was to diminish the whole protest movement, because it was not 'Russia-oriented'. Another goal could be to create a negative image of the participants and supporters of the Euromaidan for Russian viewers and to show the actions of the current government as non-violent. There is also almost no independent media in Russia, so all the events described are from the interests of the owner of the company. Furthermore, not all the incidents were described fully or carefully, so it could be supposed that one goal was to hide some facts and not show the whole picture.

The goals of the German media were focused on the German viewers, and they neutrally inform viewers about events in the Eastern part of Europe, and say what the EU does to solve this situation. Since Germany was not involved in the situation, its media was just observing all the incidents and show them more neutrally than others.

This analysis allows the author to claim that the neutrality of the German media connects with the official neutral position of Germany in this protest movement. From the position of the representative of the EU, they just neutrally reported about events at the Maidan. The negativeness of the Russian media could be explained as the 'loss of the territory under Russian influence'. The other explanation is to show the participants in a 'dark light' to dramatize the situation and make it worse in the eyes of Russian viewers. The Russian media is also oriented on their own TV-audience, so they create a negative image of Ukrainian protesters. The Ukrainian media covered the incidents fully and delivered a detailed picture of Euromaidan.

References

#Evromaidan (2013, December, 13). In: *Ukrayinska Pravda*. Retrieved from http://www.pravda.com.ua/articles/2013/12/13/7006365/.

15 tysyach studentiv vyrushyly do Yanukovycha vymahaty asoziaziyi z ES (2013, November, 27). In: *TSN*. Retrieved from http://tsn.ua/kyiv/15-tisyach-studentiv-virushili-do-yanukovicha-vimagati-asociaciyi-z-yes-322407.html.

18 lyutoho 2014 roku uchasnyky Evromaidanu vvazhayut pochatkom naykryvavishykh podiy (2014, February, 18). In: *TSN*. Retrieved from http://tsn.ua/video/video-novini/18-lyutogo-2014-roku-uchasniki-yevromaydanu-vvazhayut-pochatkom-naykrivavishih-podiy.html.

Azarov ziznavsya, shcho vidklav asoziaziyu z EZ na vymohu Rosii (2013, November, 26). In: *TSN*. Retrieved from http://tsn.ua/politika/azarov-ziznavsya-scho-vidklav-asociaciyu-z-yes-na-vimogu-rosiyi-322178.html.

Aretz, Eckart (2013, December, 2): Massenproteste in der Ukraine 'Janukowitsch ist nicht das Problem'. Retrieved from http://www.tagesschau.de/ausland/ukraine-proteste102.html.

Artemjev, Alexandr (2014, November, 12): Rossiyane veryat tolko novostyam federalnykh smi o sobytiyakh na Ukraine. In: *RBC*. Retrieved from http://www.rbc.ru/politics/12/11/2014/5460bfd5cbb20f7879b2a48b.

Besporyadki v Kieve: Meriya zakhvachena, metro zakryto (2014, February, 18). In: *Vesti*. Retrieved from http://www.vesti.ru/doc.html?id=1297825.

Do Evromaidanu pryamuyut titushky z Mariinskoho parku (2013, November, 29). In: *TSN*. Retrieved from http://tsn.ua/kyiv/do-yevromaydanu-styaguyutsya-titushki-z-mariyinskogo-parku-322853.html.

Do Kyeva planuyut zvezty proplachenykh evroshakhtariv ta titushok (2013, November, 23). In: *Ukrayinska Pravda*. Retrieved from http://www.pravda.com.ua/news/2013/11/23/7002812/.

Eskalation in der Ukraine: Mindestens 26 Tote bei Straßenschlachten in Kiew (2014, February, 19). *Tagesschau*. Retrieved from http://www.tagesschau.de/multimedia/video/video1373802.html.

Evromaidan Revoluciya Hidnosti. Povna khronolohiya! (2013, November, 21). Retrieved from https://www.youtube.com/watch?v=KWs62YiXPDA.

Freie Welt: Nemezkii SMI – rupor Washingtona, a ne Berlina (2016, August, 26). Retrieved from https://russian.rt.com/inotv/2016-08-26/Freie-Welt-Nemeckie-SMI-.

Fule nathnenyi rishuchistyu Ukrainy u pytanni prynyattya evrozakoniv (2013, November, 20). In: *TSN*. Retrieved from https://tsn.ua/politika/fyule-nathnenniy-rishuchistyu-ukrayini-u-pitanni-priynyattya-yevrozakoniv-321180.html.

Großheim, Berndt (2013, November, 24): Massendemonstrationen in der Ukraine 'Wir sind nicht die Sowjetunion'. Retrieved from http://www.tagesschau.de/ausland/ukraine434.html.

Information Broadcasting Service. Retrieved from http://media.1plus1.ua/ua/group/production/service-information-broadcasting.

Iz ubitykh v centre Kieva dostali pulyu i kartech (2014, January, 23). In: Vesti. Retrieved from http://www.vesti.ru/doc.html?id=1210147.

Holova Kabminu rozpoviv, shcho plany shchodo evrointehraziyi Ukrainy ne zminyuyutsya (2013, Novermber, 20). In: *TSN*. Retrieved from http://tsn.ua/politika/azarov-rozpoviv-pro-plani-ukrayini-schodo-asociaciyi-321169.html.

Holova SBU rozpoviv, koly i yakymy shlyakhamy Yanukovych vtik z Ukrainy (2014, April, 5). In: *TSN*. Retrieved from http://tsn.ua/politika/golova-sbu-rozpoviv-koli-i-yakimi-shlyahami-yanukovich-vtik-z-ukrayini-343726.html.

Khronika poslednikh dnei: razyarennye tolpy demonstrantov gromyat Kiev (2013, December, 2). In: *Vesti*. Retrieved from http://www.vesti.ru/doc.html?id=1161955.

Kievskie studenty bastuyut iz-za priostanovki evrointegracyi (2013, November, 26). In: *Vesti*. Retrieved from http://www.vesti.ru/doc.html?id=1159993.

Kiselev, Maksim (2014, February, 20): Boi v Kieve: 'Pravyi sektor' diktuet usloviya prekrashcheniya nasiliya. In: *Vesti*. Retrieved from https://www.vesti.ru/doc.html?id=1305319.

Klichko pytalis ne pustit v Kiev poborotsya za Evrosoyuz (2013, November, 24). In: *Vesti*. Retrieved from http://www.vesti.ru/doc.html?id=1159079.

Krei, Alexander (2015, December, 30): NDR jubelt über steigende 'Tagesschau'-Quoten. Retrieved from http://www.dwdl.de/zahlenzentra-le/54084/ndr_jubelt_ueber_steigende_tagesschauquoten/.

Kryvave Vodokhreshcha v Kyevi (2014, January, 20). In: *BBC*. Retrieved from http://www.bbc.com/ukrainian/news/140119_kiev_rally_19january_nk.shtml.

Laack, Stephan (2013, December, 2): Demonstranten harren in Kiewer Innenstadt aus. Retrieved from http://www.tagesschau.de/multimedia/audio/audio114862.html.

Levada (2014, November, 12): Rossiyane veryat tolko novostyam federalnykh smi o sobytiyakh na Ukraine. Retrieved from http://www.leva-da.ru/2014/11/12/rossiyane-veryat-tolko-novostyam-federalnyh-smi-o-sobytiyah-na-ukraine/.

Litovko, Natalya: Russia 24: Televidenie bez granic. *Vesti*. Retrieved from http://www.vesti.ru/doc.html?id=1009258.

Lyudy hotovi stoyaty na barykadakh Evromaidanu azh do Rizdva (2013, December, 13). In: *TSN*. Retrieved from http://tsn.ua/kyiv/mishki-zi-snigom-na-barikadah-yevromaydanu-peretvorilisya-na-brili-lodu-325272.html.

Lyudy postavyly ultymatum: vidstavka Yanukovycha do ranku (2014, February, 21). In: *Ukrayinska Pravda*. Retrieved from http://www.pravda.com.ua/news/2014/02/21/7015590/.

Machtkampf in der Ukraine: Zahlreiche Tote bei schweren Straßenkämpfen in Kiew (2014, February, 20). *Tagesschau*. Retrieved from http://www.tagesschau.de/multimedia/video/video1374072.html.

Medvedev ne isklyuchil vvedeniya sankzyi protiv Ukrainy (2013, November, 20). In: *Vesti*. Retrieved from http://www.vesti.ru/d-oc.html?id=1157483&cid=5.

Mehr Moskau, weniger Brüssel (2013, November, 21). Retrieved from http://www.tagesschau.de/ausland/ukraine418.html.

Messner, E. E. (2004): Vsemirnaya myatezhevoina. Moscow: Kuchkovo pole.

Mitinguyushchiye vozveli na Maidane barrikady (2013, December, 2). In: Vesti. Retrieved from http://www.vesti.ru/doc.html?id=1161986.

Na kyivskyi Evromaidan vyishlo vzhe ponad 100 tysyach ukrainciv (2013, November, 24). In: *TSN*. Retrieved from http://tsn.ua/kyiv/na-yevromaydan-viyshlo-vzhe-100-tisyach-lyudey-321742.html?g=article&m=383893633.

Neag, Mihai Marcel (2016): A New Typology Of War – The Hybrid War. In: Military Art and Science, S. 14–20.

Novoyaz 2013. Retrieved from http://www.public.ru/press_slovo_2013/.

Pershi heroyi Nebesnoyi sotni (2013, January, 22). In: *TSN*. Retrieved from http://tsn.ua/ukrayina/pershi-geroyi-nebesnoyi-sotni-minuv-rik-z-dnya-zagibeli-nigoyana-ta-zhiznevskogo-404293.htmlv.

Priostanovlenie associacyi Ukrainy s ES mozhet vylitsya v ugolovnoe delo (2013, November, 21). In: *Vesti*. Retrieved from http://www.vesti.ru/doc.html?id=1158153.

Ruck, Ina (2014, February, 28): Öffentlicher Auftritt in Russland. Zur Rede von Janukowitsch. *Tagesschau*. Retrieved from http://www.tagesschau.de/multimedia/video/video1376000.html.

Segodnya – godovshina diktatorskikh zakonov 16 yanvarya 2014 (2014, January, 16). In: *TSN*. Retrieved from http://ru.tsn.ua/video/video-novini/segodnya-godovschina-diktatorskih-zakonov-16-yanvarya-2014.html.

Sokolov, Nikolaj (2014, February, 19): V centre Kieva etoy nochyu ne spali. In: *Vesti*. Retrieved from https://www.vesti.ru/doc.html?id=1299548.

Specvypusk TSN pro Evromaidan za 1.12.2013 (2013, December, 1). Retrieved from https://www.youtube.com/watch?v=b-FcUhMUikY.

Sredstva massovoy informacyi teryayut doverie ukraincev (2015, July, 1). Retrieved from http://prokuratura.org.ua/?p=36960.

Stalinski, Sandra (2014, January, 28): Staatsmacht hat die Kontrolle verloren. Retrieved from http://www.tagesschau.de/ausland/ukraineinterview100.html.

Stöber, Silvia (2013, November, 21): Unter dem Druck des Kreml. Retrieved from http://www.tagesschau.de/ausland/euosteuropapolitik100.html.

Storonnikov evrointegracyi izbili v Dnepropetrovske (2013, December, 2). In: *Vesti*. Retrieved from http://www.vesti.ru/doc.html?id=1162066.

Tyahnybok narakhuvav u Kyevi 5 tysyach titushok-provokatoriv (2013, December, 2). In: *TSN*. Retrieved from http://tsn.ua/politika/tyagnibok-narahuvav-u-kiyevi-5-tisyach-titushok-provokatoriv-323255.html.

Ukraine: Police firing live ammo in Kiev clashes (2014, February, 20). Retrieved from https://www.youtube.com/watch?v=yCzIIFAsGk4.

Unter Mitarbeit von Birgit Virnich (2013, December, 3). *Tagesschau*. Retrieved from http://www.tagesschau.de/multimedia/sendung/tt5132.html.

Virnich, Birgit (2014, February, 18). *Tagesschau*. Retrieved from http://www.tagesschau.de/multimedia/sendung/tt5282.html.

V RF vitayut rishennya Kabminu pryzupynyty pidhotovku do pidpysannya uhody pro asociaciyu (2013, November, 22). In: *Vesti*. Retrieved from http://tsn.ua/politika/u-rosiyskiy-dumi-radiyut-zrivu-yevrointegraciyi-ukrayini-i-vvazhayut-ce-golosom-zdorovogo-gluzdu-321503.html.

Yak Ukraina otrymala Nebesnu sotnyu. Khronika nayvazhchykh dniv Maidanu (2014, February, 20). In: *TSN*. Retrieved from http://tsn.ua/ukrayina/yak-ukrayina-otrimala-nebesnu-sotnyu-hronika-nayvazhchih-dniv-maydanu-41069-1.html.

Yanukovich zhivet u druga pod Rostovom (2014, February, 28). In: Vesti. Retrieved from http://www.vesti.ru/doc.html?id=1332629.

Za otricanie nacistskikh prestupleniy na Ukraine budut sazhat (2014, January, 16). In: *Vesti*. Retrieved from http://www.vesti.ru/doc.html?id=1198340.

Additional Part

The WWI Propaganda Clichés Applied to the Modern Russo-Ukrainian Conflict over the Donbas and Crimea Regions

Ivan Basenko

Abstract: *This article reveals a resemblance between WWI propaganda and contemporary Russo-Ukrainian propaganda techniques. This research is based on the examination of each wars' media campaigns and covers enemy objectification and the deception of atrocities. In particular, it establishes the strong parallels between the WWI era demonization of the German Kaiser Wilhelm II and the more recent criticisms of the Russian President Vladimir Putin. Furthermore, the study claims that, when Russian media reported 'atrocities' by Ukrainians in 2014, they were actually comprehensively replicating the Great Wars falsification techniques. Therefore, the article suggests that the WWI historical experience is useful in the analysis of the modern information war.*

Keywords: *Propaganda, media campaign, the image of an enemy, atrocity, WWI, the Russian military intervention in Ukraine*

Introduction

The concept of propaganda as an instrument to disseminate ideological truths originated from Pope Gregory XV's Counter-Reformation bull 'Inscrutabili Divinae Providentiae Arcano' (1622) and first saw an extensive secular application during the French Revolution. However, it was not until the First World War that the term had acquired its modern sinister connotation: propaganda, particularly of falsified atrocities and patriotic, mass-mobilizing spectacles, bolstered an unprecedented military conflict between nations (Auerbach & Castronovo, 2013). This study uncovers some WWI propaganda techniques that were revived in the contemporary information war over Russian military intervention in Ukraine.

While the case study is limited to the principal examples of enemy objectification and the deception of atrocities, it should be noted that more similarities exist. For instance, there is a parallel between the Great War concept of a hostile culture and the present-day decommunization process in Ukraine, and another parallel between the Entente's economic blockade of

Germany and the international sanctions imposed against the Russian Federation. By establishing such resemblances, this article utilizes the Great War experience in the analysis of today's Russo-Ukrainian conflict over the Donbas and Crimea regions.

The evidence for the WWI analysis is from prominent Kyivan daily press from 1914-1916. At that time Kyiv was a center of the imperial borderland region of the Southwestern Krai. Despite the region's predominantly Ukrainian ethnic composition, Russians constituted the city's influential majority (Lazanska, 1999). State ideology as well as Russian public opinion claimed the region to be a core part of Russia and integrated the Ukrainians into the All Russian national project (Miller, 2008). The Kyiv press performed as a key media actor, closely connected to national politics. It is noteworthy to mention that the media represented a solely Russian point of view, since printing in the Ukrainian language had been officially banned at the beginning of the war (Mukomela, 2010).

The study reviews the most significant Russian language newspapers: the far right *Kiev*, the conservative *Kievlyanin*, and the liberal and socialist *Kievskaya Mysl*, *Poslednie Novosti* and *Gazeta Kopeyka* tabloids. The supplementary references to this historiography provide the European context of WWI media warfare. The comparison to modernity is built upon the distinguished media campaigns of 2014-2016, inter alia, the Ukrainian demonization of the Russian President Vladimir Putin and Russian falsification of atrocities.

The WWI Experience of Enemy Objectification

An atmosphere of optimism for the forthcoming grand military clash was typical in pre-1914 Europe. Since the 1870s, opinions of war had been debated amongst politicians, artists and philosophers, influencing a broad audience via popular fiction and printed media (Fergusson, 1999). Nevertheless, a real conflict was deemed highly improbable – it was both irrational for the globalized economy and destructive to civilization. Thus, the populace perceived the arms race and warmongering rhetoric as regrettable, yet ordinary tools of geopolitical struggle (Hobsbawm, 1989). In particular, this mood was common for Russo-German relations. Although the Russian public opinion was concerned with German militarism, expansionist trade and foreign policy (Bogomolov, 2015), it also acknowledged the need for beneficial cooperation and praised the innovative German culture (Obolenskaya, 2000). In general, the media distinguished the peaceful and industrious German people from the outrageously imperialistic ruling class, identified as the Prussian Junkers or members of Pan-Germanic political groups. The latter were profoundly criticized in Russia. However, the rules of decorum basically prevented the press from attacking Kaiser Wilhelm II (Busch, 2006).

The outbreak of the war drastically magnified Russia's aversion towards the belligerent 'Prussian elites'. With German aggression utilized as key moral capital, the media started a campaign of accusations. They placed sole responsibility for the 'European catastrophe' onto the German Emperor – an autocratic ruler, a plenipotentiary to wage war and notoriously known for bellicose public statements (Bogomolov, 2015). At the outset, the idea of war's absurdity prompted many to question the mental health of the Kaiser. Journalists suggested that Wilhelm might have accidently lost his nerve under the pressure of another international crisis[1] (Savenko, 1914), was a victim of degeneracy disease (*Kievlyanin*, 16 December 1914) or a purposeful 'World's Herostratus' (Bespalov, 1914).

Simultaneously, the Russian media developed the notion of the Kaiser's malign ambition for world domination. This provided the public with the earliest image of a common foe and established a righteous cause to go to war. In order to instill public repulse the press had accumulated all possible negative descriptions of Wilhelm II. Specifically, he was stigmatized as the 'bloodthirsty conqueror' (Sibirskiy, 1914), 'a Man, who flooded Europe with blood' (Figaro, 1914 a), a 'cynic' who had shamelessly annexed Belgium, a 'thug' (Miheev, 1914), a 'narcissistic tyrant' (Harold, 1914) and a 'wild beast' (Figaro, 1914b). Theatrical exaggerations allowed the media to draw the ultimate image of Wilhelm as a destroyer of civilization – a 'descendant of the barbaric Attila' (A.I., 1914), an 'insane Nebuchadnezzar of the XX century', the 'Nero' and 'Caligula' of the time (Nivich, 1914), a 'demon of the war' (Janu, 1914), 'Satan's tool' (Shcherbachov, 1914 a) and 'the German Mephistopheles' himself (*Kiev*, 10 September 1914). This kind of disparagement was frequently compounded with a grim irony,

---

[1] The references to the WWI newspaper articles are presented in the original Julian calendar.

thereby serving as an instrument of public reassurance and maintaining confidence for victory.

In August of 1914, emphasis on the Kaiser's personality marginalized the role of the German nation in starting the war. This indicated a lack of initial enmity towards the Germans as well as the common incomprehension of the horrors of that war. Occasionally, the newspapers anticipated a triumphant entry into Berlin and Vienna by the Russian army, to wreak 'an elegant vengeance' of dethronement on their 'impudent rulers' (Figaro, 1914 c). However, a discussion arose later on how to treat the belligerent nation.

Following official propaganda, Russian conservative media presented the war as an existential clash between Germandom and Slavdom. On the contrary, much liberal media exclusively blamed the warmongering Prussian authority. They expected 'the German democracy' to quickly recover from governmental deception and overthrow the country's 'criminal' elite (Bogomolov, 2015). In the most extreme instance, Kievskaya Mysl even claimed that the war was 'fratricidal': 'And behind the German Sultan stands the honest, hardworking, beautiful German nation, in its helpless despair, shedding the tears of sorrow it observes how on its behalf the robber's knife is raised against its brothers…' (Yablonovskiy, 1914 a). However, by the end of 1914, the war experience and the propaganda about atrocities had sufficiently dispelled this interpretation. Instead, the press had recognized the enemy's collective responsibility: an image of 'the apocalyptic beast' ought to be expanded to the whole of Germany, whose '…armed hordes, were pouring out of their beloved Fatherland into the West and East' (*Kievlyanin*, 2 December 1914). On the whole, the 1914 Russian media campaign had formed a complex explanation for the causes of the war. Besides the Kaiser, it also condemned the ill-willed German government, business and military elites, political parties, intellectuals and the commonalty. Eventually, these various groups fused into a single image of the German enemy (Judin, 2012). Significantly, this set of anti-German clichés constituted the basis of propaganda for the entire period of the Russian Empire's involvement in WWI.

The Objectification of an Enemy in the Modern Russo-Ukrainian Conflict: The Ukrainian Case

Russo-Ukrainian relations of the pre-war decade were overshadowed by a number of disputes: the Tuzla island controversy of 2003 was followed by the Kremlin's antipathy of the Ukrainian 'Orange Revolution' in 2004 and the two 'gas wars' of 2005/06 and 2008/09. Furthermore, the 2010 election of the allegedly loyal Ukrainian President Viktor Yanukovych did not alter Russia's policy as its government launched an export blockade against Ukraine in 2013 (*National Security and Defense*, 2014).

Yet, neither these intergovernmental tensions nor the Russian Federation's military aggression against Georgia in 2008 had effectively shaken Ukraine's positive image of Russia. According to the Kyiv International Institute of Sociology (Paniotto, 2016), the national sympathy level has remained at 80% until the end of February 2014. Although complex, this phenomenon could be generally attributed to the extent of Russian soft power in Ukraine (Bogomolov & Lytvynenko, 2012). Until recently, many among both the Russian political elites and the population perceived Ukraine as a part of their country's own identity.

This national myth derived from the old imperial 'triune Russian nation' and the Soviet 'fraternal nations' paradigms. Likewise, it asserted strong historical and cultural ties between Russia and Ukraine and prompted Russia's idea of 'reunification' (Kappeler, 2014). By taking advantage of a strong Russification legacy, Russia had effectively influenced its Ukrainian audience through various channels, such as the Russian Orthodox Church, the mass media, formal and informal business networks and non-governmental organizations (Bogomolov & Lytvynenko, 2012). Indirectly, the very same factor determined Ukraine's attitude towards Russian political elites. According to the national poll of the sociological group 'Rating' taken on the eve of Euromaidan in October 2013, a positive evaluation of the President Vladimir Putin (47%) still exceeded the negative one (40%) (*Rating Group Ukraine*, 2014).

The radical shift of attitude occurred in March of 2014, following the Russian Federation's annexation of the Crimea. Aware of the de-facto authoritarian Russian political regime (*Freedom House*, 2014), both the Ukrainian and international community accused President Putin of violating Ukraine's territorial integrity. Similarly to the WWI experience, an ill-willed political decision led to a worldwide media campaign of condemnation. Significantly, the metaphorical language remained identical: Putin was portrayed as a war's inciter, Joker – 'the world's enemy', a 'maniac' or 'devil'; new parallels with 'Hitler' and 'Stalin' substituted the outdated images of 'Attila' and 'Neron' (*Tyzhden*, 11 March 2014). Kuznetsova (2014) establishes the causal effect between the aggressive actions of Russia and an increase of the use of the Putin-Hitler media metaphor. While it is the most powerful comparison in a political discourse, this metaphor indicates the international perception of the Russian leader's ultimate threat to the world's security and stability. In Ukraine, the public frustration with Putin's policy also prompted the invention of a deriding, nationwide slogan: 'Putin – khuilo' (i.e. 'Putin is a dickhead') (*TSN*, 4 April 2014). Scandalous episodes of its overt utterance in politics and showbusiness received profound media coverage. Consequently, Ukraine's negative attitude towards Putin reached 76% by April 2014 (*Rating Group Ukraine*, 2014) and remains as high as 80 % in 2016 (*24tv*, 22 July 2015).

There is also a resemblance between 1914 and 2014 media perceptions of the enemy nation. In Ukraine's case, the public's disgust of Russian political elites did not instantly lead to the rejection of the Russian nation. Although gradually decreasing, in May 2014 the local sympathy rate towards the Russians still exceeded the enmity rate (52 vs 38%) (Paniotto, 2016). Presumably, the traditional Ukrainian perception of the neighbouring 'fraternal nation' shaped these results. The media reflected public opinion by presenting the alternative 'other Russia' – democratic, supportive for Ukraine and irreconcilable towards Putin (*Radio Svoboda*, 21 September 2014). However, by 2014 the initial expectations of Russian society's ability to stop the conflict had proved empty (*TSN*, 11 August 2016). Evidence of Putin's astonishing popularity in Russia forced many Ukrainians to break with the imposed fraternity myth with Russia and establish their own cultural distinction[2].

By January of 2015, war escalations resulted in a high of 63% of Russia's loathing. This came from reports of a Russian artillery bombardment

[2] For example, the poem by Anastasia Dmytruk, extolling the Ukrainian virtue of freedom as opposed to the 'Russian servility' became symbolic in the national media space (*24tv*, 30 June 2014).

across the border and the Russian army's explicit military invasion in August of 2014 (Paniotto, 2016). At this point the Ukrainian Parliament has officially recognized the Russian Federation as an aggressive country (*TSN*, 27 January 2015), thus suspending the protracted media discussion on the status of the conflict (Bukovskyi, 2014). Similarly to WWI trench warfare, nowadays the Russo-Ukrainian conflict continues in a series of tactical frontline clashes[3]. However, despite these casualties, the recent national poll indicated a minor decrease in the animosity towards Russia. Apparently, the war has become routine.

WWI Atrocity Propaganda

The media's exposure of enemy atrocities became the integral part of the horror of WWI and hateful propaganda. Alongside national fervor, it played a key role in 1914 through the mobilization of the war effort in both the Entente and Central Powers (Senyavskaya, 2006). According to Hayward, (2010) atrocity stories originated from either imagination or reality, yet deliberately exaggerated the incidents. Not only the special propaganda bureaus but also journalists susceptible to sensationalism and popular rumours had contributed to the creation of atrocity propaganda. In particular, a recent survey by Horne and Kramer (2001) established a controversial nature to the 'German atrocities' on the Western Front. On the one hand *Deutsches Heer*[4] had performed crimes against the civil population by killing approximately 6 thousand civilians and destroying up to 20 thousand houses over the course of the 1914 offensive. On the other hand, all the iconic media stories of the German's 'Hun barbarity', such as 'nurse mutilations', a 'baby without hands' or the 'crucified soldier' incident had all been generally recognized as fake by the end of 1920s (Ponsonby, 1928).

The Russian atrocity propaganda followed this general pattern. Upon the enemy's invasion into Russian Poland, the media presented the local German barbarity as analogous to Belgium's story. It used the incident in a

---

[3] According to the newspaper Tyzhden, since the beginning of 2016 alone more than 6 hundred Ukrainian soldiers have been killed or wounded as a result of Russian daily ceasefire violations (*Tyzhden,* 15 June 2016).

[4] Deutsches Heer – Imperial German Army between 1871 and 1919.

border town near Kalisz as the first major symbol of enemy terror, instigating a nationwide campaign (Engelstein, 2012). Significantly, at the early stages of the war, these atrocities were reported primarily due to the spontaneity of the press's patriotism.

However in April of 1915, the Russian government took charge of the campaign by establishing the Extraordinary Commission of Inquiry. It investigated German violations of the laws and customs of war, divulging the subsequent results via the country's mass media. Despite the general veracity of the data, commission reports were often criticized for a lack of consistency: official propaganda combined human misery with the bravado of martyrs' 'heroic boldness' (Astashov, 2014). Extensive reiteration of German atrocities and their divergence from the real wartime experience soon caused a gradual decay of the public interest. By the end of 1916, the overall weariness of the war had reshaped society's attitude towards the Germans as a 'cruel beast' into the humanized perception of the Germans as equal victims of the futility of war (Senyavskaya, 2006).

The atrocity propaganda in the Kyivan press embraced three subtopics, namely the brutality of *Deutsches Heer* at the frontline, its crimes against the civil population in the occupied areas and the misdeeds against the prisoners of war in Germany. Stories from the battlefield told of Russian soldiers being captured, horribly tortured and murdered, which innately nourished the public's fear and hatred, thus preventing the very idea of surrender (*Kiev*, 16 September 1914). At the same time, such episodes promoted national heroism by glorifying the warriors' ability to withstand all the torments with honour and loyalty (*Kievlyanin*, 26 September 1914).

Also, the press criticized Germany's technical superiority in weaponry. Among other things, the expanding bullets, chemical weapons, zeppelins and submarines were labeled 'immoral', thus allowing the media to justify Russia's backwardness and its right for reciprocal retaliation (ibid, 20 August 1914; Sif, 1914). The coverage of the German atrocities against civilians was identical for both the Western and Eastern Fronts. Ordinarily, it included dramatic scenes of the enemy committing brutal rapes (*Yuzhnaya kopeyka*, 5 August 1914), mutilations and murders, blasphemy (*Kievlyanin*, 13 October 1914), detention of hostages (G-ij, 1914), plundering and vandalism of the world's cultural heritage (Arkadin, 1914; Shcherbachev, 1914 b).

In the same manner, the media revealed the outrageous treatment of interned Russian citizens originally overtaken by Germany in the war (Abdrashitov, 2012). With their ultimate release, at the beginning of 1915 the focus had shifted onto the fate of Russian prisoners of war (Nagornaya, 2012). By utilizing the atrocity rhetoric, the press had effectively undermined the prewar stereotype of the 'cultured German nation' and introduced the new image of the common 'Teutonic ogres' (Skrynchenko, 1914). However, this did not lead to an uncontrolled escalation of wrath. The press dissuaded the public from committing atrocities as reprisals by claiming it was a sign of weakness (Chagovec, 1914; Korchev, 1914). The media contrasted Prussian barbarity with the concept of Russian spirituality in order to nurture a mood of moral superiority (Yablonovskiy, 1914 b). Consequently, a just international court-martial was considered to be the best revenge against the enemy's crimes (A–v., 1914; Ezhov, 1915). Furthermore, the atrocity propaganda lacked consistency while the media had occasionally presented the opposite, humanized image of the enemy. For instance, the newspapers did mention positive situations from German civilians' kind heartedness and the enemy soldiers' battleground chivalry (*Kievlyanin*, 19 November 1914; Mayskiy, 1914; *Kievskaya Mysl*, 6 January 1915).

The Atrocity Propaganda in the Modern Russo-Ukrainian Conflict: The Russian Case

The 2014 media campaign of the alleged 'genocide against the Russians and Russian speakers in Ukraine' should be examined as an acme of the Kremlin's continuous anti-Ukrainian discourse. Since the Orange Revolution of 2004, Russia has been waging an information war against Kyivan political reorientation towards the European Union / NATO global actors. Well established in the Ukrainian media space, Russian TV channels broadcasted the old Soviet propaganda clichés about the 'vicious and decaying West' and the 'Nazi-collaborative' Ukrainian nationalists. They aimed to divide Ukrainian society into two irreconcilable groups, presented as the 'good' pro-Russian majority and the 'malicious' pro-Western, Russophobic minority. Despite the campaign's general failure, Moscow succeeded in influencing a number of Ukraine's Eastern regions with a traditionally strong pro-Soviet identity (Barabash, Bordjugov & Kotelenec, 2015).

This new tension occurred in the late 2013, when, following the start of Euromaidan protest movement, Russian media reverted to its usual strategy of calumniation. Yet, the triumph of the '*Revolution of Dignity*' in 2014 marked the end of President Yanukovych's regime, which was supported by Russia, and led to Ukraine's ultimate withdrawal from the Moscow sphere of influence. In these circumstances, Russia's mass communication has spread the demonizing rhetoric over the whole of Ukraine, claiming the Kyiv authority is illegitimate, 'gripped by the fascists' and endangering the country's Russian population (Dutsyk, 2015).

According to the open source investigation of the NATO StratCom Centre of Excellence, Russian media acted in coherence with the official authorities. StratCom concludes that the Russian Federation has employed a profound deception tactic in order to distract and delay opponents and international public opinion. Under the pretext of these fabricated 'genocide' accusations, it has annexed the Crimea. Later on, the same rhetoric accompanied the Kremlin's disguised military intervention to the Ukrainian Donbas (*The NATO StratCom Centre of Excellence*, 2014). Interestingly, the Russian experts on propaganda, Barabash and Bordyugov (2015), acknowledge the principal role of the atrocity campaign to sustain Russia's public support for the hybrid war in Donbas. On the contrary, Ukrainian propaganda was largely founded on the basis of Russia's military aggression and its promotion of the pro-Russian separatists.

The National Institute for Strategic Studies argues that Russia's falsified propaganda is responsible for deliberate disinformation and an unreasonable instigation of hatred among the population of the occupied territories. By blocking the alternative Ukrainian TV broadcasting, Russian occupational authorities in Crimea and Donbas ensure the domination of the fabricated version of events (Isakova, 2014).

Similarly to the WWI case, the modern Russian atrocity campaign is build upon a reiteration of dramatized and improbable, yet emotionally affected stories. For instance, Russian state TV's First Channel constantly depicts the 'atrocities of the punitive squads of the Kyiv Junta'. In particular it became notorious after the fake story about the 'crucified Russian baby', allegedly executed by the Ukrainian military (Chumakova, 2014). Later, it also alleged that Ukrainian soldiers had been ordered to kill civilians and were fighting in order to earn, as promised, 'a parcel of land and the two slaves' (Shishkin, 2014).

Another state channel, Russia 1, broadcasted a prime-time political program, mentioning that '[Kyiv] Junta had raped a female retiree during her epileptic seizure and robbed her afterwards' ('Vecher s Vladimirom', 2014). Similarly, the Russian Federation attempted to win international support by forging false accusations against Ukraine over the Malaysia Airlines Flight 17 catastrophe. Yet, the international open source investigation of Bellingcat uncovered that it was the Russian anti-aircraft system *Buk* responsible for the airliner shootdown (*Bellingcat*, 2016). In return, the Ukrainian media exposed such cases as evidence of Russian falsification (*TSN,* 4 November 2014). However, the question of war crimes in the zone of conflict remains open: in a recent annual report, Amnesty International claimed both Russia and Ukraine were responsible for the violence (*Amnesty International,* 2016).

Contrary to WWI, Ukraine prosecuted its combatants that were accused of violating the law. This spurred a heated public discussion. Many observers believed the government misused judicial inaccuracies during peacetime, thus persecuting former paramilitary volunteers for their 'unauthorized' participation in national defense. Nevertheless, some of the trials also include marauding, kidnapping and sexual assault charges (Kostyuk, 2015).

At the same time, the Russian media adhered to the WWI principles of the war coverage. They presented the Russian-controlled forces in an exclusively positive light, attributing all the misdeeds to the Ukrainian military. Yet, as a general rule, any disinformation eroded over time (*The NATO StratCom Centre of Excellence*, 2014). Similarly to the WWI case, nowadays Russian falsified propaganda is experiencing a gradual decay. In order to sustain it, Russian authorities and media invent new fake atrocity storylines. The latest example of such creativity could be the official Moscow accusations of the alleged 'Ukrainian subversive groups' attack in Crimea (*Interfax,* 10 August 2016).

Conclusion

The First World War and the modern Russian hybrid war in Ukraine diverge in both the origin and essence, yet they share the common propaganda techniques of presenting an enemy. Out of a variety of examples, this article reveals the two significant cases of WWI legacy – the media campaigns of enemy objectification and atrocity deception.

In 1914, mass communication across Europe had transformed society's initial shock into a patriotic fervour by asserting righteous, defensive causes of struggle. In particular, the Entente Powers introduced a demonized image of the German Kaiser Wilhelm II as of the ultimate conflict instigator. In the Russian Empire, this image became the focal point of propaganda due to the surprise of the war and the original lack of enmity towards the German nation.

In 2014, the very same factors conditioned the Ukrainian campaign against Russian President Putin. As yet restrained by the myth of Russian 'fraternity', the Ukrainian media presented Putin as another malign autocratic ruler, solely responsible for Russia's military aggression in Crimea and Donbas regions. However, in the course of each war a more generalized image of the enemy was developed. As a result, nowadays Ukrainian public opinion has recognized the Russian nation's liability for the Kremlin's policy and commonly identifies Russia with an enemy-state.

Similarly to the WWI case, the media's campaign about 'the enemy atrocities' had played a crucial role in the mass mobilization Russo-Ukrainian hybrid war. At first, Moscow fabricated 'the Russian genocide in Ukraine' thesis, utilizing it as a key justification for the Crimea annexation. Later on it launched a profound media campaign of the 'Ukrainian atrocities' in Donbas, designed to both gain internal support for the war and to alienate the Russian occupied population from Ukraine.

In comparison to WWI, the contemporary Russian campaign has proved to be much more centralized and coherent. Although overtly false, it has reached its goals due to constant reiteration, total domination and its primary audience's predisposition. In the end, these similarities of the WWI situation allow us to analyze and predict the impact of the propaganda techniques in the modern Russo-Ukrainian war.

References

Abdrashitov Je. E. (2012). Rossiyskie poddannye v Germanii v avguste 1914 g. i formirovanie obraza germanskogo vraga v gody Pervoy mirovoy voyny [The Russian citizens in Germany in August of 1914 and the formation of the German enemy's image in the course of WWI]. *Nauchnye vedomosti Belgorodskogo gosudarstvennogo universiteta*. 21 (120), 170 – 178.

Astashov, A. B. (2014). 'Zverstva' voysk antirusskoy koalicyi v 1914–1918 gg.: voennyi opyt i propaganda [The 'atrocities' of the anti-Russian coalition's armies in 1914–1918: combat experience and the propaganda]. In I. N. Novikova, A. Ju. Pavlov, A. A. Malygina (Eds.), Pervaya mirovaya voyna, Versalskaya sistema i sovremennost: sb. statey (pp. 65–72). S-Petersburg: SPbGU.

Auerbach, J., & Castronovo, R. (2013). Introduction: Thirteen Propositions about Propaganda. In J. Auerbach and R. Castronovo (Eds.), The Oxford Handbook of Propaganda Studies (pp. 1–18) Oxford – New York: Oxford University Press.

Barabash, V.V., Bordyugov, G.A., Kotelenec, E.A. (2015). Gosudarstvennaya propaganda i informacyonnye voyny. Uchebnoe posobie. [The state propaganda and information wars. A tutorial]. Moskva: AIRO-XXI.

Bogomolov, I. K. (2015). Obraz protivnika v russkoy periodicheskoy pechati 1914-1915 gg. [The image of the enemy in the Russian press 1914–1915]. Moskva: RGGU.

Busch, M. (2006). Wachsende Aggressivität gegen das Wilhelminische Reich Russische Presse stimmen von der Jahrhundertwende bis 1914 [The growing aggressiveness against the Wilhelmine Empire. The Russian press case study from the turn of the century to 1914]. In D. Herrmann (Ed.), Deutsche und Deutschland aus russischer Sicht 19./20. Jahrhundert: Von den Reformen Alexanders II bis zum Ersten Weltkrieg (pp. 239–257). München: Wilhelm Fink Verlag.

Engelstein L. (2012). 'A Belgium of our own': the sack of Russian Kalisz, August 1914. In M. David-Fox, P. Holquist, A. M. Martin (Eds.), Fascination and Enmity: Russia and Germany as Entangled Histories, *1914–1945* (pp.13–38). Pittsburgh: University of Pittsburgh Press.

Ferguson, N. (1999). The Pity of War. New York, NY: Basic Books.

Judin N.V. (2012). Sozdanie obraza vraga v propagande stran Antanty v nachale Pervoy mirovoy voyny (avgust-dekabr 1914) [The creation of the image of the enemy. The Entente's propaganda at the beginning of the WWI (August – December 1914)]. *Izvestiya Saratovskogo universiteta.* 12 (3), 50–58.

Hobsbawm, E. J. (1989). The Age of Empire, *1875-1914*. New York: Vintage Books.

Lazanska, T., (1999). Narodonaselennya Ukrayiny [The population of Ukraine]. In V. H. Sarbey (Ed.), Ukrayinske pytannya v Rosiyskiy imperiyi (kinets XIX

– pochatok XX st.) [The Ukrainian question in the Russian Empire (the end of XIX – the beginning of XX c.)] (pp. 61–123). Kyiv: Instytut istoriyi Ukrayiny.

Miller, A. (2008). The Empire and the nation in the imagination of the Russian nationalism. In A. Miller (Ed.), The Romanov Empire and Nationalism. Essays in the Methodology of Historical Research (pp. 161–180). Budapest – New York: Central European University Press.

Mukomela, O. (2010) Na zlami vikiv: Ukrayinska zhurnalistyka na pochatku XX st. [At the turn of a century: the Ukrainian journalism at the beginning of the XX c.]. Kyiv: Hramota.

Nagornaya O. (2012) United by the barbed wire: Russian POWs in Germany, national stereotypes, and international relations, 1914–1922 In M. David-Fox, P. Holquist, A. M. Martin (Eds.), Fascination and Enmity: Russia and Germany as Entangled Histories, 1914–1945 (pp. 39–58). Pittsburgh: University of Pittsburgh Press.

Obolenskaya, S.V. (2000). Germaniya i nemcy glazami russkikh (XIX vek) [Germany and the Germans from the Russian perspective (XIX c.)] Moskva.

Ponsonby, A. (1928/1942). Falsehood in Wartime: Propaganda Lies of the First World War. London, Bradford & Dickens.

Senyavskaya, E. S. (2006). Glavnyi protivnik v mirovykh voynakh: Germaniya v soznanii rosseyan [The main enemy in the two world wars: the Russian perception of Germany]. In E. S. Senyavskaya (Ed.), Protivniki Rossii v voynakh XX veka: Evolyuciya 'obraza vraga' v soznanii armii i obshchestva (pp. 62–123). Moskva: ROSSPJeN.

The Russia-Ukraine conflict: current situation, consequences, prospects (2014) (The analytical report by the Razumkov Centre). *National Security and Defense*, 5–6 (148–149), 2–39.

Newspapers

A. I. (1914, September, 19). Villi i Atilla [Willy and Attila]. *Kiev*, p. 2.

A–v., P. (1914, August, 9). Chem borotsya s tevtonskimi zverstvami? [How to counteract the German atrocities]. *Kiev*, p. 2.

Arkadin, F. (1914, September, 16). Nemcy vo Lezhe [The Germans in Liege]. *Kievskaya Mysl*, p. 1.

Bezpalov, P. (1914, August, 1). Manyak [The Maniac]. *Poslednie Novosti*, p. 3.

Borba so zverem (1914, December, 2) [Struggle with the beast]. *Kievlyanin*, p.1.

Chagovec. V. (1914, September, 15). 'Revansh' [The revanche]. *Kievskaya Mysl*, pp. 1–2.

Chai i kofe (1914, November, 19) [The Tea and Coffee]. *Kievlyanin*, p. 2.

Dva degenerata – Franc Yosif i Vilgelm II (1914, December, 16) [The two degenerates – Franz Joseph and Wilhelm II]. *Kievlyanin*, p. 2.

Ezhov, A. (1915, January, 6). Dlya budushchego rascheta [For the future retribution]. *Kievlyanin*, p. 4.

Figaro (1914 a, September, 4). Vilgelm s palmovoy vetvyu v ruke [Wilhelm with a palm branch in the hand]. *Kiev*, p. 1.

Figaro (1914 b, August, 25). Myatushchiysya kayzer [The anxious Kaiser]. *Kiev*, p. 1.

Figaro (1914 c, September, 8). Obmanutye nadezhdy [The Dissapointment]. *Kiev*, p. 1.

Garol'd (1914, August, 18). Rifmy dnya. Gastronom [The rhymes of the day. The Gourmet] *Kievskaya Mysl*, pp. 1–2.

G-ij, G. (1914, Octover, 9). Iz voennykh epizodov [From the combat episodes]. *Kievskaya Mysl*, p. 1.

Ikh sistema vesti voynu (1914, August, 20) [Their system of waging the war]. *Kievlyanin*, p. 3.

Istoriya rycarstva (1915, January, 6) [The story of chivalry]. *Kievskaya Mysl*, p. 3. (1914, December, 31).

Janu, S. (1914, August, 17). 'Demon' [The Demon]. *Poslednie Novosti*, p. 3.

Korchev, A. (1914, August, 18). Rycarstvo [The chivalry]. *Kiev*, p. 1.

Koshchunstva nemcev (1916, October, 13) [Blasphemy of the Germans]. *Kievlyanin*, p. 2.

Nivich, J. (1914, September, 20). 'Sverkhchelovek' [The Overman]. *Kiev*, p. 2.

Malenkiy feleton. Faust i Mefistofel (1914, September, 10) [A small satirical article. The Faust and Mefistofeles]. *Kiev*, p. 3.

Mayskiy, V. (1914, December, 7). V gospitale [In the hospital]. *Kievskaya Mysl*, p. 2.

Mikheev (1914, August, 29). Malenkiy feleton. Vilina kasha [A small satirical article. Willy's porridge]. *Kiev*, p. 3.

Nadrugatelstvo nad polskimi zhenshchinami (1914, August, 5) [Harasment of the Polish women]. *Yuzhnaya kopeyka*, p. 4.

Savenko, A. (1914, July, 24). Mysli i vpechatleniya. LXII. Karera gosudarstva-vyskochki [Thoughts and impressions. LXII. Career of the upstart-state]. *Kievlyanin*, p. 2.

Shcherbachev, S. (1914 a, August, 30). Malenkiy feleton. Nemeckaya basnya [A small satirical article. The German fable]. *Kiev*, p. 3.

Shcherbachev, S. (1914 b, September, 11). Varvary (k razrusheniyu Reymskogo sobora) [The Barbarians (dedicated to the destruction of the Reims Cathedral)]. *Kiev*, p. 2.

Sibirskiy, P. (1914, July, 21). Siluety zhizni [The Silhouettes of Life]. *Poslednie Novosti*, p. 3

Sif (1914, December, 24). Varvarskie priemy [Barbarous methods]. *Yuzhnaya kopeyka*, p. 2.

Skrynchenko, D. (1914, August, 1). Vot tak kultura!.. [That is the culture!..]. *Kiev*, p. 2.

Soldatskaya prisyaga (1914, September, 26) [The soldier's oath]. *Kievlyanin*, p. 2.

Peremirie [The Truce]. *Kievlyanin*, p. 2.

Vyrezannye yazyki i blagouhayushchie cvety (1914, September, 16) [The cut off tongues and fragrant flowers]. *Kiev*, p. 1.

Yablonovskiy, A. (1914 a, August, 3). Nemeckiy sultan [The German Sultan]. *Kievskaya Mysl*, p. 2.

Yablonovskiy, A. (1914 b, August, 4). Nemeckie neistovstva [The German rage]. *Kievskaya Mysl,* pp. 1–2.

Internet sources

5 things you should know about the Russian attitude towards Putin, – The National Interest (2015, July, 22). *24tv*. Retrieved from http://24tv.ua/5_reche-y_yaki_potribno_znati_pro_stavlennya_do_putina_u_rosiyi__the_national_i-nterezt_n595501.

Amnesty International (2016, February, 23): Report 2015/16: The state of the world's human rights. Retrieved from https://www.amnesty.org/en/documen-ts/pol10/2552/2016/en/.

Attitude of Ukrainians to world leaders. January 2016 (2016, February, 10). Retrieved from http://ratinggroup.ua/en/research/ukraine/otnoshenie_ukrain-cev_k_mirovym_lideram_yanvar_2016.html.

Bellingcat (ed.) (2016, July, 15): MH17 The Open Source Investigation, Two Years Later. Retrieved from https://www.bellingcat.com/wp-content/uplo-ads/2016/07/mh17-two-years-later.pdf.

Bogomolov, A.; Lytvynenko, O. (2012): A Ghost in the Mirror: Russian Soft Power in Ukraine (Chatham House Briefing Paper). Retrieved from https://www.chathamhouse.org/sites/files/chathamhouse/public/Research/Rus-sia%20and%20Eurasia/0112bp_bogomolov_lytvynenko.pdf.

Bukovskyi, D. (2014, July, 16): Should Ukraine launch a war with Russia instead of the Anti-Terrorist Operation. In: *DSnews*. Retrieved from http://www.dsnews.ua/politics/chi-varto-ukrayini-zamist-ato-pochinati-viynu-z-rosieyu--16072014123200.

Celyami ukrainskikh diversantov v Krymu byli zhiznenno vazhnye obekty (2016, August, 10) [The Ukrainian subversive groups aimed to strike the essential objects in the Crimea]. In: *Interfax*. Retrieved from http://www.inter-fax.ru/russia/523000.

Chumakova, J. (2014, July, 12): Refugee from Slavyansk recalls, how she had witnessed an execution of the baby-son and the wife of the militiaman. *Russia 1*. Retrieved from https://www.1tv.ru/news/2014/07/12/37175-bezhenka_iz_sl-avyanska_vspominaet_kak_pri_ney_kaznili_malenkogo_syna_i_zhe-nu_opol-chentsa.

Deshchytsya appeased the protesters under the RF embassy in Kyiv and sang a song about Putin (2014, June, 15). In: *Dzerkalo tyzhnya*. Retrieved from http://dt.ua/POLITICS/deschicya-zaspokoyuvav-mitinguvalnikiv-pid-posolst-vom-rf-u-kiyevi-ta-zaspivav-pisnyu-pro-putina-145156_.html.

Dutsyk, D. (2015, January, 10): The twilight of the Russian journalism. Propaganda-2014. In: *Telekrytyka*. Retrieved from http://osvita.mediasapiens.ua/monitoring/ru_zmi/sutinki_rosiyskoi_zhurnalistiki_propaganda2014/.

Freedom House: Nation in Transit. Russia 2014. Retrieved from https://freedomhouse.org/report/nations-transit/2016/russia.

Isakova, T. O. (2014): Propaganda that instigates national and ethnic hostility: the problems of identification and countermeasure. Analytical report. Retrieved from http://www.niss.gov.ua/articles/1756/.

Kappeler, A. (2014): Ukraine and Russia: Legacies of the imperial past and competing memories. In: Journal of Eurasian Studies 5(2), S. 107–115. Retrieved from http://www.sciencedirect.com/science/article/pi-i/S1879366514000062.

Kostyuk, B. (2015, August, 10): The Ukrainian authorities should change their attitude to the military volunteers – the lawyers. Radio Svoboda. Retrieved from http://www.radiosvoboda.org/a/27181338.html.

Kuznetsova, E. (2014): Underlying Meanings of the Hitler Metaphor in Western Media. In: *J Mass Communicat Journalism* 4(10). Retrieved from http://dx.doi.org/10.4172/2165-7912.1000230.

Paniotto, V. (2016, June, 22): Dynamics of changes in the attitude of the population of Ukraine toward Russia, and in the attitude of the population of Russia toward Ukraine: April, 2008 – May, 2016. Retrieved from http://www.kiis.com.ua/?lang=eng&cat=reports&id=632&page=1.

Poltorak has informed about the war casualties of the Ukrainian Army in 2016 (2016, June, 15). In: *Tyzhden*. Retrieved from http://tyzhden.ua/News/167525.

Putin on the front cover of the international media (2014, March, 11). In: *Tyzhden*. Retrieved from http://tyzhden.ua/Gallery/104596.

Rada has recognized Russia as a state-aggressor (2015, January, 27). In: *TSN*. Retrieved from http://tsn.ua/politika/rada-viznala-rosiyu-krayinoyu-agresorom-405409.html.

Russia's protest movement against the war in Ukraine and Putin's falsehood (2014, September, 21). *Radio Svoboda*. Retrieved from http://www.radiosvoboda.org/a/26598518.html.

Rating Group Ukraine (2014, May, 5): Nostalgia for the Soviet Union and the attitude to separate persons. Retrieved from http://ratinggroup.ua/en/research/ukraine/nostalgiya_po_sssr_i_otnoshenie_k_otdelnym_lichnostyam.html.

Shishkin, O. (2014, November, 2): 70 ago the Soviet forces had liberated Ukraine from the fascists. *Russia 1*. Retrieved from https://www.1tv.ru/news/2014/11/02/28303-70_let_nazad_sovetskie_voyska_osvbodili_ukrainu_ot_fashistov.

Should we strike Ukraine? 'Moscow's Echo' launched a controversial poll in reference to the Crimea (incident) (2016, August, 11). In: *TSN*. Retrieved from https://tsn.ua/politika/chi-varto-vdariti-po-ukrayini-eho-moskvy-vlashtuvalo-skandalne-opituvannya-schodo-krimu-714412.html.

The evening with Vladimir Solov'ev (2014, November, 23). *Russia 1*. Retrieved from https://russia.tv/video/show/brand_id/21385/episode_id/1148439/video_id/1102419/.

The NATO StratCom Centre of Excellence (2015): Analysis of Russia's Information Campaign against Ukraine. Retrieved from www.stratcomcoe.org/download/file/fid/3213.

The Russians had interpreted the poem as an act of aggression, yet, it is about the freedom – author of the We will never be brothers (2014, June, 30). *24tv*. Retrieved from http://24tv.ua/rosiyani_spriynyali_virsh_yak_agresiyu_ta_vin__pro_svobodu__avtorka_nikogda_mi_ne_budem_bratyami_n459160.

Top 5 of the horrible Russian media fake stories about the 'atrocities' of the Ukrainian military (2014, November, 4). In: *TSN*. Retrieved from http://ru.tsn.ua/ukrayina/top-5-uzhasayuschih-feykov-rossiyskih-smi-o-zverstvah-ukrainskih-voennyh-394753.html.

Track 'Putin kh*ylo' has become famous in the Web: the coolest video and coubs (2014, April, 4). In: *TSN*. Retrieved from http://tsn.ua/tsikavinki/trek-putin-h-ylo-stav-hitom-internetu-naykrutishi-video-ta-koubi-343606.html.

The Role of the Weimar Triangle States in the Settlement of Conflicts in the Post-Soviet Space: The Russian Factor

Olga Rusova

Abstract: *In this article is a careful consideration of two of the most broad-scale conflicts in the territory of the former USSR in contemporary times, namely – the war in Georgia of 2008 and the Ukrainian crisis of 2014. The task of this research is to define the role of the EU in its efforts to resolve these crises through peaceful means. This has taken the form of the Weimar Triangle. The imposition of economic sanctions and an international boycott are used as the main leverages to impact the aggressor state. The article contains a comparative analysis of the importance of these two conflicts for the European security system and how the bilateral relations between Russia and EU member-states influence its foreign policy. The aim is also to analyze how the EU is going to realize its policy in the East, and what economic and political perspectives it has particularly for Ukraine.*

Keywords: *Weimar Triangle states, EU, the Ukrainian crisis, foreign policy, settlement of conflicts, economic sanctions*

The collapse of the Soviet Union, the foreign policy reorientation of the ex-socialist states toward the EU and NATO, and the democratic transformations in the former Soviet republics facilitated and intensified a security dialogue between the United States, Western Europe and Russia. This kind of cooperation was not only based on common interests in the defense sphere, but also on building sustainable and mutually beneficial economic ties. However, there are a lot of inconsistencies and tensions between Europe and Russia about the role of the latter in a number of military conflicts in such countries as Moldova (1992), Georgia (2008) and Ukraine currently.

After the EU's enlargement in 2004, there was a special focus on Eastern foreign policy. Then the Union started to share common boundaries with Ukraine and Belarus, which used to be considered subject to the Russian sphere of influence. In this situation a need arose to involve these countries in Europe-wide processes, but at the same time not guarantee their full EU membership in the very near future. Thus, the idea of the 'European Neighbourhood Policy' emerged. According to the European Security Strategy, the central task of the project involved the creation of the so-called 'security and stability belt' in the immediate vicinity of the EU (European Security Strategy, 2003). Apart from the post-Soviet states, the proposed program also covered the Mediterranean region (North Africa and Israel). A complex approach was used as the basis for building of relations between these countries and the EU.

However, the governments of the participating countries saw their cooperation with the EU in different ways. Also, in this context an inadequate attention was given to the 'Russian factor'. The enlargement of the EU through the accession of Ukraine, Moldova, Belarus, Georgia, Armenia and Azerbaijan, even in the long term, would conflict with the political interests of Moscow. The development of economic and political ties between the former Soviet republics and the West, and in particular their cooperation in military affairs (the majority of the EU member-states are also members of NATO), was regarded by Russia as an attempt to oust its influence from this region. In the provisions of the Russian military doctrine of 2010, the number one external military danger was the potential of the North Atlantic Treaty Organization to affect global functions (Russia's Military Doctrine, 2010). According to the document, these functions (including the enlargement of the organization) violate the rules of international law since the military infrastructure of NATO's member-states approach Russian borders.

The political situation in Ukraine and Georgia raised fears, too. In 2003 and 2004, 'color revolutions' took place there and resulted in pro-Western politicians coming to power. These events evoked in the Russian political leadership the sensation of a 'gradual loss' of the region. Consequently, the military conflict in August 2008 between Georgia and Russia, became a show of force to the Western world that the present-day Russian Federation comes short of military capabilities of the USSR, but is still a strong regional power and will protect its strategic interests. Russian political elite circles still used categorical concepts of the 'Cold War' period, where the United States and NATO are given the importance of a key player in matters of the international and European security. Russia perceives Europe as its most important economic partner and a vast market outlet for Russian oil and gas. But the post-Soviet space is the area where West and East political interests converge.

In all the conflicts that have arisen in this area since the independence of ex-Soviet republics until 2008, Russia participated in direct or indirect ways. These conflicts include clashes in the South Ossetia and Abkhazia, the conflict in Nagorno-Karabakh between Armenia and Azerbaijan, and the secession of Transnistria from Moldova. The official position of the Russian leadership refuses to recognize itself as a party in such conflicts, choosing the role of a peacemaker and simulating activities aimed to resolve conflicts. Therefore, the main task of the Weimar Triangle countries and other EU member states was to involve Russia in a real peacekeeping process. But such ideas are unrealistic, since a settlement in any of these conflicts meant Russia would lose control over those countries. Since the EU and the Weimar Triangle's initiatives have been implemented, Moscow should change its course in foreign policy. However, the EU member-states should also forge a common stance regarding Russia as an international actor.

In the 2000s, the strengthening of economic and political ties between the EU and Russia was evident. Both sides expressed their willingness to cooperate on security issues. Even the start of the war in Georgia in August 2008 failed to cause significant damage to the reputation of the Russian Federation and its political leaders. At the time, the military conflict coincided with the beginning of the global economic crisis. So, for Germany, France and other EU states, dependent on the gas supplies from Russia, it was extremely unfavorable to impose sanctions against it, as this situation could affect their own economies in a substantial way. The Russian leadership also did not wish to push their state on the edge of diplomatic blockade. That's why the Russia's president, Dmitry Medvedev, approved the project of a peaceful settlement of the conflict in the Caucasus, proposed by his counterpart Nicolas Sarkozy, rather quickly.

In the course of the crisis, the countries of the Weimar Triangle became split. Meanwhile France and Germany did not support the idea to use tough sanctions against the Russian Federation, while Poland, the Baltic States, and Britain demanded more decisive actions in relation to the aggressor state. But, as the Russian government fulfilled the majority of its obligations on the peaceful settlement – namely, a ceasefire, the withdrawal of troops from most parts of the occupied territories, a deployment of a contingent of foreign observers, and the beginning of international negotiations in Geneva – the pressure on the country was diminished. As a result, the EU resumed talks on the signing of a new EU-Russia agreement in December 2008 (Snigyr, Mikal, Mkhitaryan, Garjacha, Savin, Kaplunsky, 2009).

It may be affirmed that after the Russian-Georgian conflict, relations between Russia, France, Poland and Germany did not changed significantly and Europe's dependence on Russian energy products was not reduced. The sanctions against Russia were not imposed, but the very possibility of their use had a negative impact on investments and led to a foreign capital outflow from the country of $129.9 billion dollars according to the estimates by the Bank of Russia (Tsydria, 2009). As a whole, the Russian military campaign in Georgia can be considered successful, because it managed to achieve the desired goals and to still avoid many negative implications. The political situation in the Caucasus region was destabilized and the image of Georgia as a transit country undermined.

Even before the outbreak of hostilities, Georgia and Ukraine were refused the Membership Action Plan, which is the first step in joining NATO. In particular, Germany and France took a stand against providing these countries with MAP. The personal attendance of Vladimir Putin at the NATO Summit in Bucharest in April 2008, was a strong signal that the future membership of Georgia and Ukraine in the North Atlantic Alliance is unacceptable for Russia (Shakirov, 2014) and is perceived as a 'direct threat' to its national security. Therefore, Europe did not dare to deepen cooperation with the two countries within the NATO framework in order to maintain important strategic relationships with Russia. Consequently, the events of August 2008 clearly showed EU foreign policy priorities.

The Ukrainian crisis, which began in late November 2013, has become a kind of test of the relations between Weimar Triangle countries and Russia. Namely the foreign ministers of Germany, France and Poland contributed to the establishment of a dialogue between the government and the opposition forces in Ukraine and to the signing of the cooperation agreement on the 21st of February 2014. From a diplomatic point of view, their mission was quite successful. But right after that, V. Yanukovych fled to Russia, the political opposition came to power and the EU switched its attention to the new crisis that broke out in Crimea. That is why, to a certain extent, the applied efforts were in vain. On the 31st of March in Weimar, Frank-Walter Steinmeier, Laurent Fabius and Radoslaw Sikorski made a joint statement on the situation in Ukraine. The foreign ministers have condemned Russia's annexation of Crimea and acknowledged a threat to the territorial integrity of Ukraine coming from the Russian Federation. In turn, they undertook the commitment to ensure that Eastern Partnership countries will never have to make a tough choice between a rapprochement with the EU or a wider co-operation with Russia in the future. Also they encouraged Russian authorities to stop the further degradation of the situation in Ukraine and supported a dialogue of the two states (Joint Statement on Ukraine of the Weimar Triangle Foreign Ministers F.-W. Steinmeier, L. Fabius and R.Sikorski, 2014).

The head of the Polish Foreign Office, R. Sikorski, assured earlier in February that Poland, France and Germany rejected the Russian arguments in favor of the annexation of Crimea. They adhere to the opinion that there is no right for a ground invasion of one sovereign state, even in order to protect the citizens of the other one. The Western European states preserve this position even now. F.-W. Steinmeier, R.Sikorski and L. Fabius were sure that the Weimar Triangle had to play a key role in developing cooperation with the EU's Eastern neighbors and that the Ukrainian issue would return Europe to its status as a peacemaker (Perepadja, 2014).

If the crises in Ukraine had declined and the military operations in the East of the country had not been launched, it could be possible to agree with this statement. But the escalation of the conflict finally weakened the position of the Weimar Triangle states. There was no wish to take part in military operations to preserve the territorial integrity of Ukraine.

Later on, the European states moved away from the tripartite approach to solve the Ukrainian crisis and switched to the all-European level. Meanwhile Russia's aggression against Ukraine was growing, and the stance of Weimar Triangle countries towards the imposition of sanctions differed greatly. Germany's reluctance could be explained by the fear of the prospective economic losses and job cuts in joint Russian-German companies. For France, this meant a failure of the million contracts for a delivery of the 'Mistral warships', the economic downturn and a further decreasing of the president F. Hollande's support within the country.

Warsaw acted on the basis of the most radical sentiments, which is why it was gradually excluded from the negotiation process on the Ukrainian issue. France and Germany had fears that because of such a strong support of Ukraine and an anti-Russian attitude, the Polish side would hinder an agreement with the Russian government. In this situation, Poland decided to accede to the Washington-London axis. The former Polish ambassador in Germany, Janosz Reiter, notes that in the context of the crisis in Ukraine, the level of approval of NATO's activities and the alliance with the United States rose sharply, and the feeling that Poland may also be at risk ran high. According to expert opinion, such sentiments are evident in Western Europe too, especially in Germany. But as Poland is the closest among the EU states to the battlefields, the realization of the problem went much faster (Reiter, 2014). In case of the advances of militiamen (supported by Russia) along the territory of Ukraine, the Russian Federation could receive access to the borders of Poland and attack it. The 28 EU states will coordinate their positions regarding the new crisis on the level of European security. However according to Article 5 of the Washington Treaty on collective defense (The North Atlantic Treaty, 1949), Poland must receive military assistance, but this commitment directly involves the USA in the conflict.

A relative consensus between the Weimar Triangle states was found only in July 2014. The death of 300 passengers on an Asia Minor airlines plane while it was in the sky above Ukraine showed that the Ukrainian crisis is not an internal conflict, but a serious challenge to European and global security systems. Germany and France, as the main driving forces of the EU, had to discard the position of 'appeasement' of Russia and to stand together with Poland and Great Britain to impose tougher sanctions. The plane crash became a so-called 'game changer' and heralded a transition of the Ukrainian crisis to the bitterest phase since its beginning.

In an interview with Frankfurter Allgemeine Zeitung, Germany's Chancellor Angela Merkel stressed that Russia came back to the old way of thinking, which divides the world into spheres of influence. And it does not conform with today's principles of state-to-state cooperation, emerged after the end of the Cold War. Also the Chancellor stated that the annexation of Crimea contradicts the principles of international law and reproached Russia in the 'destabilization of the situation in certain parts of Ukraine. That is why the German government absolutely did not agree with some aspects of Russia's internal political development' (Bannas, Kohler, 2014). Expressing such an opinion, the chancellor emphasized the importance and efficiency of the imposing sanctions against Russia.

In turn the Foreign Minister of Germany, F.-W. Steinmeier, explained that sanctions are used as part of a strategy to increase pressure on Russia about the Ukrainian issue. The economic sanctions, as in the case of Iran, must return Russia to the negotiating table, even if they are painful for Europeans (Block, 2014). The real steps in this direction followed right after a declaration of Germany's official position. In early August 2014, the German group 'Rheinmetall' announced that it would not build a training center for the Russian army. The German Ministry of Economy recalled the relevant licence, which had been granted by the previous government. The contract cost was estimated at 100 million euro. Sigmar Gabriel pointed out in his remarks that it is 'not about money, but about people's lives' (Kanevskyi, 2014). These actions by the German leadership show that there cannot be compromise on the issue of European security and the government should take even the most unpopular measures to provide that security. It indicated the end of a certain phase in world politics, as well as in bilateral Russian-German relations. J. Reiter believes that an attempt to integrate Russia into the Western world has failed, and there is no hope for a quick return to the previous model of cooperation (Reiter, 2014). That is why it is necessary to preserve the unity of the Western world and an adherence to its principles.

For this reason the Prime Minister of Poland, Eva Kopacz, echoed the previous argument. Her purpose was to carry out a pragmatic policy in relation to the events in Ukraine. For Poland and its citizens the key task was to end the armed struggle and the consolidation of the Ukrainian state. Eva Kopacz promised to give assistance to Ukraine for its economic, political and military transformation, but stressed that, above all, the success of a reform process is the responsibility of Ukrainians themselves (Bajor, 2014).

Also, the Polish Government gave a special place in its foreign policy (September 2014 – November 2015) to the cooperation between the Weimar Triangle states. The first countries that Grzegorz Schetyna, as the Polish Minister of Foreign Affairs, visited were Germany and France. During the official meeting in Paris, G. Shetyna and his colleague L. Fabius, paid great attention to the relationship between the Warsaw-Berlin-Paris axes.

It was also noted that the Weimar Triangle is important in order to ensure security in Europe hic et nunc. The Foreign Ministers also expressed their support for a non-hostile settlement of the conflict in Ukraine, recognizing that this process requires permanent political decisions (Heads of Polish and French diplomacy are for the peaceful settlement of conflict, 2014).

It seemed that the trilateral dialogue was revived, but the system of international relations is often like an equation with multiple variables. And when one them suddenly changes its course, the entire system can falter. That is exactly what happened after the scheduled parliamentary elections in Poland in 2015. The majority of votes elected a national-conservative party ‘Law and Justice’ and brought with it a sharp turn in the state’s foreign policy. The new Minister of Foreign Affairs, Witold Waszczykowski, in his speech to Sejm named the United Kingdom as the most important of Poland’s partners concerning European issues. So, Germany and France (and the Weimar Triangle as a whole) do not approve of such declarations. But how the Poles see their cooperation with Brussels in the near future, especially after Brexit, is also an open-ended question.

Unfortunately, the present-day political situation in Germany and France is not in favor of the Weimar Triangle. The Ukrainian crisis is not on the agenda either. Germany is suffering from the migrant crisis and has a small space to manoeuvre. France is almost paralyzed, because of the presidential election in 2017 and a leap in popularity of the national-conservative party ‘National Front’, headed by Marine Le Pen. The relations between France, Germany and Poland fall short of any structural integrity, and the political fragmentation of the EU does not help tackle this problem either. Today, the Weimar Triangle as a political entity goes through another stage of low political activity. The 25-years of experience for the trilateral cooperation could not make the Weimar group resistant to cyclical changes in national policies of France, Germany and Poland. There is no clear understanding among the political elites of these three countries that if they sustain their sub-regional partnership, this will convert into a deeper Europe-wide integration. For Ukraine and Georgia, it is also crucial ‘to reanimate’ the Weimar Triangle, since it is an important component of coordination and realization of the European Neighborhood Policy, which will play a defining role in the rapprochement of the Eastern European and Caucasian states to the EU norms and standards. Poland’s vital interest is to stabilize its’ Eastern borders, and at the same time support the efforts of France, which is moving in the same direction regarding North Africa. It is expected that Germany will accept this division of responsibilities (Koszel, 2016, p. 82).

Conclusion

Comparing the activities of the Weimar Triangle during the military conflicts in Georgia and Ukraine, there was a more active involvement from France, Germany and Poland in the process of ending the Ukrainian crisis. In the aftermath of the Russian invasion of Georgia, the Weimar Triangle countries and other EU members, in fact, accepted Russia's 'special rights' for this region. But the situation in Ukraine unfolded in a different way. For the first time in the history of united Europe, a military conflict broke out so close to its own territory. Furthermore, the first street protests on Maidan began in response to V. Yanukovych's refusal to sign the EU Association Agreement and were perceived as a desire of the Ukrainians to belong to Europe not only geographically. But Europe underestimated the role of the Russian factor in the internal destabilization of Ukraine. De facto the Kremlin was ready to initiate military actions on Ukrainian soil, to sacrifice its political reputation in order to maintain its influence there. But the international community did not agree with the new dividing lines in Eastern Europe.

In February 2014, the Ministers of Foreign Affairs of Germany, France and Poland arrived to Ukraine to conduct negotiations with the Ukrainian authorities and even achieved a signing of the agreement on the settlement of the crisis between the ex-president Viktor Yanukovych and the opposition leaders. The Weimar Triangle framework was one of the most convenient and suitable for this diplomatic mission: France and Germany as the pioneers of the European integration process, and Poland as a former member of the socialist camp, as well as a mentally closer strategic partner of Ukraine, which is constantly supporting its pro-European aspirations. Such significant efforts of the Weimar Triangle states can be considered an attempt to demonstrate their political influence at the regional level. Even still, each of the three countries had their own attitude to the situation in Ukraine and had their own concerns with sanctioning Russia.

The aggressive foreign policy of Russia also led to certain disagreements within NATO, which is also responsible for security in Europe. Most of the EU countries had to take one side or another, similarly to the situation with Iraq in 2003, by either acceding to an alliance with the United States or France and Germany. In case of Germany, it was evident that the country was trying to hold a medial position. Germany did not want to sour relations either with NATO or with Russia (Wergin, 2014), fulfilling its commitments to both partners. But before the plane crash on the 17th of July 2014, there was a clear bias towards the support of Russia and an unwillingness to impose the third package of sanctions. All these events took place at the same time as chilly relations between the United States and Europe. This tension was connected to the scandals over the bugging of the political leadership of such states as Germany and Poland by the American intelligence agencies. But it worth it to say the Ukrainian crisis reminded many Europeans that the threats to European security posed by Russia can hardly be met without US military forces (as a part of NATO).

The military conflict in Ukraine pointed at the inefficiency and soft spots of the existing European and global security systems. There is no more room for local wars in a globalized world. A regional crisis can easily turn into a military threat of global dimensions. The recent events in Ukraine must become an impetus in search of new and more efficient forms of cooperation in the security sector. And the Weimar Triangle countries have the required potential to advance such an initiative. But the lack of political will in Berlin, Paris and Warsaw keeps this problem from being brought to the attention of enough states, both within the EU and beyond it.

References

Bajor, P. (2014): The New Polish Government. What Can Ukraine Expect? In: *UNIAN*. Retrieved from http://www.unian.info/politics/992709-the-new-polish-government-what-can-ukraine-expect.html.

Bannas, G.; Kohler B. (2014, May, 16): Russland wendet sich wieder altem Denken zu. Die Bundeskanzlerin im F.A.Z.-Gespräch. In: *FAZ*. Retrieved from www.faz.net/aktuell/politik/kanzlerin-merkel-im-f-a-z-gespraech-russland-wendet-sich-wieder-altem-denken-zu-12941544.html.

Block, N. (2014, May, 16): Außenminister Steinmeier weist Kritik an seiner Ukraine- und Russland-Politik zurück. In: *Thüringische Landeszeitung*. Retrieved from http://www.finanzen.net/nachricht/aktien/Thueringische-Landeszeitu

ng-Vorab-Meldung-Aussenminister-Steinmeier-weist-Kritik-an-seiner-Ukraine-und-Russland-Politik-zurueck-3571528.

Carnegie Endowment for International Peace (2010): Russia's 2010 Military Doctrine. Retrieved from http://www.carnegieendowment.org/files/ 2010russia_military_doctrine.pdf.

European Union External Action (2003): European Security Strategy 'A Secure Europe in a Better World'. Retrieved from http://www.eeas.europa.eu/csdp/about-csdp/european-security-strategy/.

Federal Foreign Office (2014): Joint Statement on Ukraine of the Weimar Triangle Foreign Ministers Frank-Walter Steinmeier (Germany), Laurent Fabius (France), and Radoslaw Sikorski (Poland) in Weimar. Retrieved from http://www.auswaertigesamt.de/EN/Infoservice/Presse/Meldungen/2014/140331_Gemeinsame_Erkl%C3%A4rung_zur_Ukraine.html.

Heads of Polish and French diplomacy are for the peaceful settlement of conflict (2014). *Radio Poland*. Retrieved from http://www.polradio.pl/5/38/Artykul/1831040.

Kanevskyi, D. (2014, August, 4): Germany refused to build the training centre for the Russian army. In: *Deutsche Welle*. Retrieved from http://www.dw.de/німеччина-відмовилася-будувати-тренувальний-центр-для-російської-армії/a-17829468.

Koszel, B. (2016): Trójkąt Weimarski: bilans i perspektywy współpracy 1(XVIII), pp. 65–82.

NATO (1949): The North Atlantic Treaty. Retrieved from http://www.nato.int/nato_static/assets/pdf/stock_publications/20120822_nato_treaty_en_light_2009.pdf.

Perepadja, A. (2014): The eastern neighbors will be offered the integration into EU economic space. Retrieved from http://www.eu.prostir.ua/news/262513.html?print.

Reiter, J. (2014): The West should not compromise. *Radio Poland*. Retrieved from http://www.polradio.pl/5/132/ Artykul/182928.

Shakirov, O. (2014): The 2008 War in Georgia: Lessons for the Crisis in Ukraine. Retrieved from http://www.globalinterests.org/2014/04/24/ the-2008-war-in-georgia-lessons-for-the-crisis-in-ukraine/.

Snigyr, O., Mikal, A. Mkhitaryan, N.; Garjacha, J.; Savin, S.; Kaplunsky, O. (2009): The impact of the Georgian-Russian conflict on the security situation in Ukraine and its strategic interests in the Black and Caspian Sea region. Retrieved from http://www.old.niss.gov.ua/monitor/june2009/16.htm.

Tsydria, B. (2009): The Russian-Ukrainian (American) gas war. In: *InoSMI*. Retrieved from http: //www.inosmi.ru/translation/246734.html.

Wergin, C. (2014, May, 5): Why Germans Love Russia. In: *The New York Times*. Retrieved from http://www. nytimes.com/2014/05/06/opinion/why-germans-love-russia.html? _r=0.

Ukraine's Position on the Russo-Ukrainian Geopolitical Agenda

Olena Starikova

Abstract: *This article is devoted to an empirical observation of the territorial crisis in Eastern Ukraine from a geopolitical perspective. In this article, special attention is paid to the actors involved in the conflict and their attitudes to Ukraine. The aim of the article is not only to analyse the conflict, but also introduce possible scenarios and opportunities to the settlement thereof. The paper assumes that the most probable scenario is that this conflict is going to be a constant, low-grade war between Ukraine and terrorist groups supported by the Russian Federation. It addresses practical recommendations and steps for the Ukrainian government to fulfill in order to build adequate foreign and domestic policy. The article also contains practical recommendations for the Ukrainian government in order to overcome social and international political tangles.*

Keywords: *geopolitics, Ukraine, the Russian Federation, settlement, scenarios*

Theory

In this work, two geopolitical schools will be examined: *the Western Geopolitical School,* which is deemed necessary because of its foundational character, and *the Russian Geopolitical School,* which should be considered because Russian geopolitical paradigms have influenced Ukrainian geopolitical thought, due to their proximity. Moreover, the consideration of the Western School should have an emphasis on early German geopolitics, since it is fundamental to early and contemporary Russian geopolitics. This is the reason why these two schools should be compared and studied. Furthermore, it is necessary to use this mixed approach towards a theoretical understanding.

The term 'geopolitics' was first coined by Rudolf Kjellén – a Swedish exponent of the Western geopolitical school – in his 'State as a living form', in which he, based on the methodology of Friedrich Ratzel, formulated the organic state theory. He believed that states pass through different stages of their development, similarly to how to organisms owe their existence to the universal law of struggling for existence. States and nations, according to Kjellén (1916), struggle for existence and for space. He claimed that 'a place is not a spontaneous instinct of conquest, but a natural and necessary growth for self-preservation'.

A significant contribution to the development of Swedish geopolitical knowledge was the formulation of the autarky law. The state, according to Kjellén, should be neither entirely industrial nor entirely agrarian, because the state is endangered to become hostage to the policy of other states, depending on the global balance of forces. From an economic perspective, in order to sustain stability, the state should be self-sufficient, defending the premises of autarchy. This also presumes a strong isolation from international affairs, leaving, however, a space for the state's development, which has later formed into the theory of the living space.

The theory of the living space was first coined by Friedrich Ratzel (1907) and later used in further research by Karl Haushofer. The basis of the theory is that the state is considered as a live organism which demands expansion as it evolves. In Ratzel's 'Laws of the Spatial Growth of States' he has also set forth the seven laws of expansion which are necessary for the state to grow territorially. It is important to say, that the understanding of the living space can go through alterations in different ways.

Even though the ideas of classic German geopolitics concerning the theory of the living space have been widely criticised, they are still popular among the East European scientific block. The similarities between the classic German geopolitical school and the contemporary Russian geopolitical school are comparable. The theory of ethnogenesis and ethnic cycles that Lev Gumilyov (1992) has formulated continues in the same thread as the German state-organism approach, while partly applying the ideas of geographical determinism, which was previously considered by Ratzel, Kjellén and Haushofer. Gumilyov, followed by Oswald Spengler and Arnold Toynbee, distinguishes the cycles of civilizations and cultures, as well as respective ethnic groups. Nation, state and religious communities, in his view, follow the pattern of living organisms. Naming the phases of the states he resembles Kjellén's ideas of the cycles of the state.

According to Inga Zhukova (2006), there are four possible geopolitical paradigms of any state's development, namely:

1. The imperial geopolitical paradigm, which presumes constant and extensive development of such actors in the international system. This model of international relations provides absolute centralism and the key role of its development is attributed to resource supply.

2. The geopolitical paradigm of nation-states, which stands for the establishment of the whole nation, which constitutes the absolute majority of the population of the territory. Such a paradigm denies the existence of national minorities and suggests the building and maintenance of strong nationalistic moods in the society.

3. The block geopolitical paradigm is a type of coexistence of several political actors uniting for the attainment of common goods or against a common threat. This phenomenon was often used from the late 40s to the end of the 90s of the 20th century.

4. The network or network-centrist geopolitical paradigm, which is characterized by an extensive system of relationships between its elements. Such a system best reflects the structure of a globalized world in which the actors present a hierarchical structure in different international systems. The network model also presumes the existence of powerful centres of the network system which unites elements around it, but it corresponds more to the multi-oriented world order than to the imperial model itself.

With the application of the German Classic School's ideas to Zhukova's geopolitical paradigms, it is easy to observe that the concepts of living space are best applied on the imperial growth paradigm and are less successfully, but still possibly applied to the nation-state geopolitical paradigm.

In order to attain better understanding of the territorial crises in Ukraine, special attention should be paid to the attitudes of the actors directly involved with the development of the situation. It is vital to understand current geopolitical trends and to be aware of individual state policies. When analysing contemporary premises of the geopolitical perspective of the Russian Federation, the necessity of an extensive territorial development may be indicated on one of the two paradigms adopted by the government of the state. However, it should be said that the ideological background for their foreign policy has also come through considerable alterations.

For example, during the press conference devoted to the EU-RF relations on 10th May 2005 President V. Putin stated that he had no claims for the Crimea or Klaipeda (2005). With the shift of ideological and political paradigm, the foreign policy of the Russian Federation has also changed. By referencing the historical geopolitical paradigms mentioned by Zhukova, it is worth mentioning that the geopolitical positioning of the Russian Federation resembles a metropolitan centre which is open for the transformations of peripheral territories. This statement can be made based on the 7th law of expansion by Ratzel (described before).

Speaking of the '*Russian World*', Marlene Laurelle (2015) believes that the notion of the word 'world' in this concept should be understood as the continuity of the Byzantine, Greek and Roman traditions of calling the territories under their influence as their worlds. It has also presumed the imperialistic geopolitical paradigm spoken of above: it is related to 'broad territories under the influence of one centre' and compares it to the British Commonwealth (ibid, p. 23). According to Laurelle, it also has two dimensions and should be studied as an element of both public and foreign policy. It is a mean of soft power, which uses the elements of uniting compatriots, as well as public diplomacy tools.

Possible Scenarios of the Development of the Crisis

Speaking of the supposed scenarios, there are several possibilities. These are: a) gradual abatement of the military and social conflicts, détente; b) latent or low-intensity conflict with infrequent escalations, conservation of the conflict; c) constant full-scale spreading of combat[1].

The first (a) scenario touches upon the détente of the conflict. The gradual de-escalation of the conflict on the Eastern territories of Ukraine is popular not only among the common Ukrainian population, but also among some scientists. For example, in the summer of 2015, a survey was published by the Kyiv International Institute for Sociology (2015), which sought to determine the public mood towards the possibilities of settling the conflict in the East of Ukraine. The absolute majority of Ukrainians (56,8%) believe that the most suitable option to resolve the conflict is the continuation of

[1] The latter will not be considered in the context of the paper.

the Minsk negotiations. The second highest result (28,3%) was for the continuation of the military's counter-terrorist operation.

Journalist Anastasiia Moskvychova (2016) refers to Oleksiy Melnyk, the expert on the security matters of the Razumkov-Centre, who believes that the escalation of the conflict is not beneficial either for Ukraine or for the Russian Federation.

However, there are serious concerns about the probability of this first scenario. First of all, there is no reason for or evidence that the Russian Federation will change its foreign policy concerning Ukraine. Since the Russian Federation is one of the most active participants in the conflict, it should be regarded as one of the main determining factors in this scenario. Russia is quite famous for installing unrecognized republics with a distinct pro-Russian attitude. This conclusion is made based on the experience of the events in Transnistria, South Ossetia and Abkhazia in order to impose the destabilisation of the region[2]. It may be mainly connected with a foreign policy vector other than close cooperation between a state and the Russian Federation itself.

The reason why a change in the Russian Federation's foreign policy towards Ukraine is highly improbable, is because Ukraine's foreign orientation, domestic policy and territorial integrity openly contradict the strategic

---

[2] The Strategic and Security Studies Group has issued a publication, named 'Tanks of August' (2009), devoted to the conflict in Transnistria. According to the authors' statements, in 1992 Moldova has suffered geographical losses due to after having chosen a strong pro-Romanian foreign strategy from the 14th Army of Russia (2009). In April 2008 Georgia was promised NATO membership as was explicit from the Summit Declaration of the Organization in Bucharest (2008), and in August 2008 Georgia has also faced military intervention of the Russian troops. According to the official comment of the Ministry for Foreign Affairs of the Russian Federation, 'There was a need to take urgent and effective measures to prevent bloodshed and keep the situation within legal and peaceful framework. [...] The Russian Air Force aircrafts carried out a brief flight over the territory of South Ossetia [...] (to) prevent the development of the situation on the force scenario'. This comment, however, was made a month before the full-scale military actions of the two sides of the conflict, which indicates on the preliminary character of this flight operation. Another factor to which the authors draw the attention to is that has indicative character thereon is the level of preparation of the Russian troops and their technical equipment.

view of the Russian Federation, which related closely to the theories observed above. For example, according to the theory of the life space, expansion of the Russian Federation is justified. Moreover, the territorial integrity of Ukraine now endangers the sustainability of the borders of the Russian Federation, as both of the actors' territorial integrity presumes the inclusion of the Crimean Peninsula. In regards to this, Frants Klintsevich, Principal Deputy Head of the 'Yedinaya Rossiya' political party[3], stated that: 'any calls for the return of Crimea we see as an encroachment on the territorial integrity of Russia' (2015). The situation is such that a mere compromise is impossible due to the two actors' positions and territorial demands towards each other.

However, Ukraine and the Russian Federation's territorial claims are not the only challenges for political and military stability in the area. The enlargement of NATO is such a great threat, and, as Vladimir Putin has openly mentioned during the XX St. Petersburg International Economic Forum in 2016, the training of Ukrainian regular armed forces by NATO, as well as a non-agreement of the organisation's policy with the authorities of the Russian Federation brings Russia's militarisation to life. This is also explicitly mentioned in the new Military Doctrine of the Russian Federation of 2014[4].

Article 14 of this new Military Doctrine leaves no space for Russia's policy towards Ukraine to change from an alternative discourse of power, which is highly supported by the population.

The second (b) scenario stands for a peaceful settlement within six months in 2017 (which makes it Jan-Jul'2017). A great challenge to a relatively quick peaceful settlement for the two actors' bilateral relations is that the framework to enable a settlement has collapsed. One of the basic international agreements between Ukraine and the Russian Federation – 'Of Friendship, Cooperation and Partnership…' dated 31th May 1997 – has

[3] is currently empowered in the Russian Federation.

[4] Article 14 Paragraph A: 'extending of the power capacity of the North Atlantic Treaty Organization (NATO) [...] building military infrastructure of the countries Members to NATO close to the borders of the Russian Federation, as well as further expansion of the block' (June 2016).

been violated in 21 out of 41 articles[5]; the cooperation with the CIS has been minimised, and, subsequently, with the Free Trade Zone too. This is explicitly stated in the interpretation article on the MFA of Ukraine.

When speaking of factors that impede the peaceful resolution of the conflict, the perceptions of citizens in both the Russian Federation and Ukraine towards each other should also be mentioned. For example, the Kyiv International Institute of Sociology and Levada Centre, uses methodology, exercises joint efforts towards research frames and the attitudes of social groups. In order to illustrate the bilateral relations of the citizens of the Russian Federation and Ukraine it is better to refer to the Chart provided by the Levada Center and KIIS:

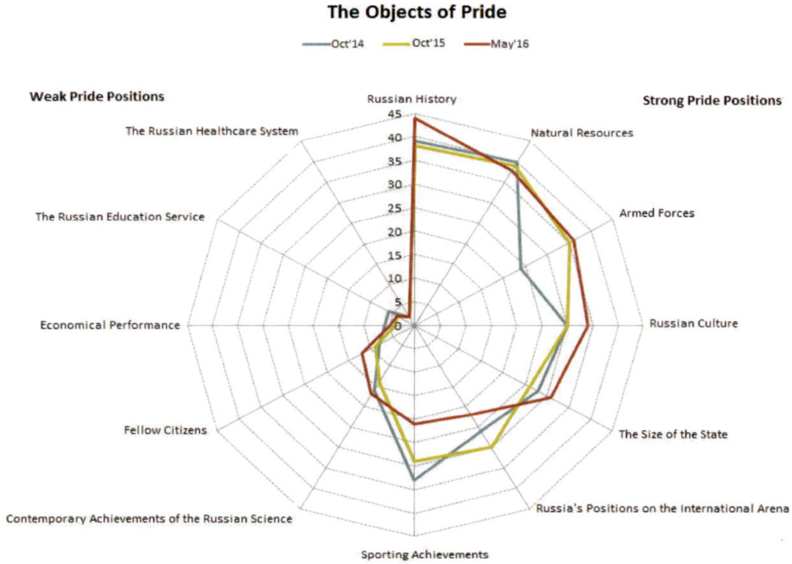

Figure 1. The Russian and Ukrainian Citizens' Opinion Comparison

One of the greatest threats towards peaceful settlement is how both sides underestimate between the official Ukrainian power and the locals of the Donetsk and Luhansk regions. As it is explicitly stated in the complex survey done by the International Centre for Policy Studies (and their partners),

[5] Namely, 1-7, 9, 10, 12-17, 19, 24, 25, 28, 29, 33.

inhabitants of the occupied territories in Donetsk still perceive themselves as Ukrainians. This conclusion can be drawn from this ICPS's survey done in 2015: 48,8% (the majority) of locals agreed that the Donbas region should remain within the geographical borders of Ukraine. While 19,8% of the respondents stated that the region should be independent, and 14,8% of those replied that it should belong to another state. However, 37,8% of locals perceive themselves as the citizens of Ukraine and 35,2% of them have a stronger regional identity[6].

Ukrainian decision-makers, as well as common citizens, have made mistakes for the goals and methods of the Donetsk residents. The mistakes result from misunderstandings and synonymizing these goals with the heads of unrecognized republics that are actually unrepresented by the population of the Donetsk and Luhansk regions. A reasonable question arises regarding the support and legitimacy of the unrepresented government. Zimmer (2007) notices that due to historical circumstances and a willingness to prioritize the industrial, and once profitable, region, there has been a lack of political will and civil society. It can be explained in such a way that relative civic passiveness and beliefs in the intensification of extreme right activists (28,5% of the Donetsk people claimed to fear nationalistic groupings) have formed a special environment which allowed the terrorist[7] government to seize and maintain power.

---

[6] The idea and the genesis of prevailing regional identity are well explained by Kerstin Zimmer in her article 'Trapped in past glory. Self-identification and self-symbolism in the Donbas' (2007). She states that over decades the identity of the locals has changed so much that they have lost the connection with any political unit. Because of rapid industrial development and constant need for labor from any part of the world, it has become of a habit not to speak about their origin. This phenomena is known and referred to by Zimmer as 'Tutoshnii-ness'. More of the reasons for such merged identity of the region could be also found in Zimmer's PhD thesis (2006), which shadowed identity is a double-edged factor, which makes it also challenging for the both sides of the conflict to manipulate with the state identity. Nevertheless, such appeals for state or nation identity may be unnecessary if the Russian Federation is planning to use the Donbas as a mere factor of destabilisation of Ukraine and of the European Union.

[7] The term 'terroristic' is used with the reference to the comment of the Chief Advisor to the Security Service of Ukraine M. Lubkivskyi dated 15th January 2015. According to the Penal Code of Ukraine (Article 258-3), the Security Service of

Another problem is the lack of research. Apart from separate interviews for theses in the sciences, there have only been think tanks' sociological surveys, focusing on general regional identities and sociological studies. Special and problem-centred surveys were not taken until late 2014-2015, and scarcely any public meetings were held by the Ukrainian government with the Donetsk people, but the vectors of foreign and domestic policies were prioritised nevertheless.

The Role of Cooperation and Alliances

In order to have an additional (and more critical) view on the observed scenarios, the role of alliances and cooperation between Ukraine and other countries should be mentioned in order to find solutions to the conflict.

For example, Michael Staack believes that there is no quick political solution to the matter, however, his work 'The Ukraine Crisis – A New Division of Europe' is dedicated to the re-integration of EU-RF relations and is important for the critical review of this paper. According to his research, bearing in mind that Ukraine is dependant both on European and Russian economies, a trilateral approach is a must in order to start moving towards reconciliation. He assumes that gaining economic stability is a primary task and the first step to settling the crisis. Staack criticises Ukraine's ambition towards NATO and EU membership as the result of Ukraine's continuing tensions with the Russian Federation. He believes that the second stage in this process is for Ukraine to return to a non-alignment status and also be guaranteed its territorial integrity by the major powers (such as the Russian Federation and the European Union). Such a strategy would be successful for the conservation of the conflict but not for its settlement.

There is also an explicit cleavage in the friendliness and unfriendliness from the population in the Russian Federation towards Ukraine. The percentage of the respondents who named Ukraine an 'unfriendly country' has increased from 11% in 2013 up to 30% in 2014 and has reached its peak in 2016 with 48%. It has become the second[8] most 'unfriendly state' among

---

Ukraine has qualified the activity of the organizers and active participants of the separatist movements as illegal and terroristic.

[8] The first 'unfriendly state' is the USA with 72% (in 2016).

other countries. This is supposedly the aftereffect of a lack of correspondence as well as the domestic policy of the Russian Federation.

It seems that the Russian Federation is regularly using military intervention as a tool to destabilise the region as well as to chasten the other regime. The non-alignment status does not prevent the region from conflicts, as is observed from the experience of Moldova. Moreover, there was no rhetoric of Ukraine's attainment of NATO membership in 2013. The discourse of enlargement of the organisation became popular only in 2014 and it was not massively supported until the intervention of the Russian Federation, as can be seen from the statistics provided by the Razumkov Centre (2007-2015). The support for NATO 'as the best means of guaranteeing security of Ukraine' has grown nearly three times in two years[9].

It is peculiar though that Ukrainians have never perceived themselves as being able to be powerful enough to build a defensive military potential alone. According to the same survey, even when the ideas of the non-alignment status were quite widespread[10], they had always been shadowed by the convictions of collective security (45,6% in April 2012: 13,0% for NATO and 26,2% for pro-Russian and pro-CIS military alliances). What is more, the Budapest Memorandum, which was signed in 1994, was meant to enshrine security as well as sovereignty and territorial integrity safeguards from the United States of America and the Russian Federation, making the scenario of guarantees impossible.

V. Dziobak (2015), one of Ukraine's higher officials, has also claimed in his interview for the *Khvylia Magazine,* that the peaceful resolution of the conflict is possible and, what is more, both sides of the conflict are ready for it. He presumes that the conflict is mature enough to be settled with the assistance of mediating third parties. According to his expertise, the very understanding by the actors that the conflict is at a dead-end makes it possible to develop new strategies and agreements towards international cooperation. He has also set forth practical steps for each of the sides to the conflict, which might satisfy both parties in a limited scope, with a space

---

[9] In April 2012 only 13,0% of Ukrainians supported this idea, whereas in May 2014 the rate of support reached 32,6% and maintained at 45,7% in November 2015.

[10] Peak – 42,1% in April 2012, context: midpoint of the Presidency of V. Yanukovych who has promoted and codified Ukraine's non-alignment status

for compromise. Some compromises (such as the RF's enabling Ukraine to restore territorial integrity and control over the Crimean Peninsula and simultaneously demilitarising the region) are deemed impossible, but others are considered a limited solution. In particular, V. Dziobak suggests NATO's strategic partnership with Ukraine without granting membership to the organisation, using the example of cooperation with Israel. Another interesting initiative is concluding a treaty between the Russian Federation and Ukraine for the purpose of a long-term lease of the peninsula on the model of cooperation between China and Great Britain for the territory of Hong Kong. Nevertheless, these initiatives contradict the Military Doctrine of the Russian Federation referred to earlier.

In 2014, the 5th German-Ukrainian Forum was held in Vienna with the support of the Future Business Ukraine initiative, where Dr. R. Lindner and K-G. Wellman (Member of the Bundestag) have navigated two Round Tables and have signed two Memorandums called 'Peace and Development in Ukraine'. The 1st Memorandum contains fifteen practical aspects towards stabilising the political and economic crisis in the region. This document presumes that, inter alia, there should be a peaceful resolution of the conflict with the signing of the number of agreements towards the status of Crimea in order to guarantee different kinds of human rights. The premise of the document, explicit in Article 15, is that the stabilisation of the current situation and providing reforms in Ukraine is the trend and the task in which both the EU and the RF are interested. The 2nd Memorandum consists of seventeen steps and economic encouragements mostly for the Ukrainian agricultural sector of the economy. And it also assumes that the peaceful settlement of the crisis is possible and must be carried out by the fulfilment of the Minsk Agreements, as is evident from Article 3 of the Memorandum. Nevertheless, the lack of fulfilment of the Minsk Agreements is one of the key factors which directly indicates a dead-end scenario. This status quo has been repeatedly pointed out by all the parties to the treaties, blaming each other for violating the provisions of the non-use of weapons. What also indicates the probable conservation of the conflict is that there are no attempts to further the dialogue by initiating alternative negotiations or alternative plans as for the settlement of the conflict.

However, the ideological underpinnings of the 'brother relation' between the two countries has also collapsed with the military conflict, which is explicit from the mutual deterioration of relations measured by the Kyiv

International Institute of Sociology[11]. This argument can also be illustrated by the demolition of the 'Nations Cohesion' monument in the centre of Kyiv, which is devoted to the union of the 'brotherly nations of Ukrainians and Russians', and the further transfer of the monument to the museum for totalitarian regimes. Such deterioration of ideological components is the greatest threat towards quick restoration of relations between Ukraine and the Russian Federation. Previous official ideology of the 'strategic partnership', 'brotherly relations' and 'good neighbourhood policy', set forth in numerous joint agreements, has lost its sense.

As it was said before, a compromise between the Russian Federation and Ukraine concerning territorial claims is impossible. However, this is not the only sphere which stalls quick resolution of the conflict. The head of the Institute for Strategic Studies, V. Horbulin, has claimed (2015) with the reference to A. Yatseniuk (Prime Minister of Ukraine in 2014-2016), that Ukraine has lost at least 20% of its economic potential. Such factors as the forced militarisation of Ukraine's economy[12]; considerable shortage of exporting potential[13]; reduced revenues of budgets of all levels by reducing the tax base, as well as increasing the pressure on the budget due to the growth of social insurances for the combatants, displaced persons and refugees; destabilisation of the banking system have all led to a 40 billion Euro shortage for Ukraine's budget in 2013-2015 (exchange rate: 1 EUR=30 UAH, the equivalent of 1,2 trillion Ukrainian hryvna).

The conflict has also caused significant human losses. According to the Echo Factsheet by the European Commission, as of the end of December 2015, approximately 3,1 million people in Ukraine have appeared to be in need of humanitarian aid, 21,085 people were wounded and 9,187 people were killed. The rates of unemployment have increased for both occupied cities. In 1HY'2016 the person per vacancy index, which is used to calculate the competitiveness on the market, has risen up to 24 persons per hiring place in Luhansk and to 50 people per vacancy in Donetsk. In comparison to this situation, in Kyiv those indices constituted 3 persons per vacancy in the same observed period. Such conditions have led to considerable losses in Ukraine's economy not only for the purpose of production rates, but it

---

[11] For further details, consult Figure 1.

[12] 16,0% of the budget and 5,0% of the GDP in 2014.

[13] -13,5% in 2014 vs. 2013 and -39,9% in Jan-Aug 2015 vs. Jan-Aug 2014.

has also cost a considerable amount of money. As of June 2016, the Ministry of Social Policy of Ukraine reported on 1 785,740 refugees and displaced people from the East of Ukraine and Crimea who have applied for such a status to the Ministry and for whom 47 203 533 Euro were distributed in 1 HY'2016 (the equivalent of 1 416 106 thousand Ukrainian hryvna; 1 EUR ≈ 30.0 UAH). The percentage of provision of the households constituted 93%.

Even though a mere quarter of the citizens of the Russian Federation agree that Russian troops are on Ukraine's[14] territory, the officials of the Russian Federation do not claim the state to be a party in the conflict in Ukraine, which disables the international discourse of the compensation for the damage caused by the Russian Army.

It is evident that there must be more actors involved in the conflict than two. All the analysed documents state that in order to embrace the resolution of the conflict a third mediating party is necessary. Such an explicitly mediating party is associated with the European Union, which has held numerous three- or more-sided negotiations. However, the Union's inner crises, which have overlapped and created more issues for both European and international society (as well as lack of evident outcomes resulting from decisions) have cooled the public interest towards the Ukrainian crisis, according to M. Kalb. The decrease of the political interest towards the crisis in Ukraine is also evident from the number of the Security Council Meetings concerning the situation in Ukraine: there were 21 meetings in 2014 and only 7 in 2015. The dynamics of meetings in 2016 are even worse: if there were 1,4 meetings per month in 2015 on the average, this index has decreased down to 0,58 meetings per month in 2016.

Conclusions and Recommendations

Having summarized all the possible scenarios, it seems the most probable one concerns the freezing of the conflict in the next 3-5 years. There is no evidence of the Russian Federation changing its foreign vector doctrine, moreover, the restoration of the territorial integrity of Ukraine endangers the political sovereignty of the Russian Federation itself. The Minsk and

[14] Levada Center 2016, the indices vary from 25% to 29% with the margin of error being ~4,1%.

Minsk-2 agreements have no alternative so far and they have not been fulfilled by either conflicting side. The Russian Federation does not admit it is a part of the conflict in any way, which means that there is no possibility of Russia paying reparations for the damage.

As the gap between executive summaries of state analysts and the results of contemporary opinion polls is considerable, there should be a greater communication and cooperation between the Ukrainian government and local civic population about the freed territories. Also, the destruction of the legal structure between Ukraine and the Russian Federation has enabled the two states to formulate a completely new approach towards regulating disputed territories. There should also be negotiations to restore business activity in the region as well as provide the means to exclude negative anthropogenic factors on the environment.

As the freezing zone scenario is the most possible one, a dialogue on the restoration of the financial infrastructure in special areas of Donbas might begin when the steps to reintegrate the regions are undertaken. To this end, support is necessary for the initiative to restore trade relations between the zone that is under the control of terrorists, as well as other areas of Ukraine. The government should facilitate the reintegration of the areas under conflict into a single energy market of Ukraine. The implementation of the rehabilitation and reintegration of infrastructure (transport, communication lines, grid, etc.) should also be introduced.

References

A Mercenary from Caucasus Complains that Local People Avoid Joining the Appraisal (2014, July, 19). Retrieved from http://news.bigmir.net/ukrai-ne/834189-Kavkazskij-naemnik-zhaluetsja--chto-zhiteli-Donbassa-ne-idut-v--opolchenie-.

Barabanov, M.; Lavrov, A.: Tseluyko, V. (2009): The Tanks of August. Moscow: Center for Analysis and Strategic Technologies.

Dziobak, V. (2015, January, 4): Unconventional means of the Russian-Ukrainian conflict settlement. Retrieved from http://hvylya.net/analytics/politics/nestandartni-zahodi-podolannya-rosiysko-ukrayinskogo-viyskovogo-konflik-tu.html.

European Comission (2016): Humanitarian Aid and Civil Protection. Retrieved from http://ec.europa.eu/echo/files/aid/countries/factsheets/ukraine_en.pdf.

Gerasymchuk, S. (Ed.) (2009): Transnistrian Issue: The Ukrainian Perspective, pp. 203–210.

Gumilyov, L. (1992): From Rus to Russia. Moscow: FTM.

Horbulin, V. (Ed.) (2015): Donbass and Crimea. The price for the Return. Retrieved from http://www.niss.gov.ua/content/articles/files/Razom_kRym_donbas-4ab2b.pdf.

International Centre for Policy Studies (2016): The results of the sociological survey provided in Donetsk and the Donetsk region, (9-12). Retrieved from http://icps.com.ua/assets/uploads/files/national_dialogue/poll_for_regions/1-0_survey_donbas_ua.pdf.

Kalb, M. (2015, September, 7): Putin won his war in Ukraine. In: *The Washington Post*. Retrieved from https://www.washingtonpost.com/opinions/putin-won-in-ukraine/2015/09/07/02a0283c-5341-11e5-933e-7d06c647a395_story.html.

Kjellén, R. (1916): Die politischen Probleme des Weltkrieges. Leipzig: Teubner.

Klintsevich: Any calls for the return of Crimea we see as an encroachment on the territorial integrity of Russia (2015, March, 22). In: *RIA News*. Retrieved from http://ria.ru/world/20150322/1053883529.html.

Laruelle, M.: The 'Russian World' Russia's Soft Power and Geopolitical Imagination, pp. 3–6.

Levada (2016, July, 1): Electoral support for the parties. Retrieved from http://www.levada.ru/2016/07/01/elektoralnye-rejtingi-partij-2/.

Levada (2016, July, 2): Allies and Foes of Russia, European Integration. Retrieved from http://www.levada.ru/2016/06/02/13400/.

Levada (2016, June, 16): Russian-Ukrainian Relations Monitoring from the Perspective of the Citizens of Both States. Retrieved from http://www.levada.ru/2016/06/16/13639/.

Levada (2016, June, 30): June Ratings of Approval and Trust. Retrieved from from http://www.levada.ru/2016/06/30/iyunskie-rejtingi-odobreniya-i-doveriya-6/.

Levada (2016, June, 30): National proud. Retrieved from http://www.levada.ru/2016/06/30/natsionalnaya-gordost/.

'Maidan'. Ukraine, Crimea (2016, March, 2). Retrieved from http://www.levada.ru/2016/02/03/majdan-ukraina-krym/.

Memorandum: Erster Runder Tisch zu Wien (2014, October, 1). In: *Ost Ausschluss*. Retrieved from http://www.ost-ausschuss.de/sites/default/files/pm_pdf/1.Runder-Tisch-Wien-Memorandum.pdf.

Ministry for Foreign Affairs of the Russian Federation, Department of Information and Print. (2008, July, 10): The comment of DIP of MFA of Russia with the respect of the situation in the South Osetia [Press release]. Retrieved from http://archive.mid.ru//brp_4.nsf/sps/CCF2BD3D05F81BB1C325748200449D3D.

Ministry for Foreign Affairs of Ukraine: Permanent Representative Office of Ukraine to Coordination Institutions of the CIS. (n.d.). Retrieved from http://cis.mfa.gov.ua/ua/ukraine-cis/cooperation.

Ministry for Social Policy (2016, June, 6). Retrieved from http://www.kmu.gov.ua/kmu/control/uk/publish/article?art_id=249089206&cat_id=244277212.

Moskvychova, A. (2016): The escalation in the Donbass region is not beneficial neither for Ukraine nor for Russia. In: *Radio Svoboda*. Retrieved from http://www.radiosvoboda.org/a/27795618.html.

Narochinskaya, N. (2006, October, 9). Retrieved from http://www.perspektivy.info/print.php?ID=36200.

Nemenskiy, O. (2012): Panrussism. Retrieved from http://zapadrus.su/2012-04-11-14-59-43/2012-04-11-15-07-21/2012-05-02-16-44-55/622-lr128.html.

North Atlantic Treaty Organization, North Atlantic Council. (2008, April, 3): Bucharest Summit Declaration. Retrieved from http://www.nato.int/cps/en/natolive/official_texts_8443.htm.

Piaskovska, T. (2016, March, 11): How the attitude of Ukrainians towards Russians has changed. Retrieved from http://www.kiis.com.ua/?lang=ua&cat=reports&id=608&page=2.

Prokhorov, A. (Ed.) (1978): The Great Soviet Encyclopaedia. Moscow: The Soviet Encyclopedia (17).

Putin, V. (2015, December, 17): The Great Press-Conference of President of Russia Vladimir Putin [Interview]: Youtube. Retrieved from https://www.youtube.com/watch?v=ZpAl1oQoFno.

Putin advised Estonia and Latvia to forget their 'silly territorial claims' (2005, May, 10). In: *Lenta.ru*. Retrieved from https://lenta.ru/news/2005/05/10/putin/.

Putin's frank response to the Journalist [Interview] (2016, May, 8): Youtube. Retrieved from https://www.youtube.com/watch?v=ysWoOr1l8UA.

Ratzel, F. (1907): Zemlia i Zhizn. S.-Peterburg: Tipo-lit. T-va Prosveshcheniye.

Razumkov (2015): Ukrainian-Russian Relations from the Citizens' Perspective. Retrieved from http://www.razumkov.org.ua/ukr/files/category_journal/UA_Rosiya_8_9-2015-FINAL.compressed.pdf.

Razumkov (2015): Which model of the security would be optimal for Ukraine? (2007-2015). Retrieved from http://www.razumkov.org.ua/ukr/poll.php?poll_id=1082.

Runder Tisch zu Wien 'Ukraine in Europa: Frieden und Entwicklung' (2014). In: *Ost Ausschluss*. Retrieved from http://www.ost-ausschuss.de/sites/default/files/pm_pdf/20141103_RT_Agrar_Memorandum_DEU_final_0.pdf.

Russian World (2014). Retrieved from http://rumol.org/category/russkiymir/.

Security Service of Ukraine (2015, January, 15): Commentary by the Advisor of the Head of SBU (SSU, State Security Service of Ukraine). Retrieved from http://www.sbu.gov.ua/sbu/control/uk/publish/article?art_id=135966&cat_id=39574.

Staack, M. (2014): The Ukraine Crisis: A New Division of Europe? In: *China International Strategy Review*, pp. 9–11.

The Arch of the International Friendship in Kyiv will not be Demolished (2016, March, 23). Retrieved from http://korrespondent.net/city/kiev/3686206-arku-druzhby-narodov-v-kyeve-snosyt-ne-budut.

The majority of Ukrainians deem negotiations as the Donbass conflict settlement. (2015). Retrieved from http://gordonua.com/news/society/socopros-bolshinstvo-ukraincev-vidyat-vyhodom-iz-konflikta-na-donbasse-mirnye-peregovory-90500.html.

The Russian Federation (2014, December, 30): The Military Doctrine of the Russian Federation. In: *Rossiyskaya Gazeta*. Retrieved from https://rg.ru/2014/12/30/doktrina-dok.html.

The Russian Nationals Abroad Project (2016). Retrieved from https://xn--80aealaaatcuj2bbdbr2agjd6hzh.xn--p1ai/projects/sootechestvenniki.

The Situation in Ukraine: Quick Guide (2016, July, 20). Retrieved from http://research.un.org/en/ukraine.

To be renamed (2014, March, 21). Retrieved from https://ru.wikipedia.org/wiki/Википедия:К_переименованию/21_марта_2014#.D0.94.D1.80.D0.B5.D0.B2.D0.BD.D0.B5.D1.80.D1.83.D1.81.D1.81.D0.BA.D0.BE.D0.B5_.D0.B3.D0.BE.D1.81.D1.83.D0.B4.D0.B0.D1.80.D1.81.D1.82.D0.B2.D0.BE_.

Vowinckel, K. (1939): Zum Begriff Lebensraum. In: *Zeitschrift für Geopolitik*, pp. 638–639.

Zhukov, E. (Ed.) (1982): Soviet Historical Encyclopedia. Moscow: Soviet Encyclopaedia.

Zhukova, I. (2006): Geopolitical Paradigms as an Instrument of Global Political Processes Analysis Tool. Yekaterinburg: UrO Russian Academy of Science.

Zimmer, K. (2007): Trapped in past glory. Self-identification and self-symbolisation in the Donbass. In: Adam Swain (Ed.): Re-Constructing the Post-Soviet Industrial Region: The Donbass in Transition. London: Routledge, p. 97–121.

Zimmer, K. (2006): Machteliten im ukrainischen Donbass: Bedingungen und Konsequenzen der Transformation einer alten Industrieregion (Unpublished master's thesis). Zugl.: Frankfurt (Main), Univ., Diss.

Belarus' Stance on Conflicts between the Commonwealth of Independent States

Olga Zhuravskaya

Abstract: *In this article, the author analyzes the position of Belarus in conflicts in post-soviet countries. To understand better the essence and background of the conflicts, the author examines factors of international relations and recent trends in international organizations. The goal of the article is to demonstrate Belarus' reaction to conflicts, taking into account the priorities of Belarusian foreign policy and national interests.*

Keywords: *instability, conflicts, mediation platform, integration, negotiations, OSCE*

I. Factors of International Relations

The modern world is characterized by political and social **instability**. Every day, there is news about social unrest and terrorist attacks or clashes between militants. However, maintaining peace and security, along with the sustainable and friendly development of nations, are two of the UN's major purposes, which was created to save generations from the scourge of war. But seventy years after the 'hot' Second World War and twenty-five years after the end of the 'Cold War' period, the international community is on the brink of a new hybrid war or large-scale conflict yet again.

Today, there are different types of **conflicts**: 'frozen' ones, 'simmering' ones, and those in an escalation phase; armed, hybrid and information conflicts; conflict of political opinions; etc. CIS[1] countries are no exception. In 1991, fifteen republics of USSR proclaimed independence and they lost their common name as a 'soviet nation'. Of course, the fall of the USSR is considered a victory for the self-identification and self-determination of nations, and the prevailing supremacy of human rights. But all these factors sometimes undermine the existing political authority and administrative-territorial system. It is a difficult and arguable question to identify the right cause.

---

[1] Commonwealth of Independent States, formed during the breakup of the USSR.

Disputes should be resolved at the negotiating table instead of the battlefield, based on the generally recognized principles and norms of international law, which every country must follow. But unfortunately, in recent years, there has appeared a growing problem: certain countries are trying to interpret the provisions of international law in their favor. Thus, **a mediation platform** and the services of a third party are necessary in order to break a deadlock of any conflict and convene the affected parties at the negotiating table.

II. Recent Trends

Today, international organizations cannot easily deal with the increasing number of conflicts. The UN organizes missions in the most dangerous and problematic regions of the world (ex: 9 missions in Africa, 3 missions in the Middle East, and also in Kosovo, Cyprus, Haiti and Pakistan), where civilians suffer greatly, the fatality rate is high and there is a struggle between ethnic groups. Very often, the UN is unable to influence its member-states, despite the numerous reforms which have been enacted in every area. There is a sharp disagreement over major issues. The matters in question are the composition of the UN Security Council[2] and the procedure of vote on Resolutions[3].

The 'frozen conflicts' exert significant impact on security and stability in the OSCE region. According to the experts of the Carnegie Center in Europe, the OSCE gained its political relevance when it acted as the mediator in the Ukrainian crisis that began in 2014. The organization turned out to be the most appropriate international organization to manage the crisis and prevent further escalation (Lehne, 2015).

The OSCE's monitoring mission in Ukraine has become an essential factor of stability, but the mission's work remains hampered by insufficient cooperation from the opposing parties. The OSCE has also assumed an important role in facilitating negotiations to implement the Minsk Agreement, which contains a road map for a political settlement. However, little progress has been made so far (ibid).

---

[2] The quantity of permanent and non-permanent members.

[3] The right of veto and ineffectiveness of decisions made.

In this regard, the Belarusian government appreciates the efforts aimed at settling these 'simmering' conflicts. For example, it plays a significant role in the resolution of conflict in the Ukraine. But in this article will demonstrate the role of Belarus as the backer of security in the European region.

III. Belarusian Foreign Policy

The recent trends in politics have vividly demonstrated that the EU and other Western countries build their relations with Belarus by taking 'the Russian factor' into account, but not because of value.

Multivector foreign policy is elaborate and requires extremely high precision. Belarus is geographically attractive to both Western and Eastern powers, and they try to involve Belarus into their sphere of influence. Belarus wants to contribute to the Euro-Atlantic security system and infrastructure, but without infringing on national interests.

Russian influence and the Russian project of the Union State, which uses a common currency between Russia and Belarus, are perceived by experts in different ways. Still the project gives economic support and a great volume of mutual trade. There are no boundaries between the two countries: both states are members of the Eurasian Economic Union, they create common regional air defense system, etc. But Belarusian history, roots in the Lithuanian-Polish region, the Belarusian language and good relations with EU countries may irritate Russian authority.

The scenario of integration with the EU is more illusory, because eurosceptics consider there is no possibility for further enlargement, and Belarus also does not put this question into the agenda. Moreover, the EU has declared an absence of democratic standards and human rights in Belarus and has developed recommendations. However, the neighbourhood policy is the best path: to participate in investment programmes and various research funds.

It is important to understand that the Republic of Belarus realizes a multivector foreign policy by prioritizing cooperation with the Russian Federation, CIS countries and the EU (*Priorities of the foreign policy of the Re-*

public of Belarus). The republic promotes the idea of '**integration of integrations'**[4]. This kind of cooperation would contribute to Belarusian economics, because their economic basis is not grounded on resources, but on trade. Economic growth is important for Belarus, in order to develop the country politically and to preserve its independence and sovereignty.

As for the question of cooperation, it is possible to say that Belarus is eager to cooperate with the EU (the Eastern Partnership of the EU was regarded in this context) and Russia on equal terms to the greatest possible extent. The recent sociological research done by the Independent Institute of Socio-Economic and Political Studies shows that 61,6% of Belarusians demonstrate a friendly attitude to Russia, 48,7% to China, and 41,1% to Kazakhstan (*IISEPS*, June 2016), while Belarus (50%), Kazakhstan (39%), and China (34%) are the 'best friends' of the Russian population (*Levada*, 02.06.2016). People of both countries take the hostile stand to similar countries: USA, Germany, Great Britain and Turkey.

IV. The Position of Belarus on Conflicts in CIS Countries

During the meeting with the heads of delegations during the 40th session of the CIS Council of Heads of Security Agencies and Special Services on 19th May, the topical issues in the CIS were discussed, namely the situation in Transnistria, Nagorny Karabakh, and Ukraine. '*We need to find an agreement. We will have to because we are in the same boat. We are not particularly welcome on the other shores. We need to make life better here*', Alexander Lukashenko stressed (*BelTA*, 2016). In his opinion, the CIS nations share a similar mentality and this will be helpful in the future. '*We know each other and know how to make life better here*', the head of state is convinced (ibid). This statement shows that Belarus tries to be a negotiation platform and a connecting link for all CIS countries, which would support further integration and development of friendly relations between members.

[4] This notion was introduced by Belarusian former Minister of foreign affairs Sergey Martynov in 2000's and it means the possible economic union of the EU and the EEU, forming economic space from Lisbon to Vladivostok.

Transnistria conflict: The analysis of bilateral relations between Belarus and Moldova shows that the dialogue is based on openness, trust, and pragmatic mutual benefit. So Moldova is the 4th partner among the CIS countries for Belarus and can be characterized as reliable. Belarus works with the autonomous territorial formation, Gagauzia, as well. It means that officially Belarus does not recognize Transnistria; this issue is not put on the agenda at the Belarusian Government or Parliament. The position of Belarus is to preserve the territorial integrity of Moldova, with Transnistria being a part of it; otherwise, it may start a war and military intervention.

However, the most vital point is not to politicize the issue of self-proclaimed territories for the sake of political aims and motives. Furthermore, there should be a sincere wish of the countries to ensure the peaceful life of the people. This is the most essential thing because every nation remembers the legacy of WWII and when the UN Charter was created, certain political and military formulas acceptable to all parties were laid down. Today the situation is changing but the founding values and principles should stay the same.

Nagorny Karabakh conflict: Presenting briefly the history of the reconciliation process in the region, it should be noted that in 1992 a conference on the Nagorny Karabakh conflict involving Armenia and Azerbaijan took place in Minsk and provided a forum for negotiations towards a peaceful settlement. Since then, the so-called Minsk Group, the permanent members[5] of which are Belarus, Germany, Italy, Sweden, Finland, and Turkey, as well as Armenia and Azerbaijan, has been working to diminish tensions and to assure the negotiation process and the cessation of the armed conflict. Still the result of its work is not significant: neither party can come to an agreement.

A recent escalation[6], which resulted in numerous casualties[7], demonstrated the precariousness of the ceasefire agreement of May 12th, 1994. Various experts are still discussing the possible reasons of this 'four-day war':

[5] On a rotating basis, also the OSCE Troika is a permanent member.

[6] 'Four-day clashes' in April 2016.

[7] Here meant around 100 victims from soldiers on each side and from civil population.

probably, it was due to an external influence (Turkey's advice) and the division of their spheres of interest (Russia vs. West), the economic crisis (low oil prices and economic decline in Azerbaijan) and the distraction of the people from domestic problems by mobilizing them around a 'national' idea. Furthermore, it must be noted that the positions of the parties in conflict and the official statements of their allies and international organizations showed multiple levels of controversy and divisions.

What counts here is the official reaction of the Republic of Belarus: firstly, the Ministry of Foreign Affairs issued a declaration about the peaceful resolution of the conflict on the basis of sovereignty, territorial integrity and inviolability of borders according to the corresponding resolutions of the UN Security Council and OSCE decisions. As a result, the Belarusian ambassador in Armenia, Igor Nazaruk, was informed by the President of Armenia that he was 'deeply bewildered' by this statement which 'does not correspond to the spirit of the Armenian-Belarusian relations' (here CSTO obligations are meant) and 'is detrimental to the negotiation process'. Belarusian president Alexander Lukashenko insisted that both sides should seek a peaceful dialogue. '*Belarus is always eager to promote the peaceful settlement of conflict at the negotiating table. Military support or any military intervention is unacceptable*' (*Ministry of Foreign Affairs*, 2016).

This tricky task requires great efforts from Belarusian diplomats and politicians; it is crucial to find balance of interests. Armenia is a partner in the EEU and CSTO, while Azerbaijan is an economic partner, and is an important centre for exporting Belarusian goods to Central Asia and the Caucasus region.

Abkhazia and South Ossetia cases: The brief scheme of this conflict is similar to the other: two republics declared their independence after the wars with Georgia in 1992-1993 and adopted their own constitutions, but they were not recognized by any country of the world. In 2006, the two republics recognized each other; moreover, self-proclaimed Nagorno-Karabakh and Transnistria recognized them as well, but not the international community or organizations.

In 2008, a military incident happened in the Tskhinvali region and Russian peace-making forces intervened to stop any violence. After that, Russia recognized both republics. In 2009, Nicaragua, Venezuela and Nauru did the same. But the EU and other countries ignored this fact, as well as international organizations (UN). Many experts think that it is the continuation of the 'Cold War' and distribution of spheres of influence. However some appeal to the Kosovo case and accuse politicians of double standards and hypocrisy.

As for the Republic of Belarus, they tend to realize a neutral policy and claim that any recognition may escalate the situation, particularly by creating a precedent that any ethnic minority group living in a region could use to proclaim sovereignty[8]. Belarusian strategy is based on a pragmatic economic approach; that is why Belarus is developing friendly relations with these two republics and intensifying economic ties and trade potential. Moreover, this state maintains good relations with Georgia. Evidence to that is the official visit of Alexander Lukashenko to Georgia on April 23rd, 2015, when he underlined the unique way of development for each country and the necessity to respect the recognized state formations with central authority. If, to judge from the president's words, there was some pressure exerted on Belarus by the West, this is why the Belarusian state does not want to become a negative factor for Russia and other countries in recognizing the self-proclaimed territories.

Ukrainian crisis: Belarus consistently facilitated the de-escalation of the crisis in Ukraine based on genuine interest in a swift resolution. The Republic of Belarus remains firmly committed to the peaceful resolution of the Ukrainian crisis, which will be facilitated by strict implementation of the Minsk agreements by all parties.

It can hardly be said that Belarus plays a visible, effective and crucial role in this political crisis (the country did not intervene into internal affairs, allocate money, sell weapons, send armed people, etc.) but Belarus qualifies for all the necessary conditions for regular meetings of the trilateral Contact Group on Ukraine and its thematic working groups. These conditions are being the neighbour of Ukraine and the Russian Federation, having a common past and Slavonic roots. These meetings have positive influence on the image of Belarusian diplomatic services and the Belarusian

---

[8] Here is meant Kosovo case that is recognized by the West and blackmailing countries into accusing Russia and sanctioning it.

state in the international arena. This proves Belarus as an isle of stability and security in the region (*Annual Review of Foreign Policy of the Republic of Belarus and Activities of the Ministry of Foreign Affairs*, 2015).

Yugoslavian conflict: Conflicts in CIS countries appeared in the 1990s after the collapse of the USSR. When this uniting force fell and the centralized government resigned, the political authority of party leaders was weak. Each republic restored its independence, but local powers were unable to suppress liberal opposition views and movements.

It should be noted that the Nagorny Karabakh, South Ossetia, Abkhazia, Transnistria conflicts have quite different origins than conflicts in the Balkans. It is necessary to enumerate the reasons for this.

Firstly, according to certain authors (*Koehler and Zürcher, 2003, p. 9*), Yugoslavia was a state with an ethno-federative system, which is why its dissolution, as a federal state and not a unitary one, had issues with the self-determination of ethnic groups or political upheavals.

Secondly, due to the ineffectiveness of the government and the failure of the communist national ideology, the new political establishment of the Yugoslavian republics was formed with strong ethnic and religious views, and a lot of local communities were created.

Thirdly, in the 1990s, the bipolar system of international relations collapsed and the Yugoslavian federation faced the terrible reality of economic crisis and a crisis of personal political authority. An example of this is that after the death of 'nation leader' Josip Broz Tito in 1980, the new presidents of Yugoslavia were unable to unite country. So six parties of the former powerful and friendly empire declared independence. Slovenia got off easy, while the Croatian, Bosnian and Kosovo wars led to ethnic cleansing, sieges and great devastation of those countries. The local government and other forces were too weak to deal with the existing situation, and the EU, being the nearest neighbour, did not have conflict management mechanisms, so international forces were active participants in the wars and some of them intervened without the sanction of the UN.

At that time, the Republic of Belarus was constructing a foreign policy oriented towards Russia (these were the first steps to create the Union state). One more priority was the initiative to create nuclear weapon free zone in Central Europe; Belarus withdrew their USSR nuclear weapons. So, the country, together with the Russian Federation, condemned NATO of illegitimate bombing in March 1999. The Parliament of Belarus issued an emergency declaration. Russia initiated the vote on the resolution accusing NATO in the UN Security Council. Only three countries – China, Namibia, India – supported it, while others[9] voted against it (Roberts, 1999).

V. Conclusions

Having analyzed the official position of the Republic of Belarus to a series of conflicts in post-Soviet countries, it is evident that the Republic of Belarus follows the principles declared in its national security concept of 2010: it is an independent, sovereign European state that does not belong to any world centers of power; it realizes peaceful foreign policy and tends to create conditions for a neutral stance. Due to its geographical position, the country is apt to changes in the geopolitical structure (*National Security Concept*).

Belarus considers it inadmissible to intervene into the internal affairs of any state or use military actions without the consent of opposing parties. It tries to fulfill various mechanisms of international security.

As for conflicts discussed, they all have differences and share common features, but the reconciliation process is always difficult and complicated.

The confrontation in Abkhazia, among others, is characterized by the prevalence of a militant titular minority, which replaced the non-titular ethnic majority. South Ossetia is an example of the sensitivity of ethnic issues, when one small nationality, due to their history, was divided between two sovereign states. In the Nagorno-Karabakh conflict, the interests of the two ethnic groups within one country and between their state formations are crossed. The Transnistrian conflict is the only one to have developed in the most civilized way. It is characterized by a small number of victims and

---

[9]Argentina, Bahrain, Brazil, Gabon, Gambia, Malaysia, and Slovenia, along with the US, Britain, France, Canada, and Netherlands.

material damage. It is a more ideological division between left and right concepts.

Common problems unite these conflicts. First, the collapse of the Soviet Union, which had a political, military, economic and ideological system that provided stability in this space for seven decades. Secondly, the sheer complexity of the settlement process was an issue (after a relatively quick termination of active phases in the first half of the 90s). These conflicts come from complex, dynamic systems and may preserve a steady 'frozen stage' for a long time without external influence. Thirdly, in the post-Soviet countries, global problems are spreading: primarily the growing gap between the wealthy and poor, demographic explosion and an uncontrolled change in the ethnic and demographic structures of population, terrorism, and drug trafficking.

In conclusion, it must be noted that the Republic of Belarus balances its interests and neighbourhood obligations. The country tries to borrow the best experiences from the West and the East and to serve as a 'safe bridge' between two opposing sides and to help in creating the economic space from Lisbon to Vladivostok.

References

Friends and enemies of the Belarus (2016). Retrieved from http://www.iiseps.org/?p=4793.

Lehne, S. (2015): Reviving the OSCE: European Security and the Ukraine Crisis. Retrieved from http://carnegieeurope.eu/2015/09/22/reviving-osce-european-security-and-ukraine-crisis/ii06.

Levada (2016, June, 2): Allies and 'enemies' of Russia. Retrieved from http://www.levada.ru/2016/06/02/13400/.

Ministry of Foreign Affairs of the Republic of Belarus (2000): Priorities of the foreign policy of the Republic of Belarus. Retrieved from http://mfa.gov.by/en/foreign_policy/priorities/.

Ministry of Foreign Affairs of the Republic of Belarus (2000): Statement by the Ministry of Foreign Affairs of the Republic of Belarus in connection with the events regarding Nagorny Karabakh. Retrieved from http://mfa.gov.by/en/press/news_mfa/ed083eeb7910baf9.html.

Ministry of Foreign Affairs of the Republic of Belarus (2016): Annual Review of Foreign Policy of the Republic of Belarus and Activities of the Ministry of Foreign Affairs in 2015. Retrieved from http://mfa.gov.by/en/publications/reports/a323c6e532e23593.html.

Nagorno-Karabakh's war. A frozen conflict explodes (2016, April, 9). In: *The Economist*.

Official webpage of the President of Belarus (2015): Official visit of the President of Belarus. Retrieved from http://president.gov.by/ru/news_ru/view/ofitsialnyj-vizit-v-gruziju-11241/.

Official webpage of the President of Belarus (2016): Meeting with the heads of delegations of the 40th session of SORB and special state services. Retrieved from http://president.gov.by/ru/news_ru/view/vstretilsja-s-rukovoditeljami-delegatsij-zasedanija-sorb-i-spetsialnyx-sluzhb-gosudarstv-uchastnikov-sng-13668/.

Roberts, A. (1999): NATO's 'Humanitarian War' over Kosovo. In: *Survival* 41(3), pp. 102–123.

Comparative Part

One Approach to the Comparative Analysis of the 'Frozen Conflicts' in the Territories of the Post-Socialist Spaces with Problematic International Recognition[1]

Kristina Khrul

Abstract: *This article is an attempt to compare the various 'frozen conflicts' from the perspective of the disintegration conflict theory. How can the right for the use of a national language in different areas of a state's life for national minorities correlate with structural, institutional, and socio-emotional recognition? This paper will compare the disintegration conflict theory through changes in 'language recognition' in the cases of Serbia, Azerbaijan, Georgia, Moldova and Ukraine, which could have influenced the rise of those conflicts.*

Keywords: *'frozen conflicts', comparative perspectives, 'language rights', disintegration conflict theory*

Introduction

The content and frame of this study is elaborated through exploring specific contentious situations (for example, 'frozen conflicts') in complexly structured regions (multicultural societies) from a comparative perspective.

Most articles in this issue focus on one aspect or conflict from the post-socialist countries. In the current article, the results of a comparative analysis of the 'frozen conflicts' in the regions of the former Yugoslavia, Transnistria, South Ossetia and Abkhazia, Nagorny Karabakh, Crimea and Donbas will be presented.

The methodology of this research is based on disintegration conflict theory, which claims that 'depreciation and devaluation of ethnically others' – or arising of conflicts in multicultural societies, in the cases analyzed – have their roots in the past, as well as in current experiences of structural, institutional and socio-emotional recognition.

---

[1] The author gives thanks to Kirill Repin for the support by topic formulation.

This paper will explain how these types of recognition correlate with the 'language rights' of national minorities and how document analysis can prove it.

Overview of Terms

First, the most used terms in the paper have to be explained. The first term which needs to be clarified is 'frozen conflict'. This item can be characterized as very problematic because of its use in mass media and because of the lack of a scientific definition. So, for example, even newly published dictionaries and encyclopedias of political science do not contain information about this term.

A more or less utilizable definition can be compiled from the descriptions of this phenomenon. So, in this paper, the term 'frozen conflict' means a situation of fighting between and/or within states. This also includes tensions between governments or groups during a non-violent phase of a conflict by keeping contentious questions unresolved and open.

Both the term and its above specification can be strongly criticized. For example, an other problematic part of the notion of a 'frozen conflict' can be seen in its ambivalence: From one side, there are conflicts 'the violent stage of which ended in a stalemate and without a peace treaty' (cf. Bebler, 2015, p. 9), can be well described as 'frozen'; from the other side, 'no situations are fully frozen' (Nodia, 2004, p. 1). Moreover, a conflict itself 'has an ambivalent nature, and can generate creative change and high levels of personal and collective integration' (cf. Cheldelin ed., 2003, p. 11). Apart from the difficulties of its application, this term is still one of the most important for analyzing conflicts in post-socialist societies, because the political systems of these countries are constantly changing, and the reorganization of their institutions, values and processes continues.

The use of the term 'post-socialist space' has to be explained as well. It is connected to how the explored regions belonged to the so called Communist or Eastern Block, or, in the example of the former Yugoslavia, to the countries in the 'Soviet '*sphere of influence*'' (Bideleux and Jeffries, 1998). The decision concerning the comparison of the conflicts in these countries was made not only because of some similarities between them, but also because of their historical (communist) background and multicultural context. Whereas the current article does not aim to explore the political regime of the former Soviet Union, the terms 'post-socialist space' and 'countries of the former Communist block' will be used synonymously.

The additional part of the title of this article, which refers to 'problematic international recognition', excludes the states from the list of post-socialist countries that had not tried to secede. Furthermore, it explains what kind of 'frozen conflicts' is discussed.

The following section is intended to show from which theoretical perspectives the roots of this kind of conflicts can be explored.

Theoretical Basis

Within the framework of this article, it is impossible to give an (even short) overview about the scholars of conflict and theories of multiculturalism[2]. For this reason, the most suitable – to the author's opinion – theoretical approach to explain the causes of conflict is briefly described below.

Although different types of conflicts, such as ethno-political, national, cultural, and historical, are considered, in all these cases one has to speak of the process of disintegration with the other state(s), or rather about failed integration within societies. That is why disintegration conflict theory was chosen.

The main idea of this approach is based on the three 'virtual' demands[3] to the state (cf. Heitmeyer and Anhut, 2008, p. 26-28):

- Social-structural (positional recognition): responsible for the access to material and cultural goods, for structural orientation in the society;
- Institutional (moral recognition): covers political and institutional participation;
- Socio-emotional (emotional recognition): belongs to the private sphere of integration.

---

[2] See more about the theories of multiculturalism in Mintzel (1997).

[3] The authors name them 'integration dimensions' (Heitmeyer and Anhut, 2008, p. 27).

The realization of these points leads to positional, moral and emotional recognition[4], as well to the identification[5] and integration with related groups and society. The rise in violence is 'a possible outlet to compensate lack of recognition' (cf. ibid., p. 29).

In the article 'Die Konflikttheorie der Desintegrationstheorie' (Anhut, 2008), there is a very complex structure, which follows that not only one factor can be stated as the reason of the emergence of a conflict (s. the figure 1). The theorist does not explain the exact cohesion between reasons and consequences of conflicts, in other words, it is still not clear how many disintegration experiences a society needs to collect in order to reach the point of 'depreciation and devaluation of ethnically others'.

As you can see on the graphic, the three 'demands' are placed in the fields of 'biographical experience' and 'current experience'. So, it can be supposed that the lack of recognition in the past and in the present has a possibility to create depreciation and devaluation of ethnically others through social competence (rather social incompetence) and inclusion. Together with the perception of the others, self-norms and mobilization factors it stimulates a collective violence.

In the current paper, this approach will be used for the analysis of conflicts in post-socialist multicultural societies. Both characteristics are important to understand the translation scheme.

---

[4] For the alternative vision of the types of recognition see more in Owen and (Tully, 2007).

[5] Other researcher of multiculturalism – Alf Mintzel – proposes alternative categories for ethnic identification: 'identification with an ecological territory; with ethnic institutions; with an ethnic culture; with historical symbols; with an ideology; with charismatic leadership' (Mintzel, 1997, pp. 119-120).

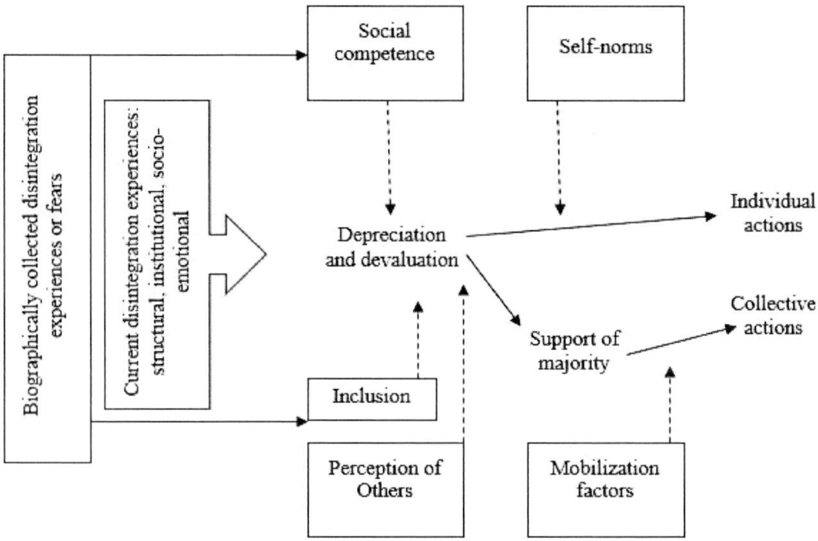

Figure 1. The translated and shortened figure from Anhut (2008, p. 386) about 'translation of disintegration experiences into xenophobic attitudes and actions'.

First of all, the kind of multicultural societies that these young post-socialist states were needs to be explained. According to Kymlicka's[6] definition, 'a state is multicultural if its members either belong to different nations (a multinational state), or have emigrated from different nations (a polyethnic state), and this fact is an important aspect of personal identity and political life' (Kymlicka, 1995, p. 18). In the case of the former USSR and Yugoslavia, it can be said that the rate of inner migration[7] was high throughout the entirety of their existences. However, they were not polyethnic states,

[6] Will Kymlicka is a political scientist and philosopher, who focuses on multiculturalism.

[7] Additionally to the voluntary migration to the USSR existed 'forced migration', during which some national minorities or social classes ('Kulaki') were displaced to other regions.

but multinational ones, because the states indeed consisted of different nations[8].

The abovementioned author writes that 'in most multination states, national groups feel allegiance to the larger state only because the larger state recognizes and respects their distinct national existence' (ibid., p. 13). This correlates with the thesis of the disintegration conflict theory, since the lack of recognition of national minorities evokes a process of their disintegration from 'big states' and, as a result, leads to the attempts of secession.

The other threat to the multicultural post-socialist societies analyzed lies in the fact of the dissolution of the states to which they once belonged and in the building of new (national) countries. A major problem is that newly formed states need time to create a new 'recognition policy'. Therefore, it is unknown to which extent and which national minorities will be recognized. Thus, the Soviet and Yugoslavian past can be seen as 'biographically collected (disintegration)[9] experience', and the new state formations as having a 'current disintegration experience'. Therefore, this research will focus on the comparison between past and new disintegration experiences for the cases of Abkhazia, Crimea, Donbas, Kosovo, Nagorny Karabakh, South Ossetia, and Transnistria.

What kind of recognition was affected after the dissolutions of Yugoslavia and the USSR is a very broad question. The literature about disintegration conflict theory does not deliver enough explanation about possible research objects for tangible cases. In other words, it is complicated to formulate what can be analyzed, for example, in the case of a lack of moral recognition. For the solution of this situation there was one issue that correlates with all types of recognition and plays an important role for national minorities: the language[10]. Using the example of Quebec, Will Kymlicka explains that it is important for the recognition of national minorities and for

---

[8] The author distinguishes between *national minorities* and *ethnic groups*: the first includes 'distinct and potentially self-governing societies incorporated into a larger state', the second are 'immigrants who have left their national community to enter another society' (ibid., p. 19).

[9] Only a profound historical research can show, in which case it comes to the disintegration.

[10] Read more about connection between language, culture and identity in Réaume (2000) and Haarmann (1986).

cultural reproduction not only to have some classes in their languages, but also be able and admitted to use it in other state institutions: at work, in newspapers, in the education system, etc. (cf. Kymlicka, 1999, p. 59). This shows that, the 'language issue' covers social-structural, institutional, and socio-emotional demands to the state.

Thus, this paper will focus on the official recognition (from the side of the state[11]) of national minorities by 'language law'. This last term is aimed at laws, which contain information about the regulation of the use of languages of national minorities. The analysis frames compares 'the recognition in the past' and 'the current recognition', so here the last 'language laws' of Yugoslavia and of the USSR (resp. of corresponding republics) and the first 'language laws' after dissolutions will be analyzed. In this regard the main question that has to be answered is: How did official language recognition of national minorities change after the collapse of the USSR and Yugoslavia in the countries of Azerbaijan, Georgia, Moldova, Serbia[12] and Ukraine?

Methodology

The analysis of 'language laws' needs a special method of analysis. In this short part, the methodological approach that is the most suitable for this analysis will be explain. The document analysis approach was chosen to explore the recognition of 'language rights' of national minorities in constitutions and/or associated laws, because it is more applicable for these kinds of sources.

One of the procedures of document analysis was described by Przyborski and Wohlgrab-Sahr (2014). They name the four following steps:

- Thematic procedure, selection of text passages, transcription;
- Formulating interpretation;
- Reflecting interpretation;
- Comparative analysis and type creation (cf. ibid., p. 292-304).

---

[11] The author's research experience shows that many processes connected with law (for example, in Russia and Ukraine), exist in 'juridical' and 'practical' realities.

[12] In this region the 'Kosovo case' will be explored.

This approach includes the most important (for this analysis) parts: selection of the text pieces, which regulate the use of languages of national minorities, their explanation (formulating interpretation) and assessment of their meaning for national minorities. The last important part is the comparison of the results.

	Past		**Current**	
	Constitutions	'Language laws'	Constitutions	'Language laws'
Y	Constitution of SFR of Yugoslavia, 1974		Constitution of Yugoslavia, 1992	
S		Law 'about languages of nations of the USSR', 1990		
		Law 'On the Functioning of the Languages Spoken in the Territory of the Republic of Moldova'[13], 1989	Constitution of Moldova, 1994	
			Constitution of Azerbaijan, 1995	Law on the state language, 1992
			Constitution of Georgia, 1995	
		Law 'about languages in the Ukrainian SSR', 1989	Constitution of Ukraine, 1996	Law 'about the languages in the Ukrainian SSR', 1989 (lost validity in 2012)

Figure 2. Analyzing documents

The table above was created for a better illustration of the analytical frames and analyzing sources, in which the documents are arranged according to their type, country affiliation and time of adoption. On the basis of this

[13] Unfortunately, the text of this law was not found.

figure, working tables[14] for the analysis will be created, whose results will be presented in the next part of this paper.

Results of the Analysis

By the analysis of the constitutions and laws on the languages two characteristics attracted attention: firstly, in the 'common' documents to the official (or state) languages belongs Russian ('USSR case'), the others are the languages of minorities; the 'national' documents of republics provide the politics of new states, in which the meaning of terms 'language of majority and minority' are changing their places[15]. In other words, in different documents there are different objects of recognition.

'Yugoslavia-Serbia Case'

The first difference between the cases of the former USSR republics and the republic of Serbia is that the new Constitution of Independent Serbia was not adopted until 2006, almost 14 years after the dissolution of Yugoslavia and after conflict in Kosovo broke out. During this time, the last Constitution of Yugoslavia (1992) was valid in the territory of Serbia[16]. For that reason, this document was dedicated in this analysis to the 'current part'. In comparison with the USSR case, the 'old' document was indeed much older than the law 'about languages of nations of the USSR' (1990): The Constitution of Socialist Federal Republic of Yugoslavia of 1974. The results of the analysis of these documents are collected in figure 3.

The following conclusions are drawn from comparison. At first, the fact that the Constitution of the SFR Yugoslavia contains no mention of state language suggests a high level of recognition; the second part concerned the official language – Serbian (ekavian and ijekavian dialects in Cyrillic and Latin script), – but the languages of the national minorities could be

[14] The analysis of the documents will be realized with help of MAXQDA Software.

[15] So, for example the recognition of language rights of minorities in the law about languages of nations of the USSR is covering among others Ukrainian language. In the law about the languages in the Ukrainian SSR is the Ukrainian speaking population not 'minor' any more.

[16] Until 2003.

very well used in official context too, at least in the territories they inhabited.

Secondly, the text of the first constitution does not show a clear distinction between the 'languages of nations' and 'languages of nationalities'. But the transformation of these terms into 'languages of national minorities' in the Serbian case shows the tendency to reduce the recognition of language rights of these groups.

Yugoslavian SFR:	**Serbia**:
• no official language • all languages of nations of Yugoslavia are equal • native language can be used in court proceeding • nations of Yugoslavia have right to be educated in their languages • in the armed forces languages of nations of Yugoslavia are used, in the regions - languages of nationalities • new laws are published in authentic languages, in Albanian and Hungarian	• official language – Serbian (ekavian and ijekavian dialects in Cyrillic and Latin script) • the languages and writings of national minorities shall also be in the official use in the regions inhabited by them • native language can be used in court proceeding • national minorities can be educated in their languages • mass media can also use languages of national minorities • in the case of arrest, the reasons of the arrest have to be explained in mother tongue or in a language which the arrested person understands

Figure 3. The results of analysis in the case of Yugoslavia and Serbia

Regarding questions about education and court procedure, the constitutions are very similar: native languages can be used. Another interesting point is the practice of publishing new laws. In the first constitution, Albanian and Hungarian were explicitly mentioned together with 'authentic languages'.

Summarizing this comparison, it becomes clear that the introduction of a single official language and the degrading transformation of conditions make the second constitution (of Serbia) less commendable than the constitution of the former SFR of Yugoslavia.

'USSR-Azerbaijan-Georgia-Moldova-Ukraine-Case'

For the comparison of this case (see figure 4), it is better to start with the law on the languages of nations of the USSR. The content of the analyzed law can be described as highly recognizable. The reasons for that are: a) the distribution of power over the use of national languages to the respective republics; b) the approval of the use of national languages in many fields of the state's life (court proceeding, education, publishing of laws, official document proceeding, elections, requests to state institutions). At the same time, in some institutions the rights of national languages were limited: in the armed forces, the Supreme Court and the central mass media. The communication between soviet institutions and the republics had to be in Russian only. In the following comparison the 'USSR experience' will be used as an 'ideal case' (by keeping in mind the statement about some limitations of 'language rights' of nations of the USSR).

The first overview of the documents on the languages of Azerbaijan shows that the law concerning the state languages has been adopted before the Constitution of the newly founded independent state. Therefore even in the documents of the new state the 'use of soviet heritage' can be seen in the articles about 'the supreme soviet of the republic Azerbaijan' (article 8).

A second important difference is apparent in the divergent terms for the designation of the official language: In the law 'Turkic' was used and in the constitution, 'Azerbaijani'. The significance of the 'language issue' is confirmed by the following part of the law on the state language: 'the usage of the Turkic language as state language is one of the principal conditions for the sovereignty of the Republic of Azerbaijan' (Law on the state language in the republic of Azerbaijan, foreword). Moreover in the same part is said that 'Azerbaijani living abroad have to be motivated to get education in their native language' (cf. ibid.).

Special attention was given to terms such as 'representatives of other nationalities residing on the territory of the republic' (ie national minorities) and 'specific area' (presumably related to Nagorny Karabakh), expressing the lack of recognition for the national minorities living in Azerbaijan.

By analyzing official documents on the regulation of official language shows that the recognition of 'language rights' of other nationalities is lower than in the law about languages of nations of the USSR. The only right that is still granted is the right to choose the language of education.

The Constitution of Georgia, on the other hand, did not provide so much information for comparison. Nevertheless, it was possible to carve out some important points. First of all, the article on the official state language is of interest. In Georgia, the language is Georgian, and in Abkhazia, the languages are Georgian and Abkhazian. This shows a certain recognition of some national minorities. A second important point concerning the regulation of language is its use during court proceeding: 'in the districts, where the population does not have a command of the state language, teaching of the state language and solution of the issues related to the legal proceedings shall be ensured'. In other words, the knowledge of the Georgian language is one of the basic resources for resolving problems during legal proceedings.

Thus, the comparison of the 'Georgian experience' with the USSR, as well as with the Republic of Azerbaijan, can only be illustrated partly because of the lack of information in the Georgian Constitution. The only conclusion that can be made, in this case, is that the official documents about the use of languages in Georgia involve both positive and negative characteristics.

The Moldovan Constitution did not give so much information either. The following features were pointed out: the declaration of Moldovan (in Latin alphabet) as a state language; the protection of Russian and other languages by the state; the possibility to choose the language of education; the use of Moldovan (or another language accepted by the majority of participants) in court proceeding.

By comparing the Moldovan constitution to Soviet law, it is possible to claim that the Moldovan case can not be described as less recognizable although the text of the Constitution of the Republic of Moldova contains far less information on any 'language rule', because none of the above points limits the language rights of national minorities.

Another interesting peculiarity of the analysis of post-soviet countries is in the case of Ukraine, which had one law 'about the languages in the Ukrainian SSR' from 1989 until 2012, even after its independence from the USSR. It is questionable how this law was implemented, if it was, but on the official page of the Ukrainian Parliament it is written that 'this law lost its validity after the other law was inured on 03.07.2012' (*Official web portal of Verkhovna Rada of Ukraine*).

<table>
<tr>
<td rowspan="3">USSR:
• Official language – Russian (obligatory to learn)
• Recognition of languages of nations of the USSR; republics regulate the use of languages on their territories
• National language is used in court proceeding
• The education can be on the languages of the nations, 'compactly living on some territory'
• Armed forces, Supreme Court, logistic, state institutions, central mass media, communication between soviet and republican institutions – in Russian
• Publishing of laws, elections, official personal documents – in Russian and national language
• Communication with other states – in Russian and language of other state
• Requests to state institutions – in any language of nations of the USSR; responds – in the same language or in other acceptable
• Language of other nations can be used in documentation on the territory of republics according to their law</td>
<td>Azerbaijan:
• Azerbaijani (or Turkic) – official language; obligatory to learn
• Court proceeding is in Azerbaijani or in a language of majority of population in specific area
• Military force, adoption and publishing of laws, elections, requests to the institutions and responds, the work of state institutions, legal and notary proceeding – in Turkic
• Other languages can be chosen for education: in kindergartens and secondary schools can be organized separate classes for studying in another language
• Representatives of other nationalities shall be encouraged to learn Azerbaijani
• Mass media can be in Turkic and other languages; logistic – in Turkic and other accepted international languages</td>
</tr>
<tr>
<td>Georgia:
• Georgian is a state language, in Abkhazia – Georgian and Abkhazian
• Court proceeding – in Georgian; in the districts, where the population does not have a command of the state language, teaching of the state language and solution of the issues related to the legal proceedings shall be ensured</td>
</tr>
<tr>
<td>Moldova:
• State language – Moldovan in Latin alphabet
• Russian and other languages have to be protected by the state
• The language of education can be chosen
• Court proceeding – in Moldovan or in other language, accepted by the majority of court participants</td>
</tr>
<tr>
<td>Ukrainian SSR:
• State language – Ukrainian, Russian – language of communication between nations of the USSR; both are obligatory to learn</td>
<td>Ukraine:
• State language – Ukrainian
• Russian and other languages of national minorities have to be protected
• Education can be received in the language of national minorities</td>
</tr>
</table>

• Russian and other languages of national minorities have to be protected • Education (kindergartens, schools and institutions) – in Ukrainian, but can be received in other languages • Ukrainian is used in state institutions and court proceeding , on territories with other national majorities – other language can be used • The legislation process, conferences, post, telecommunication – in Ukrainian • Document proceeding, requests to state institutions and work of mass media – in Ukrainian and other languages; official statements can be translated from Ukrainian • Publishing of laws, official personal documents, 'informatics language', work of state employers – Ukrainian and Russian (obligatory to learn after hiring); responds from state institutions – in Ukrainian or other language • Children can be named in national tradition	• The Republic of Crimea has the right to develop state language and national languages • Ukrainian SSR language law

Figure 4. The results of the analysis of cases USSR, Azerbaijan, Georgia, Moldova and Ukraine

Consequently, this document cannot be assigned either to the 'past' experience or to the 'current' one[17]. Therefore, the analysis of the Ukrainian case cannot be compared with other cases.

Leaving aside the fact that the 'case of Ukraine' stays outside the comparison, it is possible to state that the Constitution of Ukraine gives no reason

[17] This is the reason for adding in the second part of the table 'Ukrainian SSR language law'.

to speak of less recognition of the ‚language rights‘ of national minorities, compared to the law on the languages of nations of the USSR. This is because the parts of the constitution devoted to the 'linguistic issue' do not include attempts of failing to recognize the 'language rights' of national minorities.

Summarizing the analytical part of this paper, it can be noted that both examples from the 'past' of the territories currently burdened with 'frozen conflicts' show an high degree of official recognition of 'language rights'. Both the constitution of the Yugoslavian SFR and the laws of 'the languages of the nations of the USSR' gave the republics the power to decide about the national languages in their respective territories. Moreover the Yugoslavian Constitution did not declare a state language (in the 'Soviet Case' it was Russian).

The analysis of the 'current' examples showed that there were only two cases (Serbia and Azerbaijan) where it can be clearly pointed out that official recognition of the 'language rights' of national minorities was lower than in the past. Since the Georgian Constitution has elements that suggest a higher level of recognition,[18] as well as elements suggesting an opposite conclusion, the case of Georgia must be considered less positive compared to the example of the USSR. The cases of Moldova and Ukraine show a high degree of recognition, which is due to the Soviet laws. It is worth mentioning that the Moldovan Constitution did not cover possible fields of language use and that the Ukrainian case[19] has juridical collisions with its first Constitution and the language law in the Ukrainian SSR.

In the last part of this analysis, the results are finally classified according to the above-mentioned theoretical approach.

Conclusion

The main question of this research was focused on the change of official recognition towards national minorities after the collapse of the USSR and

[18] But not to such an extent as in the examples of Serbia and Azerbaijan.

[19] Here it is important to add that in today's Ukraine 'the language question', especially the law 'On the principles of the state language policy' from 2012, is highly discussed.

Yugoslavia in the countries of Azerbaijan, Georgia, Moldova, Serbia and Ukraine. As the analysis has shown, the 'recognition policy' has shifted in the texts of the 'language laws' and constitutions. In two cases the negative changes were more 'visible' – in the Constitution of Yugoslavia (1992), in the Constitution of Azerbaijan (1995) and in the law 'on state language' (1992). Less changes in 'recognition policies' were seen in Georgia, Moldova and Ukraine[20].

With regard to the theoretical approach – the disintegration conflict theory, – these results point to a possible lack of 'language recognition' in Azerbaijan and Serbia, which could theoretically help bring about disintegration experiences and conflicts in related areas.

This thesis can be strongly criticized, both theoretically and methodologically. First of all, the theoretical approach does not allow precise conclusions about reasons of conflicts. Besides the 'disintegration experience in the past and in the current time', other issues such as inclusion, the perception of others, social competence, self-norms, and mobilization factors can also influence the situation. This analysis covers only one part of the whole schema – disintegration experience in connection with structural, institutional, and social-emotional recognition. Therefore, the results of this work can represent only a single fragment of the overall picture of the conflicts.

Moreover, the selection of sources can be criticized as well: In some cases the texts of the constitutions did not deliver enough data for fundamental conclusions. Therefore, the possibility of the existence of another law, which partly regulated 'linguistic question', stays open.

Another important critique consists in the difference between the declaration of rules, which control official use of languages, and the implementation these rules. Without further additional research, it is difficult to estimate how the analyzed documents were actually implemented.

Despite all the complexity of this approach, one hypothesis can be formulated from the results of this analysis: The collapse of multicultural states such as the USSR and Yugoslavia tended to lead to a reduction in the recognition of national minority rights in some newly founded countries,

[20] For the first time in their existence.

especially for the 'linguistic question'. How those have influenced the disintegration processes within those countries must be explored in future research.

References

Constitution of Azerbaijan 12.11.1995.

Constitution of Georgia 24.08.1995.

Constitution of Moldova, The Parliament of the Republic of Moldova 27.08.1994.

Constitution of SFR of Yugoslavia 21.02.1974.

Constitution of Ukraine, Verkhovna Rada of Ukraine 28.06.1996.

Constitution of Yugoslavia, The Federal Chamber of the Assembly of the Socialist Federal Republic of Yugoslavia 27.04.1992.

Law 'about languages of nations of the USSR' 24.04.1990.

Law 'On the languages in the Ukrainian SSR', Verkhovna Rada of Ukrainian SSR 28.10.1989.

Law on the state language in the republic of Azerbaijan 22.12.1992.

Anhut, R. (2008). Die Konflikttheorie der Desintegrationstheorie. In T. Bonacker (Ed.), *Sozialwissenschaftliche Konflikttheorien. Eine Einführung* (4th ed., pp. 381–409). Wiesbaden: VS, Verlag für Sozialwissenschaften.

Bebler, A. (2015). Crimea and the Ukrainian-Russian conflict. In A. Bebler (Ed.), *'Frozen conflicts' in Europe* (pp. 189–209). Opladen: Barbara Budrich Publishers.

Bebler, A. (Ed.). (2015). *'Frozen conflicts' in Europe*. Opladen: Barbara Budrich Publishers.

Bideleux, R., & Jeffries, I. (1998). *A History of Eastern Europe: Crisis and Change*. London [u.a.]: Routledge.

Bonacker, T. (Ed.). (2008). *Sozialwissenschaftliche Konflikttheorien: Eine Einführung* (4th ed.). Wiesbaden: VS, Verlag für Sozialwissenschaften.

Cheldelin, S. (Ed.). (2003). *Conflict: From Analysis to Intervention*. London [u.a.]: Continuum.

Haarmann, H. (1986). *Language in ethnicity: A view of basic ecological relations*. Berlin [u.a.]: Mouton de Gruyter.

Heitmeyer, W., & Anhut, R. (2008). Disintegration, recognition, and violence: A theoretical perspective. *New Directions for Youth Development*. (119), pp. 25–37.

Kymlicka, W. (1995). *Multicultural Citizenship: A Liberal Theory of Minority Rights* (1th ed.). Oxford: Clarendon Press.

Kymlicka, W. (1999). *Multikulturalismus und Demokratie: Über Minderheiten in Staaten und Nationen*. Hamburg: Rotbuch Verlag.

Kymlicka, W. (Ed.). (2000). *Citizenship in Diverse Socities*. Oxford [u.a.]: Oxford University Press.

Laden, A. S., & Owen, D. (Eds.). (2007). *Multiculturalism and Political Theory*. Cambridge [u.a.]: Cambridge University Press.

Mintzel, A. (1997). *Multikulturelle Gesellschaften in Europa und Nordamerika: Konzepte, Streitfragen, Analysen, Befunde* (1th ed.). Passau: Wiss.-Verl. Rothe.

Nodia, G. (2004). Europeanization and (not) resolving secessionst conflicts. *Journal of Politics and Minority Issues in Europe*. (5), pp. 1–15.

Owen, D., & Tully, J. (2007). Redistribution and recognition: Two approaches. In A. S. Laden & D. Owen (Eds.), *Multiculturalism and Political Theory* (pp. 265–291). Cambridge [u.a.]: Cambridge University Press.

Przyborski, A., & Wohlrab-Sahr, M. (2014). *Qualitative Sozialforschung: Ein Arbeitsbuch* (4th ed.). München: Oldenbourg.

Réaume, D. G. (2000). Official-Lanuage Rights: Intristic Value and the Protection of Difference. In W. Kymlicka (Ed.), *Citizenship in Diverse Socities* (pp. 245–272). Oxford [u.a.]: Oxford University Press.

List of Contributors

Nazarii Gutsul is a research assistant at the Giessen Centre of Eastern Europe Studies, and was the project-manager of the DAAD-project 'Multicultural societies and their threats. Real, hybrid and media wars in Eastern Europe'. PhD at the Justus-Liebig-University Giessen (Eastern Europe History), M.A. at the National University of Kyiv-Mohyla Academy (History), B.A. at the National Linguistic University of Kyiv (German Philology).

Academic interests: World War I, World War II, prisoners of war, displaced persons, and Ukrainian migration.

Contact information: Nazarii.Gutsul@gizo.uni-giessen.de

Kristina Khrul is an initiator and coordinator of the DAAD-project 'Multicultural societies and their threats. Real, hybrid and media wars in Eastern Europe', and the second editor of this volume. M.A. alumni at the Philipps-University of Marburg (Germany), Institute for Political Science; graduate alumni at the South Ural State University (Russia), Institute for Political Science.

Academic interests: protest movements, analysis of revolutions, 'frozen conflicts', research of international relations, media, elections, and elites.

Contact information: kristina.khrul@uni-marburg.de

Jacqueline Composanto is finishing her undergraduate degree at Pitzer College in Los Angeles, and is one of the grammar correctors of this volume.

Academic interests: Modern history, German history and literature, and the EU.

Maximilian Brisach is a master student of Eastern Europe History and Political Science at the Justus-Liebig University Giessen, and a student assistant of the DAAD project 'Multicultural societies and their threats. Real, hybrid and media wars in Eastern Europe.' Works at the Herder Institute for Historical Research on East Central Europe in Marburg, and one of the correctors of this volume.

Academic interests: Early Modern and Modern Baltic, Polish-Lithuanian and Prussian History, Securitization Studies, and International Relations.

Contact information: Maximilian.Brisach@geschichte.uni-giessen.de

Angelina Yurkova is an undergraduate from International Relations Department at the Belarusian State University of Minsk, and from the European Law Department in the University of Bordeaux IV Montesquieu.

Academic interests: European politics, French foreign policy, the EU, Eastern Europe, and international organizations.

Contact information: angelinayurkova1996@gmail.com

Tetiana Levoniuk is a final-year student studying at the Faculty of International Relations of the Belarusian State University of Minsk.

Academic interests: European politics, the European Union, Eastern Europe, French foreign policy, NATO – EU relations, and the United Nations.

Contact information: tanya.levonuk.96@mail.ru

Frederick Schröder is a M.A. student at the Free University of Berlin, Institute for East European Studies, B.A. in Political Science/Public Law.

Academic interests: Post-Soviet conflicts, Eastern Partnership countries, and Russian domestic and foreign policies.

Yuliya Abibok is a journalist and a PhD student on Mass Communications at the National University of Kyiv-Mohyla Academy in Ukraine. Her dissertation topic is 'The construction of Donbas regional identities through regional and national media discourses. Implications to the conflict'.

Academic interests: social and political psychology, ethnicity and nationalism studies, and peace and conflict studies.

Contact information: y.abibok@gmail.com

Demian Shevko is a graduate student at the National University of Ostroh Academy (Ukraine), Faculty of Political Studies and Information Management. Graduate scholarship student in the Center for East European Studies of the Warsaw University.

Academic interests: political elites in Ukraine, non-military aspects of new generation warfare, and election and political PR campaigns.

Anastasiia Lykholai is a student at the National University of Ostroh Academy, Department of International Relations (Ukraine).

Academic interests: foreign policy of Switzerland and Swiss neutrality.

Contact information: yasochka15.l@gmail.com

Ivan Basenko is a PhD candidate at the Department of History of the National University of Kyiv-Mohyla Academy (Ukraine). His PhD thesis is 'The Image of the Germans in the Press of Kyiv (1914 – 1918) '.

Academic interests: imagology, nationalism studies and mass-media communication.

Contact information: ivandoc@ukr.net

Olga Rusova is a PhD candidate at National Mechnikov University of Odesa (Ukraine), Institute of Social Sciences, Department of International Relations. She is majoring in European Studies with the focus on the Weimar Triangle States (Germany, France and Poland).

Academic interests: European integration processes, security systems, and key challenges the EU faces in a world of globalization.

Contact information: olgarusova@inbox.ru

Olena Starikova is a PhD student at the National Institute for Strategic Studies, and a student at the University of Lodz.

Academic interests: contemporary international relations and the political security of East Europe.

Contact information: olena.m.starikova@gmail.com

Olga Zhuravskaya is a post-graduate student at the Belarussian State University of Minsk, Faculty of International Relations, Department of International Relations, History of Foreign Policy. Master of historical sciences, 2015.

Academic interests: international organizations in the sphere of security, the role of NATO in the world and CIS, and relations between Belarus and NATO.

Contact information: zhuravskayavolha@mail.ru

Osteuropa

Angelique Leszczawski-Schwerk
„Die umkämpften Tore zur Gleichberechtigung"
Frauenbewegungen in Galizien (1867 – 1918)
Bd. 9, 2014, 376 S., 44,90 €, br., ISBN 978-3-643-50586-6

Daniel Dumitran
Economy and Society in Central and Eastern Europe
Territory, Population, Consumption
Bd. 8, 2013, 408 S., 49,90 €, br., ISBN 978-3-643-90445-4

Magdalena Solska
Die Systemkrise des Kommunismus und die Entwicklung der Parteiensysteme in Estland, Lettland und Litauen 1988 – 2011
Nationale Identität, Cleavage-Politik und Parteienwettbewerb in Nordosteuropa
Bd. 7, 2013, 328 S., 44,90 €, br., ISBN 978-3-643-12288-9

Wieland Köbsch
Die Juden im Vielvölkerstaat Jugoslawien 1918 – 1941
Zwischen mosaischer Konfession und jüdischem Nationalismus im Spannungsfeld des jugoslawischen Nationalitätenkonflikts
Bd. 6, 2013, 304 S., 19,90 €, br., ISBN 978-3-643-12052-6

Wolfgang Gieler unter Mitarbeit von Dirk Postler
Das Politische System von Belarus
Geschichte, Grundlagen und Entwicklungsperspektiven
Bd. 5, 2013, 184 S., 39,90 €, br., ISBN 978-3-643-11813-4

Jiří Smrž
Symphonic Stalinism
Claiming Russian musical classics for the new soviet listener, 1932 – 1953. With an introduction of Peter Solomon and Thomas Lahusen (University of Toronto)
Bd. 4, 2011, 208 S., 29,90 €, br., ISBN 978-3-643-10448-9

Jörn Happel; Christophe von Werdt (Hg.)
Osteuropa kartiert – Mapping Eastern Europe
Unter Mitarbeit von Mira Jovanović
Bd. 3, 2010, 400 S., 43,90 €, br., ISBN 978-3-643-80015-2

Zaur T. Gasimov
Militär schreibt Geschichte
Instrumentalisierung der Geschichte durch das Militär in der Volksrepublik Polen und in der Sowjetunion 1981 – 1991
Bd. 2, 2009, 216 S., 29,90 €, br., ISBN 978-3-643-10001-6

Simon Geissbühler
Babuschka Anna
Das Leben einer ukrainischen Bäuerin im 20. Jahrhundert
Bd. 1, 2007, 152 S., 19,90 €, gb., ISBN 978-3-8258-0381-0

LIT Verlag Berlin – Münster – Wien – Zürich – London
Auslieferung Deutschland / Österreich / Schweiz: siehe Impressumsseite